UNION GOVERNMENT
AND ORGANIZATION

This material was prepared pursuant to Contract #99-8-1383-42-20 from the U.S. Department of Labor by the author, who was commissioned by the George Meany Center for Labor Studies, Inc., AFL-CIO, in partial fulfillment of its Tripartite Program for Apprenticeship and Associate Degree in Labor Studies. The opinions contained in this material do not necessarily reflect those of the George Meany Center for Labor Studies, Inc., the American Federation of Labor-Congress of Industrial Organizations, or the U.S. Department of Labor.

UNION GOVERNMENT AND ORGANIZATION
in the United States

James Wallihan

Indiana University

The Bureau of National Affairs, Inc., Washington, D.C. 20037

Library of Congress Cataloging in Publication Data

Wallihan, James, 1941-
 Union government and organization in the
United States.

 Bibliography: p.
 Includes index.
 1. Trade-unions—United States—Management—
History—20th century. 2. Trade-unions—United States—
History—20th century. I. Title.
HD6508.W25 1985   331.87′0973   85-10980
ISBN 0-87179-460-8
ISBN 0-87179-461-6 (pbk.)

Printed in the United States of America
International Standard Book Number: 0-87179-460-8 (hardbound)
0-87179-461-6 (paperback)

To Charlene

Contents

List of Tables

List of Exhibits

List of Figures

List of Charts

Preface

Important turning points in the rise of the labor movement centered on issues regarding the appropriate forms of union organization and the workers that should be included within them. The CIO industrial unionism of the 1930s challenged as irrelevant to the needs of most mass production workers the exclusionary craft unionism preferred by many AFL unions. The shakeout continued for two decades until the competing federations merged in 1955 to form the AFL-CIO. But the merger did not reflect agreement on an ideal form of organization; rather it symbolized recognition that many forms may be appropriate.

This book is about the many forms developed by unions to realize their goals and their attendant functions under different conditions. While the daily "stuff" of unions as organizations may not always seem as momentous as the crises of the 1930s, a familiarity with union functions, union structures, and their uses and their limitations is essential for those who would work effectively within the labor movement, those who would adapt and change it, and those who would simply seek to understand it.

An early scholar, Robert Hoxie, once described the labor movement as "protean." Lest we assume this to be a statement about nutrition, a look in the dictionary tells us that protean means "exceedingly variable" and "readily assuming different shapes and forms." Indeed, it is the adaptability and diversity of union organizations that makes their study so fascinating. But these same qualities can frustrate those who seek easy and absolute truths, who want all generalizations to be neat. Hence qualifiers like "some," "many," and "most" should be taken as implicit throughout this book.

Despite these limitations, the diversity of forms does not cripple our effort. Useful generalizations are possible.

The book incorporates distinct elements. To build an information base, a good deal of *terminology and description* is provided, especially in the early portions. *Concepts* of structure and function are woven into an analytical framework through *classification* and *propositions*. Finally, the text identifies several *issues* of union government and organization.

The subject of the book touches two others, collective bargaining and union administration, from which it should be distinguished. Though bargaining is the primary activity of U.S. unions, this book does not focus on how unions negotiate and administer collective bargaining agreements. But, of necessity, it addresses the structures through which unions and em-

ployers bargain and the influence of bargaining on the organizational structure of the union.

Nor is this a book about union leadership and administration, understood as the nuts and bolts of how officers accomplish union tasks. But a
grasp of the broad elements of organizational structure and function is
essential to effective leadership and administration.

For the labor movement to be a cohesive whole rather than an aggrega-
tion of separate units, it is necessary to understand unions other than one's
own. A familiarity with the similarities and differences of environments and
the ways unions approach their environments not only strengthens the
bonds among unions; it can contribute to effective action within one's own
situation.

James Wallihan
May 1985

Acknowledgments

Many people helped in many ways with the preparation of this book. I want to thank them, while of course noting that responsibility for shortcomings is mine.

Of fellow labor educators, Keith Knauss of the Division of Labor Studies at Indiana University was instrumental in getting me committed to the project and in sharing his experiences with teaching material. John Bennett of Empire State College in New York was a fund of information and a helpful critic. Also aiding at key points were Chuck Craypo, Miles Galvin, Frieda Rozen, Lee Balliet, Bob Repas, Greg Geibel, and Richard Humphreys. Barbara Wertheimer, whose recent death is a major loss for labor and labor education, also helped.

Several people associated with the Tripartite Program for Labor Studies and Apprenticeship and the George Meany Center for Labor Studies contributed much. Richard Hindle, the project director, showed great imagination, sensitivity, and organizational competence in developing an innovative program. In addition to her other project responsibilities, Jacqueline Brophy of the Center Staff read drafts and made many excellent criticisms and suggestions. David Alexander and Marjorie Rachlin of the Center and Reese Hammond of the Operating Engineers union also made helpful comments on particular sections. Fred Hoehler and Russ Allen, director and deputy director respectively of the Meany Center, helped with the original conception and provided administrative support. Larry Rogin contributed valuable insights that helped me establish the initial framework.

David Floyd, Dutch Kleywegt, Dick Zorabedian, Richard Almonte, and Bert Farnham—unionists associated with the community colleges in the program—helped by providing early suggestions. Hundreds of union members and leaders with whom I've been privileged to work, especially those in the Indianapolis area, have informed me about the subject, not only by telling me about their own unions but sometimes by challenging my notions about union structure and function.

Chaneta Newbern showed tremendous patience and competence in shepherding the manuscript.

1

Introduction

The rights and interests of the laboring man will be protected and cared
for not by the labor agitators, but by the Christian men to whom God in
His infinite wisdom has given the control of the property interests of
the country, and upon the successful management of which so much
depends.

George Baer, industrialist, 1902

A worker and a supervisor engage in a fight on their employer's
premises. Several witnesses are asked to describe the incident, but
their statements settle nothing. Observers' descriptions vary as to
where they were standing, when they first noticed the incident, what
they know about the background of the dispute, and what their feel-
ings are about the combatants and about their roles in the workplace.

The situation illustrates the influence of perspectives on how
we describe reality and what we think to be true. Clearly, what we
"know" often is determined by our physical vantage point and can
be clouded by what we want to believe.

Split Images and Stereotypes

So it is with unions. These complex and, to many, controversial
institutions are the subject of diverse opinions colored by the attitudes, experiences, and economic interests of the viewers. Some of
the resulting images are out of focus and others are stereotypes
based on hearsay and a will to believe.

Stereotypes, while they may reflect a grain of truth or a single
instance, are overgeneralizations that fail to withstand scrutiny. At
its peak the membership of the Teamsters union approached two
million. Yet we can no more conclude from this that all unions are

1

large any more than we can say that they all are small because the Horseshoers union has only 300 members. Nevertheless, such distortions are encountered. We are told that unions are giant organizations dominated by "labor bosses," that they are corrupt, that they cause inflation, and that "the public" or "the public interest" will not stand for various union actions.

This abuse of the term "public" rankles many unionists, for it suggests that union members and their families, a quarter of the U.S. population, are somehow not part of the public. As if it were some faceless mass, "the public" is often cited when an editorialist, a politician, or even a citizen on the street wants to show broad support.

Opinion polls recognize that there are in fact many publics when they classify respondents by age, income, occupation, and region. But the polls themselves are often superficial or biased. Poll results will vary according to how and where a question is asked. Reported attitudes toward unions, for example, might differ depending on whether they are solicited at home or on the job.

The phrasing of a question can lead to a desired response that can be waved about to show that "the public" supports one's position. For instance, a 1977 survey conducted for the AFL-CIO showed that 56 percent of the respondents favored *right-to-work laws*, which ban agreements requiring those who receive union representation and benefits to pay a share along with dues-paying members. The responses to a separate question demonstrated that many of the 56 percent answering in favor of the laws did so without knowing what "right to work" meant. When the question was rephrased, 74 percent agreed that it was unfair "for people to receive benefits from an organization such as a labor union without paying any of the costs of getting those benefits."[1]

Polls have established a fairly good record where there are only two or three possibilities, such as preferences between presidential candidates. There is cause for skepticism, however, where complex questions of attitude and action are involved or where commissioned polls are publicized to build support.

Considering the Source

Knowing the source of a stereotype or an opinion is not sufficient reason to reject it. It is clear, however, that some groups and

---

[1]AFL-CIO, *Right to Work*, Special Report (Washington, D.C.: AFL-CIO, 1977).

organizations in society have an economic stake in promoting disaffection with unions. Nevertheless, employers are not unified in their perspectives. Although antiunion employers, the National Right-to-Work Committee, and similar groups seem to seize any opportunity to attack unions, some employers have formed stable bargaining relationships and have admitted that unions, by forcing employers to examine their own policies and practices, bring to the workplace a measure of justice and benefits that otherwise would not exist.

Contradictory expectations of unions are sometimes expressed by individual employers. When union members want more, there is a call for less democracy: Management expects the union leader to be reasonable and "control his people." At other times, especially if a weak membership is sensed, such employers expect the union to be a perfect democracy. Union leaders then hear, "Will your members really support you on this?" and "Let the people decide on it."

Salaried and other white-collar employees sometimes are influenced by the stereotyped view that unions are only for blue-collar workers. This view persists despite the fact that network news staffs, salaried physicians, airline pilots, entertainers, and other high-status, highly paid workers have unionized.

Union members differ in their perceptions according to occupational setting, family background, and individual experiences with unions. Many members, while critical of certain features of their own organizations, add that they certainly would not want to be without a union. Virtually all polls on the matter confirm that members are generally much more positive than nonmembers about the value of unions.[2]

The belief that union members are held captive by "labor bosses" was reflected at one time in federal law. A provision of the 1947 Taft-Hartley Act provided for secret ballot polls on all *union shop clauses* in negotiated agreements. (A union shop clause is a negotiated provision requiring union membership as a condition of continued employment.) The designers of the provision assumed that, given the chance, captive members would reject these clauses. But when the results of over 46,000 such referendums upheld 97 percent of the union shop clauses, the provision was dropped from the law.[3]

---

[2] For example, see Thomas A. Kochan, "How American Workers View Labor Unions," *Monthly Labor Review* 102, no. 4 (April 1979), pp. 23–31. An early statement with documentation on the influence of economic class on views of labor unions is C. Wright Mills, THE NEW MEN OF POWER (New York: Harcourt, Brace, 1948), pp. 42–3.

[3] Benjamin J. Taylor and Fred Witney, LABOR RELATIONS LAW (Englewood Cliffs, N.J.: Prentice-Hall, 1971), p. 313.

Identifying the more biased assessments of unions and their activities is relatively simple. Providing a definitive assessment is impossible, if for no other reason than the sheer number, variety, and complexity of union institutions. Still, some of the prominent features of all unions can be described and the variations among them investigated to disclose important categories of structure and action.

First comes a task that is not as simple as it first appears— defining what we mean by a union.

What's in a "Union"?

One of the conventional definitions of a labor union is "a continuous association of wage earners for the purpose of maintaining and improving the conditions of their employment."[4] This is not a bad definition to start with. It highlights three elements: *continuity*, or relative permanency of organization; a goal or purpose, *improving conditions* (presumably to include compensation); and *employment*, the economic and authority relationship between two parties, worker and employer. Since there are salaried and commissioned employees in several bona fide unions, we need not, by definition, limit union membership to wage earners.

Because it is widely believed to be the "strongest union of all," the case of the American Medical Association (AMA) is instructive. The traditional image of the AMA is one of a protective organization of doctors, quite similar to the image of a craft union. Thus the AMA is seen as restricting entry to the trade; setting standards for those who are admitted to the apprenticeship programs—the medical schools; discouraging encroachments on its jurisdiction—doctors' work; standardizing the prices physicians charge for their services; and acting as a public relations and political representative for the trade.

But this picture lacks an essential feature of all true trade unions in the United States—that of representing or seeking to represent employees in a collective bargaining relationship with employers. Indeed, most AMA members are self-employed (or employed by corporations of their own creation).

Unions of physicians do exist. The Union of American Physicians and Dentists (UAPD) is a growing organization with chapters

---

[4] Sidney and Beatrice Webb, HISTORY OF TRADE UNIONISM (London: Longmans, Green, 1911).

in several states, but whose approximately 14,000 members are concentrated in California. Another, the Physicians National Housestaff Association (PNHA), at one point claimed as members 12,000 of the 60,000 salaried interns and residents on the staffs of U.S. hospitals.[5]

Unions come in all shapes, sizes, and mixes of goals and activities. But almost without exception, unions in the United States differ from other types of organizations by virtue of their bargaining relationship with the employers of their members. The AMA lacks this trait; it is a trade or professional association.[6] The UAPD and the PNHA display the trait and, to this extent, fit our definition of a union.

There is another defining characteristic of a union—independence from the employer. An employee organization without this autonomy, or one dominated or assisted by the employer, is, despite appearances, not a real union. It is termed a *company union*.

In summary, a union is a continuous organization of employees that seeks to maintain and improve the terms and conditions of employment through collective bargaining representation with the employer (from which it remains autonomous) and through other means.

Some Qualifications

Given this broad definition of a union, some additional clarifications must be made.

(1) *Unions in all but the name.* Some organizations fit our definition but reject designation as "unions." Many such groups are found in government employment and among engineers, scientists, and other employees aspiring to professional status. Some originated as *employee* or *professional associations*, but in response to membership pressure and the activities of unions in their fields, some of these organizations began to emphasize collective bargaining as a major goal. The activities of organizations such as the Fraternal Order of Police (FOP), the American Nurses Association

---

[5] Mary A. Andrews, "Housestaff Physicians and Interns Press for Bargaining Rights," *Monthly Labor Review* 101, no. 8 (August 1978), p. 30. These physicians are often defined as students and not employees, a determination that seriously impairs their bargaining efforts. The UAPD includes in its membership both salaried employees and independent practitioners.

[6] Recently at least one AMA state affiliate (California) has made an abortive effort to represent employed physicians.

(ANA), the National Education Association (NEA), and many state employee associations are little different from those of self-identified unions such as the American Federation of Teachers (AFT) and the International Union of Police Associations (IUPA).

Groups such as the ANA have been called "near unions."[7] As their increasing emphasis on bargaining with employers suggests, many of the near unions have been in the process of becoming unions for some time, even dropping their old aversion to the term itself. The 260,000 member Civil Service Employees Association (CSEA) in New York state merged in 1978 with the American Federation of State, County, and Municipal Employees (AFSCME), indicating that CSEA members had come to see their organization as a union.

(2) *Names are poor indicators of union status.* Many long-established unions title themselves orders, associations, brotherhoods, alliances, and federations. Others, such as the Brotherhood of Carpenters and Joiners, the Steelworkers, the Rubber Workers, and the Auto Workers have "United" at the head of their titles.

(3) *There is an understandable confusion between the terms* trade *union and* labor *union.* To some people the term trade union suggests a skilled craft union while labor union suggests one whose membership includes the semiskilled and unskilled. However, unless otherwise noted, this book uses the terms interchangeably.

Basic Types

Later chapters will expand on the distinctions among different union types. At this point it is sufficient to note that a craft union is one whose members share identical occupations and skills. While few pure craft unions remain, construction locals of unions like the Operating Engineers (IUOE), the Electrical Workers (IBEW), and the Plumbers and Pipefitters usually consist mainly of journeymen who have received similar training and who have much the same skills.

An *industrial union*, such as the Auto Workers or the Steelworkers, organizes workers on an industrywide or plantwide basis regardless of skill or job classification. Where a plant is organized industrially, all workers, skilled and unskilled alike, will belong to the same union. A *craft union* will represent workers of a particular

---

[7]Derek C. Bok and John T. Dunlop, LABOR AND THE AMERICAN COMMUNITY (New York: Simon and Schuster, 1970), p. 53.

skill, often from more than one place of employment. Industrial unions are also described as *vertical* because their membership ranges up and down the occupational ladder. Craft unions, by the same logic, are termed *horizontal* organizations.

The same distinctions can be applied to unions of government employees. Thus the pure industrial, or comprehensive, model would encompass in the same union all the eligible employees of an agency or department regardless of their classification or skill. By comparison, a pure craft or horizontal union would be composed only of attorneys, skilled maintenance workers (perhaps even those of a single trade), social workers, or those in another closely related group. While many government employee unions attempt to organize comprehensively, there are numerous examples of organization by craft. Notable are unions of police, fire fighters, and teachers at the municipal level and of skilled tradespeople at many federal installations.

In practice most national craft unions are mixed: Like the Carpenters and the Electrical Workers (IBEW), they have industrial local unions in manufacturing plants and craft locals in construction.

The Labor Movement: A Preliminary Sketch

Let us now move to a broad depiction of the labor movement—its organizational lines and the goals, activities, and structures of its component unions. Succeeding chapters will add depth to this initial sketch.

Membership. Government reports for 1980 list 203 labor organizations—national unions, *international unions*, and associations (the latter mostly "unions in all but name").[8] In that year these 203 organizations reported some 22.4 million members in the United States. Of these, about 34 percent worked in manufacturing, 57 percent in nonmanufacturing, and 9 percent in government.[9]

By 1982 there were 99 unions affiliated with the major labor federation, the AFL-CIO (American Federation of Labor-Congress of Industrial Organizations), which reported about 15 million mem-

---

[8] Most international unions are distinguished from national unions only by having members outside the United States, primarily in Canada.

[9] These figures and the data immediately following are from Courtney D. Gifford, ed., DIRECTORY OF U.S. LABOR ORGANIZATIONS, 1982-83 EDITION (Washington, D.C.: The Bureau of National Affairs, Inc., 1982).

bers. Many of the remaining unionists belong to large independent unions such as the Teamsters, the National Education Association, and the Mine Workers. Fifty-seven percent of members belong to 13 unions, each with over a half-million members. There were about 70,000 local unions and 195,000 collective bargaining agreements with employers.

Union Structures and Functions. Although the international union is the major identifiable unit and the international union convention the highest source of policy, the local union is the more basic unit, because of its direct contact with the membership and the workplace. Interposed between the local union and the international, there is often a third body, commonly termed a district, region, or council. These *intermediate bodies* vary in their functions but generally perform a mix of bargaining, education, and administrative functions on behalf of the local unions in their sphere, typically a geographical area.

The local union, sometimes the intermediate body, and the (inter)national are the three formal governmental bodies of most unions. They make policy, administer the internal affairs and most of the bargaining affairs of the membership, and provide forums at which members and leaders gather. But if these were the only units of organization, unions would become isolated from their members and from one another. For most unions there are two additional levels of organization, the workplace and the multi-union federation. (See Table 1.)

At the base of any union is the workplace. In almost every workplace there is an informal network of members who communicate regularly with one another. It is this shared experience and informal organization that forms the backbone of the union. In addition there is a formal workplace organization in most unions, an organization geared to the negotiating and on-the-job representation needs of the employees. In a manufacturing plant this organization consists of what are usually termed *shop stewards* and *chief stewards*, who comprise a shop committee or grievance committee that typically works with the president and other officers of the local union to achieve bargaining goals. In construction and other scattered-site occupations, the workplace structure is less elaborate, usually limited to a single steward on a job site. The steward stays in touch with a union *business agent* who visits job sites to handle difficulties that arise.

The most comprehensive levels of organization are represented by two types of multi-union bodies. The first is the *multinational*

Table 1. The Labor Movement in Brief

Structural Level	Composition	Primary Functions	Examples of Structures and Officers/staff
Workplace[a]	Union members at same location, or with same employer	Informal bargaining Contract administration and grievance representation Communication with members	"The Shop" Chapel (in printing industry) -------- Stewards Chief stewards Chapel chairperson
Local unions	Units of (inter)national union chartered by occupation, employment, and/or territory	All functions Varied mixes depending on structure and bargaining pattern[b]	IBEW Local 481, UAW Local 600 -------- Local president, business agent
Intermediate body	Typically, office and staff assist local unions in a geographic area; may have governing body representing locals	Varies May include: Organizing Collective bargaining Education Political action Communications	Locals within a Region, District, Council -------- Director (often a national vice president) Several staff representatives
(Inter)national union	Headquarters and all affiliated bodies	All functions, varied mixes	Graphic Communications International Union (GCIU) International Association of Machinists (IAM) United Steelworkers of America (USA) -------- International president Vice president(s) General secretary-treasurer
Multi-union, national federation	Made up of all (inter)national unions choosing to affiliate	External relations Political action Legislation Internal disputes resolution PR coordination Other	AFL-CIO -------- President, AFL-CIO Executive Council Staff
Multi-national or cross-national federation	Delegates from affiliated national unions	Discuss and coordinate international labor standards Exchange legislation and bargaining information	International Metal Workers Federation (IMF) International Chemical Workers Federation (ICW) -------- President General Secretary

[a] Linked to local union, more developed in plant than "scattered site" unions.
[b] Where collective bargaining is national, local negotiates only limited issues.

union organization now emerging in the form of international (cross-national) federations of unions with similar occupational and industrial interests. Organizations such as the International Metalworkers Federation are sharing information and coordinating publicity efforts in such areas of mutual concern as bargaining, occupational safety and health, and the treatment of workers and unions by governments.

The second and, to most, the more familiar multi-union body is the national federation: In the United States the AFL-CIO (the "Federation") is often described as "the union of unions" and "the United Nations of the labor movement." The AFL-CIO is the product of a 1955 merger between two rival federations, the craft-oriented AFL (American Federation of Labor), formally dating to 1886,[10] and the industrial union-based CIO (Congress of Industrial Organizations), formed in 1936–37. The Federation has a number of headquarters departments in Washington, D.C., as well as a national field staff, and is governed by a convention which meets every two years. It also has central bodies at state and local levels.

The composition and role of the Federation are among its most misunderstood features. The AFL-CIO is made up entirely of affiliated unions and has no individual members. Its president cannot dictate internal policy or practice to the affiliates, which are always free to disaffiliate, as some in fact have. The power of the president is only as great as the affiliates will grant and is based in large part on success in providing direction not only in those areas where union goals coincide, but in areas where they conflict.

Thus it is between the international and federation levels of structure that the fundamental break in functions occurs. The internationals are responsible for the internal affairs of their affiliates and for the conduct of collective bargaining with employers. The AFL-CIO does not bargain, but is instead a service organization for its affiliates. Its primary services are legislative and political representation, public relations on behalf of the movement, coordination, and the resolution of disputes among affiliates. Secondarily, it assists with education, international labor affairs, and research.

We have described generally the meshing of union functions at each of six levels of organization.

- The workplace
- Local unions

---

[10] The AFL-CIO traces its formation to the 1881 founding of a predecessor, the Federation of Organized Trades and Labor Unions (FOTLU).

- Intermediate bodies
- (Inter)national union
- Multi-union, national federation
- Multinational (cross-national) federation

Later chapters will indicate how union environments and willful decisions lead to many variations within this framework, from the workplace through international union levels.

Union Goals

Since their inception unions have debated what their goals are, or more properly what they should be. Most theories of the labor movement contain statements about both these points, sometimes adding a third—what the goals of the labor movement, given opposing forces, can be. Marx, believing that human needs would require the creation of a socialist society, saw unions as having decided advantages for workers under capitalism, but as insufficient in themselves to sustain the full political conflict. The Webbs, British labor economists of the late 1800s, wrote that while many workers initially join unions to pursue immediate economic goals, the labor movement ultimately would have to pursue political and economic reforms such as the nationalization of industry to reach its goals. Perlman, a scholar of the post-WWI era, theorized that the labor movement developed a job-conscious thrust, seeking only minor reforms in capitalism, in response to unique conditions in the U.S. economy, the society, and its own development.

An early student of unionism, Robert Hoxie,[11] "pointed to four main types of unions, distinguishable by their environments, their goals, and their day-to-day activities.

- *Business unionism* stresses trade goals rather than distant political and social benefit goals.
- *Revolutionary unionism*, typified by the Industrial Workers of the World in the early part of this century, seeks to replace capitalist production with worker-controlled industrial organizations.
- *Uplift unionism* emphasizes enhancement of the moral and social welfare of workers through political activity and co-operative enterprises.

---

[11] Robert Hoxie, TRADE UNIONISM IN THE UNITED STATES (New York: Appleton, 1917).

- *Predatory unionism* is characterized by a leadership whose goals are economic self-aggrandizement, without regard to ethical or legal considerations, at the expense of the workers. Prime examples are the corrupt or racketeer-dominated unions occasionally encountered today.

Union goals, often updated in response to changing conditions, can be discovered in a variety of ways. International union constitutions reveal the general and sometimes more specific goals of the founders. Statements by union leaders demonstrate both ultimate goals and more immediate objectives concerning organizational matters and collective bargaining. Statements of union members often reveal their aspirations and their expectations of their unions—in short, their goals. Perhaps the best indicator of a union's goals, like those of other organizations, is what it actually does.

Avowed or stated goals are seldom sheer puffery. They are clues to a union's origins, and they usually reflect something of its industrial and occupational jurisdiction. From these statements can also be gleaned the goals that different types of unions have in common, despite the translation to each union's situation. (See Exhibit 1, Excerpts From Union Constitutions.)

The most generally stated and shared union goal is a "better way of life" for members and their families. Samuel Gompers, a founder and long-time president of the AFL, was asked what labor wanted and replied directly: "More." Gompers elaborated that he meant more than simply economic improvements; he was also referring to the desire for general advances in the quality of working conditions and society: "More learning . . . more leisure . . . more justice."

"More" remains to this day the simplest expression of union goals. An important element of the goal does consist of economic improvements, more wages and more of what wages can buy. And more of something virtually unknown in Gompers' day—benefits, once called "fringe benefits," but now a substantial part of most workers' compensation.

Wages and benefits reflect the economic goals of American labor. Another element, *working conditions*, includes the more immediate noneconomic objectives. This goal is not always as evident to the public, because conditions of the workplace are not routinely carried to the public eye, cannot be spent in the marketplace, and are not always measurable in common currency understandable to all.

Exhibit 1. Union Goals: Excerpts From Union Constitutions

The objects of the Brotherhood are: To organize workers employed within the trade autonomy of the United Brotherhood, to discourage piece work, to encourage an apprentice system and a higher standard of skill . . . to reduce the hours of daily labor, to secure adequate pay for our work, to establish a weekly pay day, to furnish aid in cases of death or permanent disability . . . and to improve the trade in every way possible.

—United Brotherhood of Carpenters (1979)

Our organization will render its support to and show its solidarity with all workers in their efforts to organize other industries.

—United Cement, Lime and Gypsum Workers (1978)

It is recognized that the problems with which this International Union is accustomed to deal are not limited to organization and collective bargaining alone, but encompass a broad spectrum of economic and social objectives. . . .

—Aluminum Workers International Union (1977)

The objects of this Association are to protect its members from unjust and injurious competition, and secure through unity of action among all workers of the industry . . . claiming, as we do, that labor is capital, and is the only capital that possesses power to reproduce itself, or in other words, to create capital. Labor is the interest underlying all other interests. . . .

—United Association of Plumbers and Pipe Fitters (1976)

Believing that the right of those who toil to enjoy to the full extent the wealth created by their labor is a natural right, and realizing that under the enormous growth of syndicates and other aggregations of capital it is impossible for those who toil to obtain the full reward of their labor other than through united action; and recognizing the fact that those who toil should use their rights of citizenship intelligently, through organizations founded and acting along co-operative, economic and political lines, using the natural resources, means of production and distribution for the benefit of all the people, with the view of restoring the commonwealth to all those performing useful service to society;
Now, therefore; We . . . pledge ourselves to labor unitedly in behalf of the principles herein set forth, to perpetuate our Association on the basis of solidarity and justice, to expound its objects, to labor for the general adoption of its principles, to consistently endeavor to bring about a higher standard of living among the toiling masses.

—International Association of Machinists (1977)

The term working conditions encompasses all features of the workplace that affect the worker: how much of what work is done by whom (workload, job assignment), when it is done (scheduling), and the circumstances in which the work is performed (health, safety, cleanliness). Working conditions narrowly defined exclude a related and important element, *control in the workplace*. Unions strive to limit employer's ability to make arbitrary judgments in job assignment, promotion, lay-off and recall, discipline and discharge, and a host of other decisions important to workers. For example, industrial unions seek a measure of control over workplace decisions through the application of seniority and grievance procedures. Control can extend to worker and union representation on management decision-making bodies, such as boards of directors, and to worker ownership.

What Unions Do

Unions carry on many different activities. Most visible to the average member are those which produce direct benefit—negotiations, grievance handling, community service, and in certain trades, job referral. Another type of activity arises from the internal politics of the union. It consists of elections, meetings, conventions, and similar forums in which members participate in governing the union. But to be effective a union must build and maintain itself as an organization. This entails bringing in members through organizing and keeping the union running smoothly through union administration and effective internal communications. Several distinct union activities are observable.

Organizing. Organizing new members, and sometimes new work opportunities, is the lifeblood of any union. The union is first brought into being through organizing. Once established it faces a task similar to that of keeping a barrel with a hole in it full of water, because the union loses members through retirement, death, plant closings, and technological change. The union that fails to deal with severe membership losses faces decline and stagnation, often becoming incapable of performing its most elemental functions. The next chapter will go into more detail on this subject.

Collective Bargaining. The main activity of unions, collective bargaining, is conventionally divided into two phases: (1) *contract negotiation* to determine the terms of an agreement and (2) *contract administration* to interpret and apply the terms of the negotiated agreement. Overlapping but broader than contract administration is *grievance representation* in which unions seek to redress worker complaints in order to obtain justice in the workplace. Collective bargaining, then, is a system of joint governance in the workplace, a means of rule making, rule interpretation, and rule enforcement.

Jurisdiction Maintenance. Lines of work demarcation are especially important where two or more unions share a job site, as in the building trades or within a manufacturing plant. Two unions may both claim a certain kind of work. Disputes also arise when employers attempt to move jobs out of the unit covered by the negotiated agreement. Policing one's jurisdiction, identifying trouble spots, and resolving conflicts without jeopardizing jobs are all part of holding a jurisdiction. A parallel situation exists when workers from different trades within a plant, all of whom belong to the same union, follow lines of demarcation assigning certain work to certain trades.

Union Administration and Governance. Administration, as used here, refers to the many routine tasks required to maintain the organization: the operation of an office (in some unions), financial record keeping, conducting correspondence, maintaining membership files, and administering benefit programs. Union governance refers to tasks such as electing officers and conducting meetings that are necessary to set policy and maintain democratic control in an organization.

Political and Community Action. The phrase "What is won at the bargaining table can be lost in the Congress" suggests one reason that political action and lobbying are integral functions of unions. In addition to this "bread and butter" incentive, many unionists participate in political and community affairs out of commitment to the "general welfare."

Organization Building. Intertwined throughout the above union activities are several processes that serve to build the effectiveness of the union as an organization. *Education* and *communications* are the vehicles for equipping members and leaders with the information and skills necessary to accomplish union tasks. These two processes also build commitment to the union and its goals and maintain cohesiveness, known in the labor movement as *solidarity*. The external application of these processes is *public relations* designed to present the union favorably to persons outside the organization who may be in a position to enhance or impede its ability to reach its goals.

A second dimension of organization building is *leadership recruitment and development*. To maintain and build its strength, a union, like any organization, must have members able and willing to move into various leadership roles. Ideally these roles form a progression of responsibilities ranging from those requiring minimal time and commitment to those with overall direction of union affairs. Future leaders require experience in different roles and, increasingly, education and training about the complex environment in which a union operates and the elements of organizational leadership.

The thread linking these varied activities is probably best described by the word *representation*. Representing worker interests and concerns in the workplace and the society is, at the core, what unions are all about.

The Many Faces of Union Organizations

Organizations can be classified according to their primary goals and activities. Thus schools are educational institutions; business and trade associations are termed economic organizations; clubs and fraternal societies are social organizations; and parties are political organizations.

These are simplistic designations because all viable organizations display features of more than one type, appealing to members on more than a single interest. Unions, for instance, are conventionally termed economic organizations. But unions also perform social functions for many of their members, the education function described earlier, and the political function necessary in today's society to realize economic and social goals.

We return to the notion of the perspectives from which something is viewed. For one whose concern is strictly wages and benefits the union may be purely an economic organization. But from the perspective of one whose family has been helped through union counseling and referral to a service agency, the union may be viewed as a social service organization. And the politician seeking to build an electoral coalition with union support may view unions as essentially political organizations. The labor movement as a whole displays all of these dimensions.

The conventional description of unions as economic organizations comes perhaps from the early interest of economists in unions as a major subject of labor economics. This designation should not obscure the many differences between unions and other organizations, such as businesses and trade associations, assigned to the same category. For in the long list of economic organizations unions seem unique.

First, unlike businesses, unions are in most respects *voluntary organizations*. They exist at the will of their members and depend largely on the uncompensated activity of members and leaders to accomplish their goals. At the opposite extreme, prisons rely on coercive sanctions to accomplish their missions. Businesses rely primarily on financial compensation to bring people into their organizations and to support ongoing activities.

The second distinction between unions and most other economic organizations is seen in the relationship between the union and the employer. While the employer cannot operate without employees, it can and often prefers to exist without a union representing the employees. The union as we have defined it does not exist without one or more employers, whose presence defines the union's membership and the main motive for joining. As Tannenbaum has noted, "the relationship of dependency and conflict with management is at the core of union action."[12] Union action is typically a response to an employer initiative.

A third distinction can be noted very simply at this point. Unions are built on the democratic model, with control from the bottom up. Businesses, on the other hand, are premised on an authoritarian model, with control exercised from the top down.

Other "faces" of unions as organizations can be summarized briefly:

Mutual Aid, Benefit, or Protective Societies. Many unions began as mutual aid societies, associations of workers with shared economic and occupational interests. Printing trades chapels (workplace organizations) date back to at least 17th century England where, much like the medieval guilds, they enforced the recognized customs of the trade, provided aid for members in need, and "promoted good fellowship."[13] Many mutual aid associations maintain death benefit funds and share trade information. Words such as "fraternal," "benevolent," and "order" suggest the social or fraternal aspects (and sometimes the Masonic origins) of certain contemporary unions.

---

[12] Arnold S. Tannenbaum, "Unions," in Handbook of Organizations, ed. James G. March (Chicago: Rand McNally, 1965), p. 710.

[13] A. J. M. Sykes, "Trade-Union Workshop Organization in the Printing Industry—The Chapel," *Human Relations* 13, no. 1 (February 1960), pp. 50-1.

Service Organizations. Unions, as service organizations, provide aid to their members and others. Many service-oriented members view their union much like an insurance agency to which they pay premiums with the expectation of returns and a guarantee of service should the need arise. In this connotation the union is seen as a separate, nonparticipatory body providing services for a passive membership. In another usage "service" is likened to "representation," as when a higher official "services" a local. In yet another sense, unions often function as service organizations when they aid the broader community.

As a *political interest group*, organized labor does more than represent the immediate interests of its members. It is the primary institutional voice for working people and an important one for consumers. Labor's activity extends from political education to candidate endorsement, electioneering and poll work, and lobbying activity at all levels of government.

Unions are *governments*, or, more accurately, two governments in one. The first is the government of the collective bargaining relationship with the contract as its "constitution." The second is the internal government of the union itself, whose relevant body of law is the union constitution and by-laws. Understanding this *dual government* and its variations among unions is essential to understanding the structure and operation of a union.[14] Particularly at the local level, leadership positions tend to be associated with one government or the other, with some officers having duties in both.

Finally, the labor movement is the major institution representing the *working class* in the United States. One can loosely define working class as all nonelite wage and salaried employees (including the unemployed) who produce goods and services. Or one can define working class by its relationship to authority, as the takers of orders. By any of these definitions, union membership remains greatest in the blue-collar and wage-labor sectors and is still less dense in the white-collar, salaried segment. In either case, the labor movement is the major force representing employees in their capacity *as employees*.

Conclusion

This chapter opened with a look at some of the more common myths and misconceptions about unions. While many of these views

---

[14] Alice H. Cook, "Dual Government in Unions: A Tool for Analysis," *Industrial and Labor Relations Review* 15 (April 1962), pp. 323–49. This concept is elaborated in Chapter 5.

can be traced to sources hostile to labor, some have other origins, such as vantage point or perspective, the "news needs" of the media, and the lack of adequate or accurate coverage in educational institutions. To understand unions, more information and a more complex perspective are needed.

Subsequent discussion began with a definition of the term "union," noting that some "professional associations" are unions in all but name since they do the same things. A preliminary sketch of the organization of the labor movement was followed by a discussion of union goals and the range of union activities. Taken together, these features distinguish trade unions from other organizations but reveal a number of ways in which they display "faces" similar to other institutions in society.

This chapter has of necessity provided a somewhat simplistic picture of American unions. In real life their histories, their forms, and their functions are as diverse as the circumstances and needs which give rise to them. Some, like the printing trades, have long traditions. Others, like the recently formed unit of players in the North American Soccer League, have virtually no traditions yet. Some unions number their members in the dozens, while a few local unions have more members than most internationals. Organizational structures and practices are even more diverse.

Yet there is a logic to all this diversity. One element of that logic—what unions and members share in goals and activities—was touched on in this chapter. Future chapters will add depth and detail to the picture painted thus far.

Review and Discussion Questions

1. Identify three stereotypes of workers or unions that you have encountered in the media or among acquaintances.

2. Can you identify any "perspectives" or other reasons contributing to these stereotypes?

3. What is the potential for, and what are the limits on, labor's ability to project an accurate image of itself?

4. What do you consider to be the three most important tasks of your union or a union with which you are acquainted? How do these tasks relate to each other and to other primary activities?

5. Chapter 1 provides an overview of union organization and action. List what in your opinion are five significant unanswered questions about the structure and operation of American unions (omitting collective bargaining activities). Consider this list a tentative agenda for the rest of the book.

Key Words and Phrases

stereotype

right to work laws

union shop clause

union

company union

employee association

trade union

labor union

craft union

industrial union

(inter)national union

local union

intermediate body

workplace organization

multi-union organization

multi-national union body

shop steward

business agent

AFL-CIO

business unionism

working conditions

organizing

collective bargaining

contract administration

grievance representation

union administration

governance

organization building

representation

voluntary organization

mutual aid (or benefit)

   society

working class

Suggestions for Further Reading

The reader who wants to investigate direct sources should look over international union magazines and newspapers and *AFL-CIO News*, the latter widely available in libraries and union offices.

2

Sources of Union Organization

Don't waste time in mourning. Organize!

Joe Hill, union organizer,
on the eve of his execution, 1915

The roots of union organization are to be found in the decisions of workers to form a union where none exists or to join an established union. These decisions are anchored in the ownership and authority relationship of the workplace, which leaves to employers the right to make unilateral decisions establishing compensation, working conditions, and other terms of employment. Hence, unionization is a collective effort to alter power in the employment relationship.

Viewed from another perspective, organizing new members is both the source and sustenance of union institutions. Without the renewal of membership to offset losses, a union's essential processes, from collective bargaining to leadership development, stagnate and its structures atrophy. The effect of such membership change is most evident at the level of a single local or international union. The effect is also seen, if less sharply, in the labor movement as a whole.

Though membership has not kept pace with the growth of the work force, the absolute number of union members in the United States has risen in most years since the 1930s. In recent decades many new members have joined more or less automatically upon their employment because of union shop clauses—provisions negotiated with employers that require union membership as a condition of continued employment. Other workers, particularly in the government sector and in service industries, have voted to join a union as the culmination of an organizing drive.

This chapter surveys three areas of relevance to unionization: (1) the circumstances in which people become union members and the methods by which unions are organized; (2) the opportunities for choice and the reasons workers vote for and join unions; and (3) the primary union organizational models, past and present. This survey is necessary not only to "learn where we come from," but also to understand the broad terrain in which unions now exist.

Formation

Most frequently a union is formed through an *organizing campaign* leading to an election conducted by the *National Labor Relations Board* (NLRB or "the Board"), established under the 1935 Wagner Act. Though this law applies only to private sector employees, similar provisions increasingly apply to government employees at all levels.

The organizing campaign begins either on the initiative of one or more employees who "shop" for a union or as a result of initial contact by a union organizer. Regardless of who initiates the contact, an inside organizing committee is usually formed and works closely with the organizer. This organizing committee, created within the workplace, is the core of the union campaign. The goal is to convince enough fellow workers of the advantages of union representation to enable the union to gain a clear majority. This majority is necessary if the union needs to win a *representation election* in order to become the certified bargaining agent and thereby get the employer to negotiate an agreement.

The initial measure of success is signed *authorization cards* stating that the employees want the union to act as their representative for collective bargaining purposes. Some cards combine application for membership in the union with the statement of authorization. While a union with signed authorizations from only 30 percent of the employees can petition the NLRB to hold an election, most unions are reluctant to take this step without a substantial majority.

No two organizing campaigns are identical, but several phases can be observed in most. Once on the scene, the organizer gets to know the people and assesses the situation. The assessment incorporates information about the employer and the operation, the sources and patterns of worker problems and dissatisfaction, and the surrounding community. Informal leaders who might become members of the organizing committee are identified.

The effective committee reflects a broad spectrum of worker concerns. The organizer works with the committee to heighten issues and gather authorization cards. Leaflets, house calls, and meetings are used, but the campaign is typically built around worker-to-worker contact during breaks and at places in and around the workplace. At some point the union decides it has sufficient support and signed authorization cards to move for recognition.

The union can present the employer with a demand for *voluntary recognition*, which most employers reject.[1] In most cases the union petitions the NLRB to hold a representation election, although this prolonged process gives the employer time to mobilize a counteroffensive. The union has an option, however, to bypass these lengthy procedures and attempt to force the employer to terms through what is called a *recognition strike*. This tactic has been effective in a few situations where the employer was not prepared or could not afford interruptions and where the workers were well organized and determined. One advantage under these conditions is that the strike denies the employer the chance to mobilize its own campaign and make use of the many stalling tactics that increasingly are used to defeat organizing efforts.

Any description of the official process contains little hint of what the employees and the union are often up against from the employer determined to remain nonunion. If the union pursues the NLRB election route, as happens in the majority of cases, it must surmount a number of organizational, psychological, and procedural hurdles beyond those it has already faced. One hurdle is the task of overcoming employee fear of retaliation, stereotypes of what unions do, misinformation about existing rights and benefits, family pressures, and simple hesitance to change the status quo.

Another hurdle to be faced is the employer's campaign. Brazen or subtle, legal or illegal, the campaign is generally (for large employers) well financed and staffed, often involving one of the growing number of antiunion consulting firms, and usually takes advantage of employees' fears and misconceptions. Activitists may face coercion and discharge (or "payoffs" to "sell out"). Veiled and open threats to job security are commonplace. A frequent employer tactic during organizing campaigns is to issue two paychecks, one

---

[1] The following discussion does not cover the many legal nuances of the recognition process and possible unfair labor practices associated with the conduct of elections and picketing.

for the amount of union dues and the other for the balance of wages, to impress on workers the "cost" of unionization. Given the employer's knowledge that an election delayed is likely to be an election lost for the union, legal maneuvers and stalls are common. Unions typically count on some *slippage*—loss of votes from employees who previously signed authorization cards.

The union may also face a variety of employer objections ranging from unfair labor practice charges filed by the employer with the NLRB to allegations that the Board does not have jurisdiction or the union does not have sufficient authorization cards. These are among the complicating factors in the procedure. Employers often dispute which employees are eligible to vote in the election—a matter of determining the appropriate bargaining unit.

The Bargaining Unit and Union Security

As the drive matures and the employer's countercampaign becomes more visible, the union seeks to hold and build its support and to obtain a favorable bargaining unit, or at least to avoid an unfavorable one. The *bargaining unit* consists of the jobs whose occupants are eligible to vote in the representation election and are eligible for representation by the union should it win. It is the elemental unit of *bargaining structure*, a complex concept[2] defined roughly as the combination of employers and unions negotiating agreements covering one or more bargaining units. It is also an important element in understanding union structure, especially the parts performing bargaining functions.

Where the employer and the union cannot agree on the composition of an appropriate bargaining unit, the NLRB conducts a hearing to resolve the matter before it sets a date for the representation election. Since the union needs the vote of 50 percent, plus one, of the employees voting to win the election, it is of course first necessary to determine who is eligible to vote—who is in the unit.

Within the guidelines established by the Board, several types of bargaining units are possible. Much depends on the type of establishment—factory, office, warehouse, hospital, retail operation, or other job site. Two general types of units are often described: the first is *comprehensive* (also termed *vertical, industrial,* or *wall-to-*

---

[2]The several dimensions of bargaining structure are elaborated in E. Robert Livernash, "New Developments in Bargaining Structure," in Trade Union Government and Collective Bargaining, ed. Joel Seidman (New York: Praeger, 1970).

wall). In a factory it typically includes all production and maintenance employees regardless of their skill or classification. Comprehensive units may even include plant clericals and groups of skilled
tradespeople. Among those excluded are supervisors and confiden-
tial employees (secretaries privy to employer negotiating matters).

The other primary type of unit is the *craft unit* consisting of
employees within a certain range of skills or classifications who are
thought to have a common identity and interests. Such units are
also termed *exclusive* or *horizontal.*[3] Examples are nurses in hospitals, technicians in broadcast stations, and skilled tradespeople in
plants.

Once the unit is defined and eligible employees identified, a
secret ballot election is scheduled. It is normally held at the workplace. If the union wins a majority of the votes (over other competing unions and the "no union" choice) and maintains its majority
after challenged ballots and any objections are processed, it is certified as the *exclusive bargaining agent.* The employer is then required by law to bargain in good faith with the union.

Then begins the effort to negotiate with the employer a contract that will improve the income and conditions of the workers. As
a rule, the stronger the union majority in the representation election, the greater its strength in subsequent negotiations. Much also
depends on the workers, the nature of the industry, and the staying
power of the employer. The process of agreeing to a first contract is
often complicated by employer delay and by unfair labor practice
charges. If the union sees that the employer is determined to avoid
agreement, the union may call a strike to force concessions.

Because it is the exclusive agent, the union is the only organization that represents bargaining unit employees. By law the union
must represent fairly everyone in the unit. In addition, all gains won
by the union must apply to everyone in the unit. Hence the union is
interested in negotiating with the employer what is called a *union
security clause* to ensure that employees represented by the union
contribute to its support. The strongest form of union security now
legal is the *union shop*, a provision requiring all employees to join
the union after a minimum of 30 days (seven in the construction
industry) in order to remain employed. An *agency shop* provision
requires that those who do not join must pay the union a fee approx-
imating dues for the representation and benefits received. If the es-

---

[3] The terminology used here to describe units is similar to that used in Chapter 1, pp. 6–7
to distinguish industrial from craft unions.

tablishment remains an *open shop*, as it must in the right-to-work states, then anyone can benefit from a union contract without contributing to the support of the union that negotiates it. Between union shop and open shop, a number of other variations are possible.

Thus far we have described the creation of a bargaining unit, but have said little about the union's own organizational structure. At some point either before or after the election, the union either charters a new local union to represent the new bargaining unit, or it adds the bargaining unit to an existing local union. If the unit consists of all production and maintenance employees of a large manufacturing plant or a utility, for instance, the international union will often charter a new local which will elect its own officers and negotiate with a single employer. If the unit is a small plant or is a relatively small craft unit, it is sometimes added to an existing local that represents similar types of units in the area. This type of local union is usually termed *amalgamated*.

Much depends also on the tradition and policy of the union and what part of the union has financed the organizing drive. If the campaign is headed by an international or regional staff representative of the Auto Workers or the Steelworkers for a unit of 300 employees, it is likely that a new local will be chartered. But if the same unit is organized by a local of the Service Employees or the Teamsters, it will probably be included in that existing local union, and a business agent from the local will be assigned to coordinate its bargaining activities.

The composition of the bargaining unit and the organization of the local union do not necessarily reveal the actual bargaining structure. In practice many different local unions and even international unions may combine to negotiate contracts with associations representing many different employers, even though the union was initially established on a small unit-by-unit basis.

Variations

Workers in the building trades and in certain other mobile site employment typically enter the union in ways different from those described above. Many are accepted into an apprenticeship program sponsored by a joint union-employer committee, join the union, and are then referred to a variety of jobs. Others work at the trade for some years and join in order to obtain work with a union contractor at union standards. Depending on the union practice and their own skills, they may or may not be granted immediate journeyman standing.

Bargaining units in the construction industry cannot be defined in the manner described earlier, because of the mobile nature of the employment. It is no simple matter to hold an election in an industry where employees may work for several employers within a year and where their primary orientation may be to their craft and their union. Consequently federal labor law recognizes other means of establishing representation in construction. Unions are allowed to sign prehire agreements with contractors, then furnish the contractor with workers through a hiring hall or a referral system. Alternately, the union might attempt to sign up the employees on the job site, then force the contractor to recognize and bargain with it. Failing this, the union might petition the NLRB for an election. The NLRB election is not typical practice, however, in the construction industry or in others where employment is scattered and mobile. More traditional, especially among the highly skilled trades, is the approach of *organizing the work* ("top down" organizing in which the employer is signed to an agreement without the employees first supporting or becoming members of the union), the opposite of *organizing the worker* ("bottom-up" organizing in which the workers join or support the union before the employer is asked to sign a union contract).

The Individual Decision and Its Setting

The fact that most workers join unions because of a union shop agreement does not indicate that, given a choice, they would not join. We do know that originally union shop provisions were negotiated with the support of the vast majority; unions prevail in sectors that were strongly organized at the outset, with some exceptions; and union members report significantly more favorable attitudes toward unions than do nonmembers.[4]

The opportunities to express support for a union in the formative stages range from commitments of active support in the organizing campaign, through voting in the representation election, to such matters as accepting leadership positions.

---

[4] Thomas A. Kochan, "How American Workers View Labor Unions," *Monthly Labor Review* 102, no. 4 (April 1979), pp. 23–31.

Why do workers support the union—or oppose it?

Economic Motives. Employees often vote for a union because they see it as an instrument for obtaining higher wages, benefits, job security, or sometimes even promotions. Others, especially if their employers pass along union-negotiated increases to unorganized employees, may believe a union cannot measurably increase these benefits.

Job Security. Fear of job loss is often a consideration, especially where employers hint at, threaten, or actually carry out plant relocations, shut-downs, dismissals, reductions in benefits, or other reprisals to discourage union support. The concern with job security clearly underlies worker attitudes in an economy where unemployment runs between 5 and 10 percent or more. Some workers view union dues as premiums that will insure them against the possibility they will be out on the street or denied benefits and conditions. As far as union support or the lack of it goes, the desire for security can cut either way.

Control and Fair Treatment. A third set of reasons involves the desire of employees for control over their own fate at the workplace and for fairness in decision making and treatment. The workplace without a union remains the major institution where adult citizens have no guaranteed voice in determining the rules governing their activities.

Social and Psychological Factors. Group pressures and the desire for friendly relations within the workgroup figure significantly in some situations. In the United Kingdom, where most union security provisions are unwritten, workers sometimes refuse to cooperate with workers who do not join the union or who work during a strike, and this kind of treatment operates as a powerful organizational tool.[5] In the United States ostracism of nonmembers and strikebreakers is less pervasive. Other social and psychological factors include the presence or absence of a sense of dignity and pride; a union tradition in the family, the community, or industry; and the presence of class, employee, or craft consciousness. Some people may simply be "joiners" or "loners."

It is the task of the union organizer to identify and heighten awareness of existing problems and turn this dissatisfaction in a positive direction—toward support for the union. On the other side, the typical employer attempts to enhance satisfaction with "what

---

[5] In British parlance the offending worker is "sent to Coventry."

is," or at least to convince employees that things will be no better with a union. Often the employer retains expensive consultants versed in the deployment of legal and psychological tactics to deter the union. The consultant's tool bag includes techniques of manipulating compensation, promotions, working conditions, images, and attitudes to serve the employer's ends.

Recent Research

Determinants of attitudes toward unions and the influences on employee votes in representation elections are not fully understood. Most existing studies suffer from poor design and tell us little about the effects of specific union and employer actions on support for unionism.

The most thorough study, conducted in the early 1970s, covered 33 NLRB elections.[6] It focused on the relatively narrow question of the effects of the campaign itself, especially the later stages, on employee attitudes and election outcomes, necessarily excluding the ways in which attitudes are shaped prior to the campaign.

The study found that 81 percent of the employees voted on the basis of the preferences expressed when they were first interviewed by the researchers and that for the remaining 19 percent there was no evidence to suggest that campaign activities, especially illegal ones, were the determining factors. Rather, the authors argue, "Employees have strong predispositions for or against union representation that are based on their attitudes toward working conditions and unions. Their ultimate votes are largely a function of these predispositions."[7]

This finding challenged Board assumptions of the time that campaign misrepresentations, threats, and promises of benefits influence votes. But the authors admit that a strong possibility of intimidation remains:

> The apparent failure of unlawful campaigning tactics to affect vote does not mean that some employees are not deterred from supporting union representation for fear of the employer's reaction. The data suggest, rather, that most employees susceptible to coercion have been weeded out before the pre-election campaign takes place. They know of many employers' hostility toward unions and of their employ-

---

[6] Julius Getman, Stephen Goldberg, and Jeanne Herman, UNION REPRESENTATION ELECTIONS: LAW AND REALITY (New York: Russell Sage, 1976).

[7] Ibid., p. 146.

er's economic power over them. Rather than risk the exercise of that
power, they decide, as soon as they learn of the union organizing campaign, to have nothing to do with the union.[8]

It is also possible that undecided voters first report themselves as
"no union" for self-protection and are subsequently intimidated to
actually vote to agree with their report. At any rate, the resulting
suggestion that the NLRB should not regulate campaign practices,
since campaigns do not change votes, would seem to deny opportunities to remove fears during the campaign.

The national survey of union and nonunion employees suggests
somewhat different influences.[9] The data indicate that fully one-
third of eligible nonunion employees now desire union representation in their workplaces. The author suggests that workers approach the decision to unionize more on their estimate of what the
union will do for them than on their general images of organized
labor. The decision to support a union is based on a *last resort calculus*, with workers turning to a union when they are greatly dissatisfied with their job or conditions, desire more influence in establishing their conditions, and believe that other forms of influence do
not work.

This survey finds a reservoir of union support among all demo-
graphic groups, including Southerners and white-collar workers. Of
nonunion workers, two-thirds of nonwhites, 39 percent of blue-
collar (compared to 28 percent of white-collar), 40 percent of
women, and 35 percent of workers in the South indicated they
would vote for union representation if an election were held at their
place of work.[10]

The election study and the national survey invite comparison.
They differ on the importance of the general image of unions in determining worker choices, with the national survey suggesting an
insignificant role.

The fact that unions currently win a substantial number of the
representation elections conducted by the Board (46 percent in
1982) would suggest either that organizers are picking the excep-
tional cases where a preformed majority already exists or that organizing campaigns do have some effect in changing attitudes, or at
least in converting latent support for unionism (beyond the one-

---

[8] Ibid., p. 129.

[9] Kochan, "How American Workers View Labor Unions," see note 4.

[10] Even stronger union support was found in a 1982 *Washington Post*/ABC News poll
aired February 5, 1982. A national survey of nonunion members showed 51 percent stating
that if "working on a job where they could join a labor union," they would do so.

third overt support found in the national survey) into active support at the ballot box.

Union Incentives to Organize

Union growth depends not only on the complex influences on workers' willingness to join unions but also on the organizing efforts of unions themselves. Organizing is an increasingly expensive process, and the prospects of union victory are less favorable than they were just a generation ago. Nevertheless, few unions will crassly calculate future dues from a prospective unit as the sole consideration for undertaking a campaign. Other incentives come into play. There may be idealistic commitments to extend the benefits of unionism to the unorganized or desires to build the organization for the sake of size and strength or to maintain its stability.

The structural imperative for unions is that unorganized workers and firms within an area or an industry undercut the bargaining effectiveness of those who are unionized. When labor costs become an important factor in competition among employers in a market or industry, organized workers can bargain only so many improvements before the employer begins to resist union demands that make it less competitive with the nonunion segment. The union must, therefore, organize those who are in competition, particularly when their compensation is lower, in order to protect and advance the interests of those it currently represents. In such cases organizing new workers is not just a matter of survival; it is a benefit to those newly organized, as well as to those already organized.

This explains the interrelationship between bargaining and organizing. Where a union cannot organize, it cannot bargain to best advantage on behalf of those it represents. And where a union cannot bargain effectively, it cannot organize. Not only does it have little to show prospective members, but it may well be bogged down in its bargaining problems.

The next section traces the historical sources of today's union structures, including the outlines of a current imbalance that has major implications for union organizing and bargaining.

Union Forms, Past and Present

While it is sometimes believed that the first unions were organized by the most downtrodden of workers, this is clearly not the case. Early efforts at self-organization occurred even before the American Revolution among strategically located craftsmen who generally enjoyed better conditions than the indentured servants and slaves who performed much of the manual labor in the colonies. These artisans were cordwainers (shoemakers), tailors, coopers (barrel makers), printers, carpenters, and other tradespeople who often used their own tools, worked in close association with their employers, and produced hand-crafted goods for a local market area. While the "free Negro" chimney sweepers of Charleston, South Carolina organized and demanded more pay as early as 1763, skilled workers were usually the first to organize, in part because they were best able to back up their economic demands by withholding their labor.

When specific grievances arose, such as a cut in wages, the artisans would organize and present demands to their employers. There were no back-and-forth negotiations or compromises as we know them today. If the workers won they gained their full demands. If they lost they accepted no less than the full wage cut. In either event their formal association usually then lapsed into inactivity, perhaps to be revived later in response to a new issue. This pattern continued well into the 1800s. Throughout this period workers faced a hostile environment, as reflected for instance in court rulings that any collective attempt to improve wages or conditions was an illegal conspiracy or combination.

In the 1820s and 1830s unions in several Eastern cities began to form *city centrals*, citywide bodies combining different trades, anticipating today's central labor bodies. The city centrals backed labor parties which pressed such issues as free public education, the ten-hour day, passage of mechanics' lien laws, opposition to imprisonment arising from debt, and bans on the exploitation of child labor.

Midway in the 19th century, several aspects of rising industrial capitalism led to a broader scale of unionism. These aspects were the growth of transportation and communications facilities, as well as technological changes that made possible broader markets; the separation of the worker from ownership of the means of production; and the concentration of production in factories whose lower-priced products undercut individually crafted items in the market. Paralleling these changes was the development of extractive and heavy industries necessary to produce the industrial equipment required for factory production.

One often hears that labor movements arise largely as a result of the changes associated with industrialization. If we distinguish between a *labor movement* as a coherent national network and its component unions, which may emerge from more specific circumstances, this generalization is relatively accurate. We have noted the temporary local organizations dating to the mid-1700s and the citywide movements that emerged in the 1820s. But it was not until midcentury that truly national unions and federations with national ambitions were formed.

The 1850s saw the formation of the first lasting national unions among printers (International Typographical Union, 1852) and iron molders (now the International Molders and Allied Workers, formed in 1859). From the Civil War to the end of the 19th century, the major building trades and several other crafts organized themselves nationally. National unions of miners, steelmakers, and railroad workers also emerged.

What forms did these early unions take? One was the *Knights of Labor* (the model for Hoxie's uplift unionism[11]), which grew from a secret society in the early 1870s to a mass organization of workers, and sometimes shopkeepers, farmers, and others considered "real producers," by the end of the decade. The organization consisted of a weak national body and a geographical unit, the *district assembly*, that combined local assemblies organized along occupational, industrial, or mixed lines. Thus a district assembly of a multicounty area might contain 30 local assemblies, some consisting of individual building trades, others of shopkeepers, and yet others of all the union employees of a single establishment. The geographical units of the city central and the district assembly made particular sense in the years before regular contact over long distances was possible. The Knights' structure was well suited to those industries and crafts that could conduct their affairs locally, i.e., in most cases local market industries.

The Knights' lack of a viable national structure, the vague reformist goals espoused by its leaders, and the absence of a coherent economic and organizational program led to its rapid demise. Sustained for a time by the enthusiasm of workers, local assemblies of the Knights often overlapped in membership with locals of existing national trade unions. During the late 1880s skilled workers in par-

---

[11] See Chapter 1, p. 11.

ticular began leaving the Knights for the more coherent structure and philosophy of the AFL.

The AFL leadership set the structure and philosophy for the craft unionism it so vigorously espoused. The principal elements of its approach were *exclusive jurisdiction* and *trade autonomy*. The Federation recognized the exclusive jurisdiction of each affiliated national union to organize and represent those in a particular type of work. In theory this jurisdiction was distinct from that of any other union. The Carpenters, for instance, were granted jurisdiction over all work involving wood construction and the Electrical Workers (IBEW) jurisdiction over all electrical installation and maintenance. Within the decentralized AFL structure each union retained the autonomy to conduct the affairs of its trade, free from interference by the Federation or any of its affiliates.

The economic philosophy of the AFL accepted the basic tenets of capitalism, demanding only that workers receive a "just" share of their produce while leaving ample profit for the capitalist. Often implicit was the notion of job ownership—that the property, the end product, and often the tools belonged to the employer, but the job itself was the property of the worker and could be bought, sold, and virtually willed through inheritance. The AFL and its affiliates focused on protecting these "rights" and pursuing goals of better working conditions and economic benefits through collective bargaining.

Under the leadership of *Samuel Gompers*, the Federation pursued nonpartisan interest-group politics, expressed in the phrase "Reward your friends and punish your enemies." Related to this approach was the philosophy of *voluntarism* which held that, while labor had a stake in certain legislation and other government action, collective bargaining and not government intervention was the proper means for pursuing better wages, benefits, and conditions.

In time the AFL became known as much for its limitations as for its stability in surviving the economic fluctuations and other problems to which its predecessors had fallen prey. The first of these weaknesses was that changing technology created almost constant stress on the original jurisdiction of its affiliates. Something once made of wood, for example, might suddenly be replaced by metal, with another union claiming jurisdiction. The second limitation (though AFL leaders thought it was an advantage) was the persistent opposition of many of its unions to industrial unionism, or organizing unskilled and semi-skilled workers along industry or employer lines. Most AFL affiliates organized only the skilled workers falling within their jurisdiction in a single plant, rejecting the remaining unskilled employers.

The craft union model first came under attack from the radical *Industrial Workers of the World* (the IWW or "Wobblies"), which scored noteworthy but impermanent successes in the decade prior to World War I. The core of the IWW was a network of traveling organizers and strike leaders who mobilized thousands of workers in mines, mills, and logging camps for major strikes, but left no viable organization behind them. The IWW espoused *one big union* and officially rejected signing agreements with employers. While it lacked the organizational stability to survive in the face of often violent opposition from employers and government, it planted the seeds of industrial unionism among thousands of workers.

With the depression of the 1930s, these and other seeds bore fruit in the form of viable industrial union organizations, eventually formed as the *Congress of Industrial Organizations* (or simply, CIO) to rival the AFL craft model. Spearheaded by *John L. Lewis* of the Mine Workers and by a number of other AFL leaders who broke with their peers, the CIO successfully organized in the mass-production auto, steel, rubber, electrical manufacturing, flat glass, and textile industries. Rather than "skimming" the skilled trades-people from a plant, the CIO unions combined them in the same local unions with the less-skilled workers.

The passage of the Wagner Act in 1935, noted earlier in this chapter in connection with union representation elections, had multiple impacts on labor. By institutionalizing a voice for workers, it gave a boost to organizing efforts. But it also brought unions and labor-management relations under greater government scrutiny and regulation, a development which many now consider a mixed blessing. The provisions for representation elections among workers helped to transform the organizational premises of the labor movement, an impact described in Chapter 4.

Each of the rival federations was under some pressure to make concessions to the model of the other. Some AFL affiliates chartered industrial local unions. The Carpenters, the Electrical Workers (IBEW), and the Machinists are examples. Contending with craft-industrial splits in some of their industrial plants, CIO unions in turn took steps to create special interest units such as skilled trades councils within their organizations.

Rival charters were issued by each federation to cover identical industries, with sometimes bitter organizational campaigns resulting. The AFL, meanwhile, never had to worry about competition from other unions in industries, such as on-site construction, where craft organization was traditional and in many ways well-suited to the environment. The CIO organized most of the mass-production industries.

The current era in unionism began with the 1955 merger of the two rivals into the AFL-CIO. In 1957 the Teamsters were expelled, and in 1968 the Auto Workers left the Federation, returning in 1981.

The major development of the 1960s was the growth of unionism among government employees—federal, state, and local—a phenomenon about which more will be said. Many of these workers had previously belonged to employee associations that did not function as unions.

The structural forms to note in this historical development are the city central, the national union, the Knights' multi-trade and -industry geographical assembly, craft and industrial unions, the "one big union" concept, and the federation of the AFL-CIO.

Each of these forms has had its trial period, with some forms now virtually extinct and others surviving to the present. Conditions greatly different from those of the trial periods may argue for reconsideration of forms discarded earlier, along with newer, untested organizational structures, as the labor movement tries to keep abreast of its needs.

Another pattern to note is that of change and adaptation between corporate structure and union structure.[12] Midway through the 19th century the basic form of union jurisdiction and hence organization followed craft or occupational lines. Labor markets, not product markets, shaped the boundaries between unions. This union alignment accorded quite well with the employer structures and technologies of the time, based as they were on small scale, hand-crafted production for local or regional product markets. Under these conditions, as long as a union organized the workers of a craft and avoided their replacement by substitutes, it could maintain a strong bargaining position.

Transportation improvements, the development of mass-production technology, and the related emergency of national product markets, though occurring at different rates in different industries, upset what employer-union structural balance existed. Except

---

[12] These developments are detailed in Kenneth O. Alexander, "Union Structure and Bargaining Structure," *Labor Law Journal* 24, no. 3 (March 1973, pp. 164–72.

in those industries such as construction and printing whose markets remained local or regional, craft union jurisdictional lines became increasingly irrelevant. New production techniques required large numbers of relatively unskilled workers. Craft distinctions increasingly blurred. A few emerging corporate giants reorganized production in their respective industries and, after bitter struggles, were often able to eliminate the control that craft workers had earlier exercised over production. Unions, attempting to organize the new industrial workers into the old craft forms, continued to fall short. Corporate structure had surpassed the ability of the current union forms to match up.

Not until the emergence of the CIO in the 1930s did unions redress this imbalance by aligning union structure with the product market and industry, as opposed to the occupation or craft. The distinction is evident in a comparison of AFL and CIO union names. Most of the former (Painters, Molders, Carpenters for example) identify a craft or an occupation; the CIO unions (such as Auto Workers, Steelworkers, Glass Workers) emphasize the product and the common name of the industry. With the growth of the CIO, the structure of unions once again, though only temporarily, encompassed the industry.

A new imbalance has since resulted from the emergence of the conglomerate form of organization and from the expansion of multinational corporations, an old form with new implications. In a conglomerate, corporate lines cross industry lines, outmoding and fragmenting the efforts of single-industry unions.

Conclusion

This chapter has examined union formation from several perspectives: as a process by which workers make group decisions; as a result of worker and union decisions; and as a matter of organizational design, that is, choosing the forms of organization.

Since 1935 the organizing process is typically, though not invariably, one of workers cooperating with union organizers to seek recognition using NLRB procedures. Researchers seek to explain the results in sometimes conflicting ways. The results reflect, in part, the motives of workers for desiring unions and the motives of unions for organizing workers. They are conditioned by opportunities and by the interplay of forces, including the employer effort. Often it is the strategically located workers with a long-term stake in their jobs who, under certain conditions, are the first to organize and remain organized. Others, though no less desirous of unionization, follow.

Unions, for their part, often organize to enhance the power of current members as well as to extend the benefits of organization to new groups.

Looking at the structural forms in which workers combine is often as important as examining how and why they are first organized. A review of history reveals a number of forms, some long-discarded. It also shows the need for unions to stay abreast of changing employer formations. The current lag results from an inability to match up with multinational and conglomerate forms of corporate structure.

Having traced the methods, motives, and structural circumstances shaping union organization, we turn in the next chapter to an assessment of the current state of organization. We will examine the extent of unionization and look at the characteristics of current members and the implications for union organizing efforts.

Key Words and Phrases

organizing campaign
representation election
authorization cards
National Labor Relations Board
voluntary recognition
recognition strike
bargaining unit
bargaining structure
comprehensive unit
wall-to-wall unit
craft unit
horizontal unit
exclusive bargaining agent
union security
union shop
agency shop
open shop
amalgamated local union

"organizing the work"
"last resort calculus"
city centrals
labor movement
Knights of Labor
district assembly
American Federation of
  Labor (AFL)
exclusive jurisdiction
trade autonomy
Samuel Gompers
voluntarism
Industrial Workers of the
  World (IWW)
"one big union"
Congress of Industrial
  Organizations (CIO)
John L. Lewis

Review and Discussion Questions

1. Speculate on the explanations for the success or failure of a union organizing campaign in a specific situation. Aside from the factors discussed in the reading, what do you think might be the effects of bargaining unit size, employer size and profitability, and community history and structure?

2. Why should well-established unions organize new members in old or new areas of employment? What effects will organizing successes have on current members and on workers as a whole?

3. Of the models of union structure discarded in the past, which, if any, do you think most merit a new "trial?"

4. Why would contemporary employers be more prone than those of four decades ago to engage expensive consultants to keep workers from unionizing or to "bust" established unions?

5. This chapter argues that unions organize in large part to protect their bargaining power on behalf of their current members. How does this logic apply, if at all, in the case of diversified general unions such as the Teamsters or the Service Employees? What might be their reasons?

Suggestions for Further Reading

Two excellent books on union organizing are: *Union Organizing and Staying Organized*, by Kenneth Gagala, and *Organizing and the Law*, 3rd edition, by Schlossberg and Scott.

There are numerous comprehensive labor histories, including *A History of American Labor*, by Joseph Rayback; *Labor in the U.S.A.: A History*; and the illustrated Department of Labor work, *The American Worker*, edited by Richard B. Morris. A more episodic treatment is *Labor's Untold Story*, by Boyer and Morais.

The history and structure of American unions can be seen through the rich variety of buttons and similar items. For a brief introduction see John W. Bennett's article, "Using Union Memorabilia as a Teaching Aid," in *Labor Studies Journal* (Fall 1978).

Complete bibliographical information for the above titles can be found in the Bibliography.

3

Union Membership and the Work Force

It is, of course, the supervised who produce the goods and do the work of the world, not the supervisors who stand and watch, and the proliferation of watchers seems to me an ominous and unhealthy development.

Lane Kirkland
AFL-CIO President, 1980

Within two centuries the labor movement evolved from a few loose and temporary associations of skilled craftsmen in the colonies into a durable network of national and local organizations comprising some 20 million people, with influence affecting millions more.

Membership growth over this period was by no means constant. Indeed, in its first century the labor movement approached extinction at several points. By 1900 total membership was at less than a million, but several unions had established themselves on a lasting basis. From each crisis the labor movement seemed to rebound to some new plateau.

The major spurt of growth which brought the movement near its present proportions occurred from the mid-1930s to the mid-1950s when membership grew from slightly over two million to almost 17 million. (See Figure 1.) Despite fluctuations, there has since been an underlying stability and modest growth in *absolute* membership, but a decline of membership in proportion to the expanding work force.

The work force has not only grown but its composition has also changed from predominantly blue-collar, manufacturing workers to predominantly white-collar and service workers. Only in the government sector has union organization kept pace with these devel-

40

Figure 1.   Membership of National Unions, 1930–82¹

Millions of members

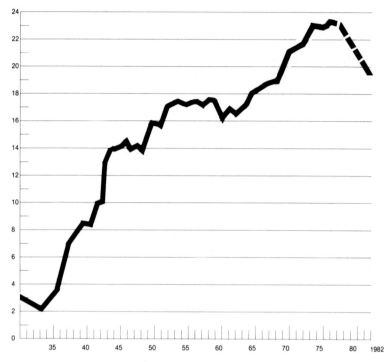

¹Excludes Canadian membership but includes members in other areas outside the United States. Members of AFL-CIO directly affiliated local unions are also included. Members of single-firm and local unaffiliated unions are excluded. For the years 1948–52, midpoints of membership estimates, which were expressed as ranges, were used.

Source: Adapted from Bureau of Labor Statistics, DIRECTORY OF NATIONAL UNIONS AND EMPLOYEE ASSOCIATIONS, 1979, Bulletin 2079 (Washington, D.C.: Government Printing Office, 1980), p. 58, and updated from data in Courtney D. Gifford, DIRECTORY OF U.S. LABOR ORGANIZATIONS, 1984–85 EDITION (Washington, D.C.: The Bureau of National Affairs, Inc., 1984), p. 2. Relevant data from the Gifford book are contained in Table 3, page 47 of this book. [The solid rule in the above figure represents BLS data; the broken rule represents data from the Gifford book.—Ed.]

opments. While changes in the composition of the work force clearly signal the potential for growth, union membership patterns have not followed these employment patterns.

Membership surges are typically concentrated in specific sectors and periods, with considerable lag between the appearance of a major group in the work force and its unionization. At the outset of the 1980s, union organization had not caught up with the shift to white-collar and service employment that had occurred over the previous three decades.

Prophets of Doom

Membership during the 1970s appeared to be on another plateau. A leveling off of membership was coupled with a continued decline in the union percentage of the growing work force. Within this overall pattern short-term fluctuations occurred, often in response to the state of the economy. One such fluctuation, a drop of 700,000 members attributable largely to the 1974–75 recession, gave rise to a chorus prophesying doom for the movement.

The source of this chorus? It may have been wishful thinking by those never friendly to labor. The tone of the chorus was embodied in magazine features with titles such as: "The Big Squeeze on Labor Unions"; "Labor's Creaking House"; "Labor on the Defensive"; and even "The Last Days of the Labor Movement".[1] This recession loss and the steady, if not precipitous, decline in the percentage of union membership were both evident. Usually omitted from the sensationalist coverage, however, was the mention that similar declines had occurred in the past only to be recouped during economic upswings and occasionally by union breakthroughs into new sectors.

A few more sanguine observers went against the media trend. *Business Week*, in an article titled "Embattled Unions Strike Back at Management,"[2] cautioned that history had made fools of past experts who forecast the disappearance of the labor movement. *U.S. News and World Report* in "While Everyone Was Writing the Unions Off"[3] pointed out that AFL-CIO affiliates alone gained more than 382,000 new members in the first half of 1978, recouping more than half the total decline of 700,000 reported earlier.

---

[1] A. H. Raskin, "The Big Squeeze on Labor Unions," *Atlantic Monthly* 242, no. 4 (October 1978), pp. 41–8; "Labor's Creaking House," *Newsweek* (December 12, 1977), pp. 83–90; "Labor on the Defensive," *Forbes* 121, no. 4 (February 1978), pp. 44–8; and Nicholas von Hoffman, "The Last Days of the Labor Movement," *Harpers* 257, no. 1543 (December 1978), pp. 22–8.

[2] "Embattled Unions Strike Back at Management," *Business Week*, no. 2563 (December 4, 1978), pp. 54–69.

[3] "While Everyone Was Writing the Unions Off," *U.S. News and World Report* 85, no. 12 (September 1978), pp. 97–9.

Playing With Percentages

Because statistics on union membership are frequently used as weapons, it is important to understand their computation. Several figures expressing membership as a percentage of the work force are used as rough measures of current and potential unionization. Each yields a different result, but all have this in common: their computation takes the form of a simple fraction expressed as a percentage. The different results depend on the selection of numerators (membership) and denominators (work force). Any reduction in the numerator, the top figure, or increase in the denominator results in a smaller percentage.

The smallest numerator is membership in unions, narrowly construed to exclude union-like associations. The largest numerator is the figure for membership in unions and associations combined.[4] The denominator can be selected from several measures of employment. The largest is *total labor force*, which includes not only executives and supervisors, but the unemployed, members of the armed forces, self-employed persons, and others not usually considered prospective unionists. A smaller figure is *employment in nonagricultural establishments*, which excludes military and agricultural employment but continues to include executives and supervisors. The smallest, but perhaps the most appropriate figure for depicting potential membership, is that of *nonsupervisory, nonagricultural employees*. An estimate developed by the AFL-CIO Research Department placed 1978 employment in this category at slightly over 70 million.[5]

Three examples using 1978 data illustrate how different selections yield quite different results that can be used to support different characterizations of union strength. (See Exhibit 2.)

While none of the figures or conclusions in the three examples is necessarily misleading, each presents a different image. As noted, the last example probably best reflects actual potential, because it excludes the rising proportion of supervisory and other nonproduction employees found in the contemporary U.S. economy. But, as

---

[4] Published figures sometimes include Canadian members and people who are represented by, but are not members of, unions. These categories are excluded here unless otherwise noted.

[5] AFL-CIO, Department of Research, Union Membership and Employment, 1959–1979 (Washington, D.C.: AFL-CIO, 1980).

Exhibit 2.   Calculating Union Membership: Three Versions

Low Percentage Membership

$$\frac{\text{Membership in unions (20.2 million)}}{\text{Total labor force (102.5 million)}} = 19.7\%$$

Conclusion: Fewer than one of five U.S. workers belongs to a union.

Higher Percentage Membership

$$\frac{\text{Union \textit{and} Association membership (22.9 million)}}{\text{Nonagricultural employment (86.7 million)}} = 26.4\%$$

Conclusion: More than one of every four workers belongs to a union.

Highest Percentage Membership

$$\frac{\text{Union \textit{and} Association membership (22.9 million)}}{\text{Nonsupervisory, nonagricultural employment (70.2 million)}} = 32.6\%$$

Conclusion: About one of every three eligible workers is a union member.

Source: Membership figures are Bureau of Labor Statistics data from DIRECTORY OF NATIONAL UNIONS AND EMPLOYEE ASSOCIATIONS, 1979, p. 59. Total labor force and non-agricultural employment figures are found in MONTHLY LABOR REVIEW 104, no. 5 (May 1981), pp. 71, 77; the nonsupervisory, nonagricultural employment figures are an estimate by the AFL-CIO Department of Research in UNION MEMBERSHIP AND EMPLOYMENT, 1959-1979.

---

long as data are gathered and reported in the same way from year to year, any of the above computations can be used to reflect certain trends or changes. One danger, however, is to make too much of a slight change or to project permanent catastrophes from temporary dips. For this is apparently what happened with the recession-caused membership dip of the mid-70s.

The fact remains that, by any of these measures, membership has been undergoing a slow decline in percentage over the past two decades, capped by a precipitous drop in key industries in the early 1980s. (See Figure 2 and Table 2 for figures up to the year 1980.)

The gravity of the recent membership decline is illustrated by data using yet another employment measure—the civilian labor force. This measure reflects the total labor force, less the resident armed forces. Over the two years 1981–82 union membership dropped by 2.6 million while the civilian labor force expanded by

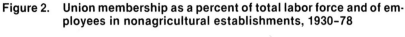

Figure 2. Union membership as a percent of total labor force and of employees in nonagricultural establishments, 1930–78

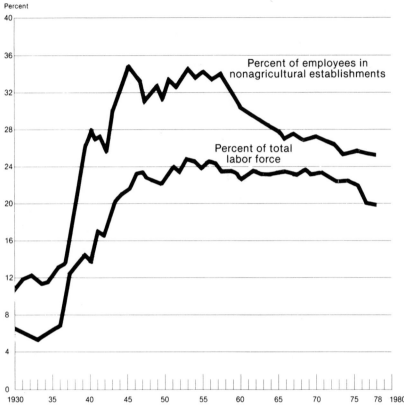

Source: Adapted from Bureau of Labor Statistics, Directory of National Unions and Employee Associations, 1979, Bulletin 2079 (Washington, D.C.: Government Printing Office, 1980), p. 60.

over three million. Table 3 shows a drop in union membership from 20.9 percent of the civilian work force in 1980 to 17.9 in 1982. Both absolute and percentage membership losses were the greatest of any two year period in the modern era.

The response of some traditionally one-industry unions to such membership losses is to seek to diversify into areas of employment growth or to merge with other unions. Both responses are elaborated further in this and subsequent chapters.

Table 2.   U.S. Labor Organization Membership, 1958–80 (in thousands)[a]

Year	Member-ship excluding Canada	Total labor force		Employees in nonagricultural establishments	
		Number	Percent members	Number	Percent members
Unions:					
1958	17,029	70,275	24.2	51,324	33.2
1959	17,117	70,921	24.1	53,268	32.1
1960	17,049	72,142	23.6	54,189	31.5
1961	16,303	73,031	22.3	53,999	30.2
1962	16,586	73,442	22.6	55,549	29.9
1963	16,524	74,571	22.2	56,653	29.2
1964	16,841	75,830	22.2	58,283	28.9
1965	17,299	77,178	22.4	60,765	28.5
1966	17,940	78,893	22.7	63,901	28.1
1967	18,367	80,793	22.7	65,803	27.9
Unions and associations:					
1968	20,721	82,272	25.2	67,897	30.5
1969	20,776	84,240	24.7	70,384	29.5
1970	21,248	85,903	24.7	70,880	30.0
1971	21,327	86,929	24.5	71,214	29.9
1972	21,657	88,991	24.3	73,675	29.4
1973	22,276	91,040	24.5	76,790	29.0
1974	22,809	93,240	24.5	78,265	29.1
1975	22,361	94,793	23.6	77,364	28.9
1976	22,662	96,917	23.4	80,048	28.3
1977	22,456	99,534	22.6	82,423	27.2
1978	r 22,757	102,537	r 22.2	86,697	r 26.2
1979	r 22,579	104,996	r 21.5	89,886	r 25.1
1980	r 22,366	106,821	r 20.9	90,657	r 24.7

[a]Totals include members of locals directly affiliated with the AFL-CIO, but exclude Canadian members and members of single-firm labor organizations.

r = revised.

Sources: Adapted from U.S. Department of Labor announcement, September 1981 (Bureau of Labor Statistics Union Survey) and DIRECTORY OF NATIONAL UNIONS AND EMPLOYEE ASSOCIATIONS, 1979. Bulletin 2079 (Washington, D.C.: Government Printing Office, 1980).

Explaining Union Growth

No single explanation accounts for or predicts membership fluctuations. A large number of studies point to several factors that seem to influence union growth.

One such influence is the business cycle—the mid-1970s membership dip just discussed is an example. Contrary to the often-expressed belief that "the worse, the better" (for unions and other progressive movements), labor seldom advances in times of reces-

Table 3.   U.S. Labor Organization Membership, 1970–82
(in thousands)[a]

| Year | Membership | Civilian labor force[b] | |
		Number	Percent members
1970	21,248	82,771	25.7
1971	21,327	84,382	25.3
1972	21,657	87,034	24.9
1973	22,276	89,429	24.9
1974	22,809	91,949	24.8
1975	22,361	93,775	23.8
1976	22,662	96,158	23.6
1977	22,456	99,009	22.7
1978	22,757	102,251	22.3
1979	22,579	104,962	21.5
1980	22,366	106,940	20.9
1981[c]	—	—	—
1982	19,763	110,204	17.9

[a] Includes active members reported by unions, but excludes Canadian members.
[b] Revised from "Total Labor Force" classification in Table 2 of the DIRECTORY OF U.S. LABOR ORGANIZATIONS, 1982–83 EDITION.
[c] Data not available.
Source: Courtney D. Gifford, DIRECTORY OF U.S. LABOR ORGANIZATIONS, 1984–85 EDITION (Washington, D.C.: The Bureau of National Affairs, Inc.,1984).

sion. (The Depression of the 1930s is an exception, and it should be noted that the advances of the period coincided with the spread of industrial unionism, the passage of the Wagner Act, and a breakthrough into a new sector, unskilled factory work.) When layoffs occur and jobs are scarce, unions have a difficult time bargaining and organizing new members. As the economy moves out of the recession, unions gain not only from increases in established units but from organizing victories that come more easily with more employment.

Another influence is the ability of unions to adapt to changed circumstances. Part of a percentage decline in the 1920s, for example, can be attributed to the failure to organize the increasing number of mass-production workers, and in the 1960s and 1970s, to slow progress in organizing the growing segment of service and white-collar workers.

Other influences on membership growth are even less predictable—the sudden breakthrough into a new sector after years of little success; the onset of war, which in the past has led to higher employment levels and to governmental desire to reduce industrial conflict, both contributing to union growth; or the passage of enabling legislation. The passage of new state legislation is often associated with breakthroughs among state and local government employees. It heightens expectations and often brings national-level organizing resources to the state.

The future growth of the labor movement is by no means assured. The next section examines in greater detail the important changes in the make-up of the labor force to which unions have not yet adjusted.

Patterns in Employment

If there exists such a phenomenon, the United States seems to be moving toward a "post-industrial" economy. Indicators of this transformation are the shift in employment from the production of goods to the dispensing of services and an accompanying growth in the percentage of women and office workers.

In 1958 service employment (excluding transportation and utilities) in the profit sector of the economy for the first time exceeded employment in goods production (mining, construction, and manufacturing). By 1982, over 65 million people worked in the service sector and only 24 million in goods production. Over the 24-year span this amounted to 25 million new jobs in wholesale and retail trade, finance, and other services, and a gain of only four million in goods production.

While the shift from goods to services depicted by these data may be startling, the goods-producing sector remains significant, perhaps out of proportion to its share of employment. This sector produces goods sold in domestic and international markets, and developments in mining, construction, and manufacturing are likely to have greater "ripple effects" throughout the economy than developments in the service sector. It is also the most unionized sector, and patterns negotiated in the goods sector influence other parts of the economy.

The causes of the shift from goods to services are many.[6] The fitful growth of manufacturing employment (blue-collar employment tends to rise disproportionately when the economy is expanding) masks at least two trends. One is the decline of employment

---

[6] The displacement of manufacturing labor into the service sector where labor processes are less susceptible to technological changes, the rise of clerical-intensive industries, and other features of "mature" economies causing this transformation of the work force are discussed at length in chapters 11–12 of Harry Braverman, LABOR AND MONOPOLY CAPITAL (New York: Monthly Review Press, 1974).

where jobs shift overseas, often to be performed by cheap labor but sometimes by comparably paid union labor. Products such as clothing, leather and electrical goods, and automobiles are increasingly manufactured abroad. Another development is the stemming of employment growth by increased productivity. Assuming no compensating employment increases, when worker output increases there is either no need to employ more workers to produce more, or the same production can be maintained with fewer workers.

More goods—whatever their source—are being sold on the market, and there is an attendant increase in the need for workers to distribute, finance, sell, and service these products.

Union Membership

Having looked at employment trends in the U.S. economy, an examination of the distribution and characteristics of union members is in order. What sectors of the economy are best organized and which least organized? Which regions and states are best organized and what changes are occurring? What are the characteristics of union members by occupation, sex, and race? To what size unions do most members belong? With these questions answered, some implications for union organizing efforts and for union structure become apparent.

Regional Distribution of Membership. New York and California have the most members in absolute terms, but when states are ranked by the highest percentage of workers organized, Michigan replaces California in the second position. (See Table 4.)

Table 4. Distribution of Union Membership by State and as a Proportion of Employees in Nonagricultural Employment, 1980

(Membership in thousands)

State	Membership[1]		Total union membership[4] as a percent of employees in nonagricultural employment	
	1980	1980 rank	1980	1980 rank
All States	22,811	—	25.2	—
Alabama[2]	296	21	21.8	27
Alaska	57	46	33.7	6
Arizona[2]	160	30	16.0	39
Arkansas[2]	119	33	16.0	40
California.....................	2,661	2	27.0	15
Colorado	227	27	18.1	32
Connecticut..................	327	18	23.0	24

Distribution of Union Membership in Nonagricultural Employment—Contd.

State	Membership[1]		Total union membership[4] as a percent of employees in nonagricultural employment	
	1980	1980 rank	1980	1980 rank
Delaware	65	43	25.2	19
Florida[2]	420	16	11.8	47
Georgia[2]	323	19	15.1	44
Hawaii	113	36	28.0	13
Idaho	61	45	18.4	31
Illinois	1,487	4	30.4	8
Indiana	649	10	30.4	9
Iowa[2]	244	25	22.2	26
Kansas[2]	146	31	15.4	42
Kentucky	290	22	24.0	22
Louisiana[2]	257	24	16.4	37
Maine	101	37	24.1	21
Maryland-District of Columbia	527	14	22.8	25
Massachusetts	660	9	24.9	20
Michigan	1,289	6	37.3	2
Minnesota	463	15	26.2	16
Mississippi[2]	135	32	16.2	38
Missouri	544	13	27.6	14
Montana	82	42	29.2	10
Nebraska[2]	114	34	18.1	33
Nevada[2]	95	39	23.8	23
New Hampshire	61	44	15.8	41
New Jersey	784	7	25.7	18
New Mexico....................	88	41	19.0	28
New York......................	2,792	1	38.8	1
North Carolina[2]	228	26	9.6	49
North Dakota[2]	42	47	17.1	36
Ohio	1,376	5	31.3	7
Oklahoma	174	29	15.3	43
Oregon	272	23	26.1	17
Pennsylvania..................	1,644	3	34.6	3
Rhode Island	113	35	28.3	12
South Carolina[2]...............	93	40	7.8	50
South Dakota[2]	35	50	14.8	46
Tennessee[2]	334	17	19.3	29
Texas[2]	669	8	11.4	48
Utah[2].........................	98	38	17.7	35
Vermont	36	49	18.0	34
Virginia[2]	318	20	15.0	45
Washington	553	12	34.4	4
West Virginia..................	222	28	34.4	5
Wisconsin	554	11	28.5	11
Wyoming[2]	39	48	18.9	30
Membership not classifiable[3]	376	—	—	—

[1] Based on reports from 125 national unions and estimates for 49. Also included are local unions directly affiliated with the AFL-CIO and members in single-firm and local unaffiliated unions.

[2] Has right-to-work law.

[3] Includes local unions directly affiliated with the AFL-CIO.

[4] Includes some retired members.

NOTE: Because of rounding, sums of individual items may not equal totals. Dashes indicate no data in category. Table is based on preliminary union survey data.

Source: Adapted from Bureau of Labor Statistics data reported in DIRECTORY OF U.S. LABOR ORGANIZATIONS, 1984–85 EDITION, Courtney D. Gifford, ed. (Washington, D.C.: The Bureau of National Affairs, Inc., 1984).

Of the ten states with the lowest percentage membership, eight have right-to-work laws in force. Whether these antiunion statutes are the cause or the effect of the low percentage of unionization is similar to the chicken-egg dilemma. It is arguable that the strong position of employers and the low percentage of unionization permit the passage of this right-to-work legislation and that, once in force, it helps to maintain the status quo which made the initial passage possible.

Union jobs are currently leaving the "graybelt," the industrial states of the north and east. Employers often move south or overseas to escape union wages and working conditions, legislation designed to protect workers from the effects of unemployment and occupational injury, and outmoded plants and equipment. At the same time they are lured by both federal and local tax incentives, right-to-work laws, and a generally antiunion climate in business, media, and government circles.

Occupational Collars. While not everyone agrees on the meaning of the terms blue collar and white collar, it is clear that by almost any definition there has been an employment shift from the former to the latter. Department of Labor estimates for 1980 put the number of white-collar union members at seven million, or over a third of total membership. These people were concentrated in unions with at least 90 percent white-collar membership—unions such as the Musicians, the Teachers, and the Education Association. A growing number of unions have some white-collar workers as members, apparently reflecting a broadening of interest in their organization. Yet overall only about 15 percent of white-collar workers are unionized.

There is, of course, significant overlap between white-collar occupations and three other membership types—women, government employees, especially teachers, and office workers.

Women in Unions. Since the early 1800s when they were hired into New England textile mills to work long hours at low wages, women have been a significant, if not always highly visible, part of the industrial labor force and, in some instances, of the labor movement. Recent developments have further contributed to their importance. Consider these changes:[7]

---

[7] Bureau of Labor Statistics, United States Department of Labor, DIRECTORY, 1979 and PERSPECTIVES ON WORKING WOMEN: A DATA BOOK, Bulletin 2080 (Washington, D.C.: Government Printing Office, 1980), p. 3.

- The number of women in the labor force rose from 18 million to 44 million between 1950 and 1980, or from less than 30 percent to 42.5 percent of the total labor force.
- Between 1954, when the government first collected information on women union members, and 1980 the female proportion of total membership rose from 17 to 30 percent.
- The proportion of women workers who are organized is increasing. From 1976 to 1978 it rose slightly to 15.2 percent, with a third of the increase credited to two unions, the Service Employees and the State, County and Municipal Employees. By 1980 almost 16 percent of working women were union members.

The government reports that in 1978 women made up at least half the membership of 26 unions. Eighteen unions remained all-male in that year. Most of these unions had memberships concentrated in occupations where entry to women is either difficult or unattractive due to a variety of barriers, including a tradition of sex discrimination. These included the Maintenance of Way Employees and the Locomotive Engineers, both railway unions, the Flight Engineers, and several unions of professional athletes.

Seven large unions reported 300,000 or more women members, accounting for 48 percent of all women in unions in 1978. The seven were the Teamsters; State, County, and Municipal Employees; the Food and Commercial Workers; the Clothing and Textile Workers; the Service Employees; the Electrical Workers (IBEW); and the Teachers. Not included in this government summary is the largest teachers union, the National Education Association (NEA), which probably has more women in its membership than any of those cited above.

Minority Membership. Nonwhite workers, especially blacks, are more likely than white workers to be union members. A 1980 survey reports 29 percent of nonwhites, compared to 22 percent of whites, in unions. Nonwhite men, at 33.6 percent, are most unionized.[8] Another source notes that between 1960 and 1980 black members of AFL-CIO affiliates increased from 6 to 17 percent of the total.[9] Hispanics are almost as unionized as blacks.

---

[8] Bureau of Labor Statistics, U.S. Department of Labor, EARNINGS AND OTHER CHARACTERISTICS OF ORGANIZED WORKERS, Bulletin 2105 (Washington, D.C.: Government Printing Office, 1980).

[9] *The Indianapolis Star*, December 29, 1980, p. 40.

These figures reflect the concentration of black and other minority workers in certain heavily organized sectors. But they probably also reflect the greater propensity of blacks to support organization where there is no union.

Membership by Union Size. Membership is heavily concentrated in the largest national unions. The Teamsters and the NEA at one point each neared two million members. The Auto Workers, the Food and Commercial Workers, and the Steelworkers also reported more than a million members for the year 1982.[10] (See Table 5.)

Concentration in the large unions appears to be a continuing trend. In 1976 the 13 unions with at least a half million members accounted for 51 percent of union members. Just two years later there were 15 unions of over a half million, now accounting for 57 percent of the total.

Nevertheless, many of the smaller unions, despite membership losses during the recession, continue to represent their members effectively. In recent years, however, the technological change and plant closings, along with employer offensives, have forced mergers among many unions, especially in printing, transportation, clothing, and services.

Since 1960 there have been more individual unions suffering membership losses than enjoying gains. Declines were felt especially by the smaller internationals and those in declining sectors, such as the railroad and clothing industries and, more recently, some of the "smokestack" industries.

Unionization by Sector. Earlier we examined trends in employment growth, noting the shift from the goods to the nongoods producing sector. Table 6 breaks out employment and union membership by 11 industrial groupings and shows a strong, but percentagewise relatively low, union presence in certain areas of traditional strength.

Mining and construction were once well organized but are now only one-third union. So too is manufacturing, although here the one-third figure accounts for some seven million members, still the largest single industrial grouping in the labor movement.

---

[10]The UAW and the Steelworkers were among the industrial unions suffering large membership declines in the early 1980s. The Steelworkers, for example, dropped from a reported 1.2 million in 1980 to slightly more than 700,000 in 1984, prompting the leadership to consider new sectors in which to organize. During this period large steel employers continued the trend to diversification into nonsteel activities, including the much-noted acquisition by U.S. Steel of Marathon Oil.

Table 5. Unions Reporting 100,000 Active Members or More, Including Canadian Members, 1982[1]

Organization	Members	Organization	Members
Teamsters (IBT) (Ind.)	1,800,000	United Electrical Workers (UE) (Ind.)	162,000
National Education Association (NEA) (Ind.)	1,641,354	Nurses (ANA) (Ind.)	160,357
Steelworkers (USW)	1,200,000	Police (FOP)	160,000
Auto Workers (UAW)	1,140,370	Iron Workers (BSOIW)	155,587
Food and Commercial (UFCW)	1,079,213	Bakery, Tobacco (BCTW)	152,100
State, County (AFSCME)	950,000	Classified School (AACSE) (Ind.)	150,000
Electrical (IBEW)	883,000	Mine Workers (UMW) (Ind.)	150,000
Service Employees (SEIU)	700,000	Sheet Metal Workers (SMW)	144,000
Carpenters (CJA)	679,000	Railway Clerks (BRAC)	140,000
Machinists (IAM)	655,221	Oil, Chemical Workers (OCAW)	125,000
Communications Workers (CWA)	650,000	Bricklayers (BAC)	120,000
Teachers (AFT)	573,644	Transit Workers (ATU)	120,000
Laborers (LIUNA)	450,442	Boilermakers (BBF)	117,642
Clothing and Textile Workers (ACTWU)	400,000	Longshoremen (ILA)	116,000
Hotel and Restaurant (HERE)	375,000	Transportation (UTU)	115,000
Plumbers (PPF)	353,127	Office and Professional (OPEIU)	112,793
Operating Engineers (IUOE)	345,000	Rubber Workers (URW)	100,175
Ladies' Garment Workers (ILGWU)	276,000		
Paperworkers (UPIU)	263,695		
Musicians (AFM)	260,000		
Retail (RWDSU)	250,000		
Postal Workers (APWU)	248,000		
Government Workers (AFGE)	210,000		
Electrical Workers (IUE)	190,786		
Letter Carriers (NALC)	175,000		
Graphic Communication Workers (GCIU)	165,000		
Painters (PAT)	165,000		
Firefighters (IAFF)	162,792		

[1] All organizations not identified as (Ind.) are affiliated with the AFL-CIO.

Source: DIRECTORY OF U.S. LABOR ORGANIZATIONS, 1984–85 EDITION, Courtney D. Gifford, ed. (Washington, D.C.: The Bureau of National Affairs, Inc., 1984).

Table 6.   Union Membership as a Percentage of Employment,
by Industry, May 1980

(in thousands)

Sector	Employment	Membership	Percent organized
Agriculture	1,455	51	3.5
Forestry and fisheries	87	12	13.8
Mining	892	286	32.1
Construction	4,982	1,574	31.6
Manufacturing	20,976	6,771	32.3
Nondurable goods	8,430	2,405	28.5
Transportation, communications, and utilities	6,048	2,903	48.0
Retail and wholesale trade	17,401	1,753	10.1
Finance, insurance, and real estate	5,152	190	3.7
Other services	26,121	4,743	18.2
Government	5,364	1,812	33.8
Federal non-postal	1,795	347	19.3
Postal	691	509	73.7
State	972	253	26.0
Local	1,906	703	36.9

Source: Adapted from Bureau of Labor Statistics, *Earnings and Other Characteristics of Organized Workers, May 1980* (Bulletin 2105).

Most unionized, at 48 percent, are the infrastructure industries—transportation, communications, and utilities. And while the reported figures show government employees overall as one-third unionized, another estimate places half of the full-time employees of state and local governments in unions.[11]

Among major categories, the area of greatest employment growth, the trade, finance, and "other services" categories, is the least unionized. This broad sector employs 48 million people, but fewer than 14 percent of them are union members. Thus, while employment growth in the nongoods sector outpaced manufacturing by a six-to-one margin over the past two decades, unionization did not expand with it. If it had, the labor movement would now be almost double its current size.

Yet the picture is not entirely bleak; there is invariably a lag between the growth of employment in a sector and its unionization. Despite the overall low percentage of unionization in the broad service sector, more than six million union members are there already, many of them white-collar workers and others thought to shun

[11] *Wall Street Journal*, May 23, 1978, p. 1.

unions. Teachers, airline pilots, and some workers in the entertainment field, among others, have been substantially organized for some time. Others, such as physicians, engineers, and office workers in many situations, are just beginning to organize. And we should not forget that the majority of government employee unionists are also "service workers," as well as being considered office workers and white-collar workers.

These people represent more than simply a beginning in the growth sectors. Their presence means that several unions have developed or are now acquiring competency in representing service, office, and white-collar workers. In addition to the teachers and pilots unions, we note such unions as the Newspaper Guild, the Musicians, the Food and Commercial Workers, the Office and Professional Employees, and the Communications Workers among those that have traditionally represented large numbers of white-collar workers. These unions are now joined by traditionally blue-collar unions, such as the Auto Workers, which have seriously begun to organize office and white-collar employees.

In the above respects the labor movement, or at least several of its unions, are indeed well positioned for a rapid catch-up in the new economy.

The Union Response: Organizing

The picture of unionism remains incomplete if we look only at employment and unionization data. To fill it out we need to examine union organizational efforts. Toward what workers are these efforts directed and with what success?

On the surface, organizing trends over the past 30 years seem as discouraging as the percentage unionization rates. Union organizing success, as measured by percentage victories in NLRB elections, has been on the downswing since the 1950s. Where unions once won over 60 percent of the elections, they now win less than half.

These data have been added to the decline-of-the-labor movement chorus noted early in this chapter. Of note is the effort to explain the decline partially as a matter of unions lacking their traditional appeal with the new employment groups—especially workers in the south and white-collar workers. The stereotype of the old South becomes almost a self-fulfilling prophecy: If one believes that southern culture is inhospitable to unionism, making it almost impossible to organize successfully, then one will not undertake to organize. The result will be no organization, which only "proves" that successful organizing is impossible.

A recent study looks into elements of these views by separating out relevant NLRB election results for the 1973–80 period.[12] When the results for Deep South states are broken down, it turns out that Alabama, Louisiana, and Mississippi are not significantly lower than the national union-victory average. North Carolina and Florida, with fewer than 40 percent victories, drag down the regional average.

Results for four states in the southwest (Arizona, Colorado, New Mexico, and Texas) are even more revealing. This region, often lumped with the south, has a generally high, rising victory rate— over 50 percent in 1979 and 1980—with over a 60 percent success rate in professional and technical workers elections.[13] Nationally, union victory rates are higher in professional, technical, and service worker units than among industrial and traditional craft unions. In this respect results in these southwestern states simply reflect the national trend. The data indicate that, where unions have endeavored to organize the growth sectors, they have met, as a rule, with considerable success.

For the past 30 years, in both industrial and white-collar representation elections, unions have experienced higher victory rates in smaller bargaining units than in larger units. For the manufacturing sector, part of the explanation seems to be that the organization of those large units which could most readily be unionized was accomplished from the 1930s through the 1950s, and the smaller and more peripheral units were left unorganized. This is consistent with the fact that average unit size is substantially larger in elections in the sunbelt states than in the more highly organized snowbelt states. And to the extent that larger units indicate the presence of larger employers, it is likely that the employer's resources for resisting unions would be greater in the larger units in any sector.

One set of inferences drawn from findings of the sort just presented is depicted in the market analysis approach. One such study begins by noting that organizing is still disproportionately directed toward declining employment sectors:

---

[12] Michael Goldfield, "The Decline of Organized Labor: NLRB Union Certification Election Results," *Politics and Society* 11, no. 2 (1982), pp. 167–209.

[13] Ibid., p. 191.

> Unions have been dragging their past traditions, their past jurisdictional agreements, their past failures, and their past successes into their current organizing efforts. The union movement's concentration has been on industries and geographic areas where unions already occupy a comfortable position but which are low growth, or no growth, in terms of employment.[14]

Instead, the author argues, unions should focus on the "higher yield" areas, those with low unionization.

To some extent this analysis seems to confuse low unionization with high yield, a link by no means automatic. Given that there are unorganized units in all sectors of the economy, it does not follow for the labor movement as a whole—and much less for an individual union with a concentration in one sector—that unionizing efforts should be concentrated in the least organized sector. In addition to variations in receptiveness and employer resistance among sectors, it should be recalled that unions organize in part to enhance their ability to represent current members. Hence for a union whose membership is concentrated in one industry to abandon that industry for another simply because it is "high yield" might be irresponsible to its members. Low unionization may suggest great potential, but it is no guarantee of yield.

This is not to say that market analysis is worthless, but only to indicate the risks of applying business techniques too rigidly to union organization. The analysis noted earlier points to the trends toward success in the emerging sectors. Only certain unions, however, are capable, through organizing, of keeping the entire movement current with changing employment patterns. Typically, these will be unions that are diversified or otherwise well positioned through past organizing efforts to concentrate in growth areas, or they will be unions with ideological commitments to a particular form of organization.

There are other indications that the near future will not reflect the recent past, that the organizing slide of recent decades will level off and even reverse. Another assessment notes:

> First, there will be a labor market glut of highly educated persons age 25–44 over the next few years, reaching 50 percent of the labor force by 1990. The consequences . . . will be more competition for available jobs and promotions, slower career growth, lower rates of increase in wages, and increased wage pressure from those 18 to 25.

---

[14] Ronald Berenbeim, "The Declining Market for Unionization" *Information Bulletin*, no. 44 (New York: The Conference Board, 1978), p. 3.

Second, we believe that employers have come to treat white-collar workers as variable costs. Whereas in earlier recessions, white-collar workers were inventoried and blue-collar workers laid off, more recent experience suggests that white-collar workers are no longer buffered from the vicissitudes of the business cycle. Taken together, these two forces could create the classic concerns of job insecurity and job consciousness among white-collar workers.[15]

Conclusion

Statistics, even simple numbers and percentages, are not the most human terms with which to describe the labor movement and the workers comprising it. They do not reveal the thoughts and emotions of workers as they work and as they participate in their unions. Nor do statistics disclose the complex motivations that underlie decisions to join or not to join, as these decisions are made by individuals, be they blue- or white-collar, male or female, white, black or Hispanic, skilled or unskilled. But these data are important.

If one is to understand the institutions of labor it is essential to comprehend their dimensions and their composition, where they are strong and where they are weak, which industries and occupations they represent. Sheer numbers do not always translate into understanding, just as they do not necessarily translate into strength. In the right place, however, they are prerequisite to both.

Before any breakthrough occurs it is likely that several barriers will have to be removed:

(1) The current climate of resistance to unionism, which includes elements of ideology, corporate policy and practice, and law, will have to be altered. One phase of this struggle is head-to-head confrontation with "union busters" and "union avoidance consultants" in organizing campaigns, but the political arena will in the end be of equal importance.

(2) The labor movement will have to develop new organizational forms and strategies to match the conglomerate and multinational employers it faces.

---

[15] Myron Roomkin and Harvey A. Juris, "Unions in the Traditional Sectors: The Mid-Life Passage of the Labor Movement," in THIRTY-FIRST ANNUAL PROCEEDINGS OF THE INDUSTRIAL RELATIONS RESEARCH ASSOCIATION, ed. Milton Derber (Madison, Wis.: Industrial Relations Research Association, 1978), p. 220.

(3) The foundational efforts and positioning that have occurred in the growth areas to date will have to be followed
by a massive change in consciousness among millions of
white-collar and office workers, resulting in a perception
that unions are the necessary means for dealing with their
problems.

Key Words and Phrases

numerator/denominator	post-industrial economy
total labor force	white collar
nonagricultural employment	blue collar
nonsupervisory, nonagricultural	self-fulfilling prophecy
employment	union "positioning"

Review and Discussion Questions

1. Would you expect to find smaller or larger unions in ten years?
More or fewer women unionists? Why?

2. George Meany once explained that he was not concerned about the
decline in the union percentage of the work force because unions still represented most of the key people. Do you agree? Why or why not?

3. To what extent are corporate structure and technological changes
responsible for changes in union membership?

4. Map an organizing strategy for one of the sectors that has low percentage unionization. With which groups of workers in what types of establishments would you start? Why? Would you begin with appeals to the
skilled, unskilled, or would your appeal be across-the-board?

Suggestions For Further Reading

Since the government in 1981 ceased biennial publication of the *Di-
rectory of National Unions and Employer Associations*, the most compre-
hensive source of data on unions and their members is the *Directory of
U.S. Labor Organizations* published by the Bureau of National Affairs.
For a discussion of changes in several industries that are having severe con-
sequences on unions, see the special issue of *Labor Studies Journal* on
"The Impact on Labor of Changing Corporate Structure and Technology"
(Winter 1979).

There are a number of books available on different categories of workers. See, for instance, Barbara Wertheimer, *We Were There: The Story of Working Women in America*, and Ray Marshall, *The Negro and Organized Labor*.

Complete bibliographical information for the above titles can be found in the Bibliography.

4

Elements of Structure and Government

> The job relationships of the members are the elemental stuff of union life. The society of union members begins with the facts of their ways of earning a living, and the government of the union grows out of the need for a rule-making authority to regulate job relations among the members and with the employer. But it is the society which comes first—the government follows.
>
> Joseph Kovner and Herbert Lahne, 1953*

Friendly rivalry among unions sometimes takes the form of humorous exchanges over competing jurisdictional claims. Carpenters have been known to claim jurisdiction over "All that is made of wood, or was ever made of wood." Communications Workers assert the right to organize anyone who uses a telephone; Electrical Workers, anyone who works under a light fixture; and the Teamsters, anyone who moves.

The Service Employees represent both hospital and cemetery workers. In their lighter moments some have stated that "If they're breathing, we'll organize them; if they're not, we'll bury them." This has also been dubbed the "womb to tomb" jurisdiction. And, of course, a card in the Roofers' Union "covers everything."

Occasionally these competing claims take on a more serious note, inviting comparison with what happens when a gold miner discovers a claim jumper or when a river changes course and an international boundary changes along with it. When jobs and, hence, livelihoods are at stake, union jurisdiction becomes a matter of survival.

---

*"Shop Society and the Union," *Industrial and Labor Relations Review* 7, no. 1, (October 1953), p. 4.

This chapter examines union jurisdictions as well as several concepts of environment, structure, and government that are used in later chapters.

Types and Sources of Jurisdiction

In common parlance jurisdiction is often used loosely to describe the current make-up of a union's membership. But there are other, more formal, meanings. *Jurisdiction is a claim on, or a grant of, the right to organize or represent a category of work or workers.* Where there is a grant, there must, of course, be another body to issue the grant. This may be a national union issuing a local's charter for a geographic area or a plant, or it may be a federation issuing jurisdictional charters to internationals. In other cases employers and government agencies influence the content of a union's jurisdiction. The documentary sources are found in constitutions, charters, collective bargaining agreements, and agency certifications and rulings. To understand the usage of the term, it is usually necessary to specify the type of jurisdiction, the level of organization, and the source of the grant, if any.

The basic distinction among types is that between *territorial* and *trade* jurisdiction. Territorial, or geographic, jurisdiction is primarily an internal matter within each international union, although it sometimes enters into negotiations with employers. Its source is in the union's organization, as reflected in its constitution and local union charters. Trade jurisdiction, sometimes called work or craft jurisdiction, is a claim upon a certain type of work, tool, material, or operation. In practice it is less subject to total union control and more open to influence by outside parties. A third notion, *industrial jurisdiction*, is the virtual opposite of trade jurisdiction, because it usually refers to an international union (such as those formerly with the CIO) claiming jurisdiction over an entire industry regardless of craft or trade.

International unions establish territorial jurisdictions when they charter locals to organize and represent members within a county, a multicounty area, a state, or even a multistate region. These charters are often accompanied by restrictions on the local's trade jurisdiction. An IBEW local, for instance, may cover all employees of a utility in an area; it may be limited to the employees of a given manufacturing plant; or it may extend to all workers in a multicounty jurisdiction, including those in the building trades.

The IBEW constitution includes this language on the subject of jurisdiction:

> Keeping in mind progress for the IBEW, and that all electrical work be done by its members, it is impractical to classify or divide jurisdiction of work in every detail between the various branches in this organization to meet all situations in all localities.
>
> Therefore, the classifications and divisions outlined below are necessarily of a general nature and LU's (local unions) whose jurisdiction with other LU's of the IBEW, or whose agreements are harmonious and conducive to the progress of the IBEW, shall not be disturbed.[1]

The provision goes on to classify the membership by trade jurisdictions: outside and utility workers, inside electrical workers, communications workers, railroad and Pullman electrical workers, and electrical manufacturing workers. Further, it gives the international union president the authority to assign and adjust local union jurisdictions. One can detect in practice, as well as from the constitution excerpt above, that local lines are not always drawn neatly and that the authority of the president to make adjustments has several implications, not only for control over locals, but for use in creating organizing incentives at the local level.

It is not unusual for international union constitutions to devote several pages to a statement of trade jurisdiction. These descriptions often consist of a broad claim followed by a detailed list of job titles, materials, and processes. Lest anything be omitted there is usually an elastic preface such as "including but not limited to" or a closing phrase such as "and all related types of work."

Preservation clauses are sometimes added. The Graphic Arts International Union (GAIU) is one of several that specifically anticipated the ravages of technology, as well it might in the printing industry:

> Such jurisdiction shall not be diminished, limited, or impaired by any technological or other change in, evolution of or substitution for any work, process, operation, or product now within the jurisdiction of the International, but any such alterations shall be encompassed by the jurisdiction of the International.[2]

The significance of these clauses varies. But a union without a constitutional claim to disputed work might well suffer within the

---

[1] Article 28, Sec. 3.
[2] Article 2, *GAIU Constitution*. In 1983 the Graphic Arts International Union merged with the Printing and Graphic Communications Union to become the Graphic Communications International Union (GCIU).

AFL-CIO and possibly in other forums where this document might be considered one factor in support of a claim.

The constitutions of at least two types of unions are distinguished by the virtual absence of language on jurisdiction. As one might expect, these are unions with either no tradition of jurisdictional difficulty or little need for concern due to the nature of their memberships. The constitutions of CIO unions were often patterned on that of the United Mine Workers, asserting a jurisdiction extending to all workers "in and around" the industry. The other type includes unions like the Air Line Pilots, the Musicians, and professional athletes unions, which limit their membership to closely related occupations. For this type of union, there is little chance of jurisdictional conflict with another union over their core memberships.

Jurisdictional Change

In its formative years the AFL granted *exclusive jurisdiction* to national craft unions in a manner similar to that of today's franchise industry. The Brotherhood of Carpenters and Joiners was franchised for the carpentry trade and the Sheet Metal Workers for the sheet metal trade. Each union was then free to parcel out its franchise in the form of trade and territorial charters to its local unions—so long as it did not encroach on the franchise granted another union by the AFL.

The problems of delineating where one union's work stopped and another's began were difficult enough at the outset. Who attached wiring or sheet metal to wood? Did each craft move its own material and equipment? If not, who did and when did they turn it over to another craft? These and myriad other questions arose from the craft basis of the construction unions. This craft orientation was traditional and in many ways well suited to the industry. The skill required in many of the trades could be enhanced by establishing apprenticeships and lines of demarcation among trades, thus avoiding both the skill and wage dilution associated with "jack of all trades" organization while also providing the employer with more productive labor.

If these initial problems were difficult, new technology compounded them. It was one thing to draw lines of demarcation in a static world, another to do so in a world that was constantly changing. New technology, involving new materials and construction methods, required constant adjustment. Sheet metal window sashes often replaced wood sashes. Concrete and steel often replaced wood. Electric and gas power replaced steam. New tools were invented. Did the union claim jurisdiction over the material, the tools of the trade, the part of the structure, or the function of the operation? Or, all of the above?

Unions responded in various ways. Some survived and grew because they were more successful in taking and holding new work. Others grew because they had broad charters, their jurisdiction was in a growing field, or they organized beyond the limits of their official jurisdictions. Yet others shriveled and merged with another union or, in some cases, disappeared.

Union Diversification

The Machinists union (IAM), founded in 1888 by skilled railroad craftworkers, expanded during the 1930s and 1940s into other industries, and it now has both industrial and craft members. And, if the Teamsters union (IBT) had restricted its focus to the drivers of horsedrawn vehicles denoted by its name, the membership would no doubt approach that of today's Horseshoers—about 300. Even the full name of the union—the International Brotherhood of Teamsters, Chauffeurs, Warehousemen and Helpers of America—conceals the fact that the IBT is now a *general union* asserting jurisdiction over "all workers, without limitation."[3] Further indication of this composition is that fewer than a quarter of the Teamsters are freight drivers. The majority are classified as "miscellaneous"—from laundry, packinghouse, and clerical workers to police, nurses, and cab drivers.

There remain only a handful of national unions whose entire memberships fall within their original jurisdictions or are reflected in their union names. Some, like the Siderographers (15 members), the Coopers, and the Horseshoers, represent what remains of a small or vanishing trade.[4]

The CIO unions formed during the 1930s were chartered for entire industries. Today most of these organizations retain the bulk of their membership in their core industries, but it is not unusual to

---

[3] See Article 2, Sec. 1, *Constitution*, International Brotherhood of Teamsters, Chauffeurs, Warehousemen and Helpers of America.

[4] Chartered by the AFL in the 1890s, the Horseshoers numbered 10,000 members early in this century, but the siderographers, printing plate artists employed by the government, rarely exceeded 100 members.

find them representing workers in unrelated industries, especially in geographical areas where they predominate. Thus, the UAW has represented hospital workers, laundry employees, and government clericals. The Amalgamated Clothing and Textile Workers Union has members in metal-fabricating plants, banks, and the Xerox Corporation. The Steelworkers union includes producers of candy, baseball bats (the famed Louisville Slugger), and, in the union's home turf of western Pennsylvania, even mushroom workers!

Many building trades unions extend their jurisdictions vertically to include workers who fabricate the materials used by the tradespeople on the job site. For instance, the IBEW, chartered originally by the AFL for all branches of the electrical industry, includes local unions of workers manufacturing electrical products. There remain many exceptions, among them craft unions that have not followed the trend toward larger and more diverse organizaton.

The official policy of the AFL-CIO is to encourage the trend toward fewer, more diversified, unions by encouraging unions to merge, a phenomenon discussed in Chapter 7.

External Influences on Jurisdiction

Thus far we have discussed jurisdiction largely as a matter of union policy and practice—strictly as an internal matter. Asserting a claim in a document and having it recognized within the labor movement, however, does not always establish it. Two groups, employers and the government, must at times be reckoned with.

Employers influence jurisdiction at three stages. First, the employer's preference concerning the composition of the bargaining unit is taken into account in either the voluntary recognition process or the NLRB election and certification process described in Chapter 2. Second, through negotiations employers and unions agree on contracts that contain *recognition clauses* detailing the jobs included in the unit and covered by the contract. Typically, industrial unions include such descriptions more as a hedge against an employer assigning work to nonbargaining unit employees than for protection against claim jumping by other unions (though this is by no means unheard of). Building trades unions, on the other hand, need such language not only to protect against the assignment of work to nonunion employees, but to other unionized crafts as well. The third occasion for employer influence is in the 10(k) hearing described below.

Government involvement in cementing jurisdictional claims occurs at two points. The first is in the bargaining-unit determination procedure. By ruling in favor of broader or narrower units, the NLRB affects union bargaining and organizing effectiveness and organizing strategies. Board policy, for instance, currently makes it almost impossible for units of skilled tradespeople to separate themselves from previously established production and maintenance units combining skilled and unskilled workers. The Board has also continued certain outmoded unit policies that erect barriers to unions facing conglomerates and other multiplant employers.[5]

The second occasion for government influence arises when two unions dispute the assignment of work and one seeks a hearing before the NLRB, called a *10(k) hearing* after the relevant section of the Act. While several criteria can be used by the Board in resolving such disputes, its decision usually accords with the preference of the employer, termed the *employer's work assignment*.

Prior to the 1935 passage of the Wagner Act, which established the NLRB, unions fought amongst themselves and with employers over existing work and over the right to organize new groups of workers. Enforcement of negotiated jurisdiction agreements depended primarily on union strength. While the AFL at times attempted to mediate disputes by enforcing its increasingly difficult to delineate franchises of exclusive jurisdiction, internal AFL politics in practice had the greatest effect on the resolution of such disputes.

The collapse of exclusive jurisdiction as the AFL's first principle of organization was precipitated by the Wagner Act provision for representation elections conducted by the government. With workers deciding which union would represent them, unions were in effect invited to compete with one another. This effectively abrogated the franchise agreements so essential to exclusive jurisdiction.

With the establishment of a government role in the unit determination and union certification process, a new measure of established jurisdiction emerged. This standard, *established bargaining relationship*, has come to anchor the Federation's jurisdictional policy. Once a union is certified as a bargaining agent by the NLRB, the employer comes under a duty to bargain in good faith with the union for the duration of any contract or for a period of one year. Using this NLRB measure, the Federation deems a certified union

---

[5] See Charles Craypo, THE ECONOMICS OF COLLECTIVE BARGAINING (Washington, D.C.: The Bureau of National Affairs, Inc., forthcoming).

to have established a bargaining relationship and thus bans efforts by other affiliates to raid the unit.

Established bargaining relationship is a more limited notion than exclusive jurisdiction, because it applies only after workers are organized and does not protect a union's claim to unorganized groups. Because an established bargaining relationship has no reference to the type of work performed, it is more flexible and more easily measured. It is not the sweeping principle of organization that exclusive jurisdiction was for the old AFL, but it accords better with the realities of technological change and with the emergence of general unions.

In sum, the important elements of formal jurisdiction include type, whether trade, geographical, or industrial; source, whether derived from union government, collective bargaining agreement with employers, or NLRB certification or ruling; and the level of organization from which it issues and to which it applies, whether a federation issuing franchises to internationals, internationals assigning jurisdictions to local unions, or even local unions establishing lines of demarcation among trades. But the concept in practice is not what it was originally conceived to be by the AFL.

Elements of the Environment

Unions establish their membership composition by claiming and organizing workers within a jurisdiction or by refusing to recognize any jurisdictional limits. In doing so, they select and sometimes shape their environments. The environment of a union consists of those external surroundings that influence its structure and operations. If we examine influences on the local, the national union office can be viewed as part of the local's environment, as are local management, other unions in the area, and area traditions. At the national level the more diverse the occupational and industrial composition of a union, the more difficult it is to specify a single type of environment.

At its broadest level the general environment consists of some influences that affect all unions or an entire class of unions. More specific influences vary with the industry, market, employer, service or product area, and occupational and employment patterns that each union encounters. Table 7 classifies some of the significant elements in each level.

The mix of environmental traits in the real world is almost as varied as the possibilities presented in the Table 7. There do ap-

---

Table 7.   Elements of Union Environments

Uniform characteristics

| Economic system | | Legal system |

| Political system | | Social/cultural systems |

Variable characteristics

Type of industry, markets, and employers
Competitive or monopolistic
Concentrated or dispersed
Capitalization required to enter
Average firm size
Conglomerates, multinationals, or small single-line firms
Predominant/international
Local, regional, or national markets
Stable, seasonal, or other market fluctuations
Alternate sources of supply and production (Can other products satisfy the demand? Are there substitutes?)
Traditions/attitudes
Extent of hierarchy

Occupation/employment patterns
Skill mix (uniform, high, low)
Training requirements
Craft separation/traditions
Tools
Casual/regular/mixed
Method of entry
Form of compensation
Worker–supervisor ratio
Type of supervision
Uniform/variable conditions
Tradition of worker organization
Employment level in firm and industry

Product/service
Fixed/transportable
Durable/nondurable
Standardized/individualized

Area
Area unemployment
Mobility
Multi-employer organizations
Customs/Traditions
Strength of worker/union organization

---

pear, however, some clusters in certain types of industries. A comparison between two such environments, the construction and the auto industries, will clarify the meaning of the term union environment and illustrate contrasting environmental patterns that influence union structure.

The Construction Industry. This industry is characterized by relative *ease of entry*, meaning that massive amounts of capital are not normally required for an employer to set up shop. This trait is associated with others: The industry has a relatively *large number of small employers* who *compete* within a *local market* area.

The nature of the product is important. The construction of a hospital or a large office building is not a "cookie cutter" or assembly-line operation. Beginning with the architect's rendering, the project is usually a one-of-a-kind effort, designed for a single location. While prefabricated materials are increasingly used, they are combined at the job site to achieve a singular result that cannot be shipped.

Workers in the industry are often *mobile among employers* and *among scattered job sites*. They obtain jobs through a union hiring hall or referral system, through contracts with other workers, or through direct contact with employing contractors. They are generally highly skilled. *Hierarchy* in the industry is minimal, especially where small contractors prevail. *Conditions* from job to job are apt to be *variable*.

The Automobile Industry. While it shares with construction the same general economic, political, legal, and social systems, the auto industry environment is almost a direct opposite of construction. Obviously even an exceptionally industrious person cannot, with a savings passbook and a small business loan, get started in auto manufacturing. The *investment required to enter* is immense. A *very few, large producers* account for almost all production. Prior to the entry of foreign producers, there was *little real competition*. The auto industry is an *oligopoly* in which prices are administered by the industry leaders. Unlike a construction worker, an auto worker in Georgia, working for lower wages, could undercut a higher paid worker in California, because the product could be shipped within a national market.

Large numbers of relatively unskilled workers and a few skilled workers labor under a single roof to create standardized products. These workers obtain their jobs through the company personnel office and often stay with the same employer at the same plant for most of their working lives.

Hierarchy and ranking in the auto industry are elaborate, running from corporate headquarters through local plant management and from supervisors into the ranks of the workers, who fill many job classifications, each with its own wage rate.

Other environments resemble one or the other of the above. Steel and rubber, for instance, resemble auto. The broadcast technician employed on a network field crew, on the other hand, is like a skilled construction worker. This person is mobile, encountering a variety of situations and conditions which he or she is trained to handle. But unlike the construction worker, the technican works for the same large employer from year to year and from job site to job site. Another example of an environment combining elements from both auto and construction clusters is commercial printing, an industry characterized by small employers, competitive pricing, relatively high skill levels, some casual employment, but fixed employment sites. Each industry and occupation will have its own mix of the elements identified in Table 7. The broad features of national economic, political, and social environments are essentially the same for all U.S. unions.

Framework and Terms

We have now defined and illustrated the concepts of jurisdiction and environment. Before detailing their influence on the structure and government of a union, it is necessary to explain further the framework and some of the terms that arise.

Organization is used in this book in two senses. One refers to the manner in which a union is founded—or organized—and by which it builds strength. The other usage is synonymous with structure, the form or shape of the union, the combinations of roles and positions people assume in the union. Structure is the form, or shape, of the organization and is often associated with *function*, the content or substance of the forms—what they do and how they do it—the *behavior* of the people who make up the organization. These functions and behaviors are encompassed within the term *action*. Action can be energetic or lacadaisical, routine or unusual.

A related concept is *process*, the flow through which something is conducted. We term the passage of food through a series of bodily organs as the digestive process. It is said that the simplest communications process is one person's mouth aimed at another's ear. Analogies and examples are plentiful. For instance, the fuse box or circuit panel in a building is a *structure* that *functions* to distribute power from a supply source to a number of outlets, as well as to protect circuits and the entire building from overloads.

A local union executive board is a policy-making (function and process) body (structure) made up of several *positions* or *roles*, such as president, vice-president, at-large member, and so on. Industrial union locals typically have major in-plant organizations (structures) made up of stewards, chief stewards, and/or committee people who serve in grievance handling, communications, contract negotiations (functions), and other capacities.

Not all structures perform functions. Some resemble the committee that was appointed but never met. This committee is perhaps formed with good intentions or perhaps to create the illusion of action. Other structures are *vestigial*. Like the human appendix, such structures may once have served a purpose, but the purpose seems to have long since disappeared. The opposite occurs when structures take on new functions—when groups assume new tasks.

Matters of structure, function, and process are intimately linked to matters of *government* in organizations. Government is an *established framework of authority for making decisions that are binding on a class of matters involving those within its jurisdiction*. Within this broad definition we can identify some governments that are more or less limited in scope and authority; some that are representative and others that are not; some with popularly determined constitutions and others which lack such documents.

Seen in this manner, unions are clearly governments. As noted in the first chapter and developed later in this chapter, unions have two distinct governments—one for *internal* affairs and the other for *collective bargaining* matters.

Governments spell out the rights and powers of units at different levels, much as powers are allocated among cities, states, and the federal government. The government of the labor movement includes members, local unions, international unions, intermediate structures and, for about two-thirds of the labor movement, the AFL-CIO. The international tends to be supreme with considerable authority over the locals and other sub-units. The AFL-CIO is a federation with extremely limited powers. Although the Federation cannot make binding internal and bargaining decisions for its affiliates unless expressly assigned these powers, it is nevertheless a government.

This perspective on the government of the labor movement and on the limited authority of the AFL-CIO helps clear away some stereotypes. Were the stereotype of AFL-CIO supremacy accurate, then the AFL-CIO could have prevented, as it would have liked to, the ascendancy of James Hoffa to the presidency of the Teamsters in 1957. But as a limited government, this was clearly beyond its powers.

Union Structure and Bargaining Structure

Union structure consists of the organizational forms of the union itself. *Bargaining structure*, introduced in Chapter 2, refers to the forms in which labor and management conduct negotiations. It is also a matter of who represents which bargaining units for what purpose and at what level of centralization and scope. One union may bargain with one employer over a single unit. Another may negotiate a contract with several employers that covers many different units. Several unions representing several units in plants owned by a single employer may engage in *coordinated bargaining* with the employer. A single international union may bargain major subjects with a single major corporation, with the settlement becoming the *pattern* for subsequent negotiations with other corporations in the industry. Local unions and local managements then bargain local supplements to cover details at individual plants. Major types of bargaining structures are described, with examples, in Table 8.

Where most workers in an industry belong to one union, that union is likely to have major, even controlling, influence on the bargaining structure. Once over-the-road trucking was organized by the Teamsters, the union was able to move toward a multi-employer bargaining structure and a nationwide motor freight agreement. Even in such situations, however, the union's own structure will have to adjust to the bargaining structure(s) of which it is a part.

Classifying Union Structure and Government

The reader who ignores footnotes should know that the following discussion draws heavily on the contributions of three students of union organization and action—Robert Hoxie, Van Dusen Kennedy, and Alice Cook. These three, while not necessarily originating all the concepts they used, have expressed them in what are probably their clearest and most comprehensive forms.

The usefulness of these concepts extends beyond the ivory tower. Teachers of union classes have found them useful in organizing their own thinking. Many union leaders have found that they shed new light on practical organizational patterns and possibilities. These frameworks have helped members and leaders to understand their unions, especially the internal power relationships and relationships with employers, thereby helping them to pin-point and correct causes of ineffectiveness. Union organizational forms require periodic updating lest they become irrelevant to the shape of their environments and to the needs of workers. Some forms exist as they do because they were originally copied from another union, then perhaps adapted; others because they are traditional; and yet

Table 8. Major Bargaining Structures

Type and description	Examples
Local, single employer: A local union negotiates a contract covering a single establishment or a set of locally integrated operations. Found most often in factory situations, but nonfactory unions sometimes negotiate single-employer agreements.	A local union of the Steelworkers negotiates a contract covering the employees of a bearing manufacturing plant; an Amalgamated Transit Union local negotiates with a transit authority as do teachers' unions with school boards.
Local, multi-employer: One or more unions negotiates with all unionized employers in a local market. Often found in nonfactory situations.	Electrical Workers local union bargains agreement with local affiliate of National Electrical Contractors' Association covering all unionized electrical work in a metropolitan or multicounty area; a local union of the Service Employees bargains with an area association of apartment owners for building service employees.
Corporationwide: One or more unions bargain with large multifacility employer to cover major contract terms at all unionized units. (Usually factory situations.)	Postal unions negotiate national contract with U.S. Postal Service; Auto Workers with each major auto producer.
Local supplements: Where "two-tier bargaining" occurs, local issues are settled between local unions and local managements. All are covered by same corporationwide agreement.	
Industrywide: One or more unions bargain with most employers in an industry. Occurs in factory and nonfactory situations. Note: Where a corporationwide agreement with a major employer sets an industry pattern, as in the auto industry, corporationwide negotiations become industrywide in effect.	Mine Workers bargaining with the Bituminous Coal Operators Association; Teamsters bargain with over-the-road trucking employers association.

others simply because they work, or come as close to working as human ingenuity can achieve.

More than two decades before the industrial union surge of the 1930s, Hoxie developed systematic notions of union origins, structures, and functions.[6] He went beyond his four-type functional classification described in the first chapter—the behavioral categorization of unions as business, revolutionary, uplift, or predatory—to

---

[6] TRADE UNIONISM IN THE UNITED STATES (New York: Appleton, 1917).

pose questions that continue to interest unionists and students of the labor movement today. Is there, he asked, a tendency for each functional type to adopt a particular type of structure, or for structures to lead to particular functional approaches? How does each type approach its environment? Indeed, is each in the beginning determined by its environment?

Drawing from this work Van Dusen Kennedy, writing in the early 1950s, presented a classification based on the association between environment and union structure.[7] Kennedy noted that while most of the literature dealt with factory unionism of the type advanced by the CIO unions, the prevalent type, especially on the West Coast at the time, was nonfactory unionism.

Kennedy's scheme isolates two extreme types of environment and two extremes of union structure, arguing that a cluster of nonfactory extremes in the environment will be conducive to the formation of nonfactory union structures. The most clearly nonfactory union environment is that of the construction industry, described earlier. The clearest factory environment is that of the auto or basic steel industries. Some unions will fall between the two extremes, exhibiting characteristics of both environments and structures. Table 9 is an adaptation of Kennedy's scheme.

Kennedy went on to argue that, not only were factory and nonfactory environments and structures associated, but each in turn produced distinctive patterns of behavior and ideology. Nonfactory unionism was found to be more economically sophisticated, more middle class, and more favorable to employers, whereas factory union postures were more militant, more working class, and less economically sophisticated. However, sharp differences of this sort across a broad range of factory and nonfactory unions seem difficult to identify. Exceptions are plentiful. (See Exhibit 3.)

As suggested in Table 9, the international union with predominantly nonfactory locals will tend to have relatively strong locals vis-à-vis the international union office and staff. This decentralization occurs particularly with nonfactory unions in local market industries where collective bargaining is also local, not national or industrywide. Local union activity centers around the business agent who operates out of an office where members stop by to pay dues or to seek job information or referrals.

---

[7] Nonfactory Unionism and Labor Relations (Berkeley, Calif.: California Institute of Industrial Relations, 1955).

Table 9. Union Environment and Structure: Kennedy's Nonfactory and Factory Classification

Nonfactory	Factory
Some environmental determinants	
Small employers	Large employers
Local market	National, international markets
Dispersed employment sites	Concentrated employment sites (plants, etc.)
Employment turnover	Employment stability
Uniform wage structure	Graded wage structure
Variable employment conditions	Uniform conditions
Union structure	
Retention of functions by locals	National and regional concentration of functions
Office centered union activities	Plant centered activities
BA dominant figure	Collective, plant leadership
Union often has hiring hall	Employer hires
Often an absence of seniority	Elaborate seniority system
Informal grievance procedure	Formal, elaborate procedure
Weak steward system	Strong steward system

Source: Adapted from Van Dusen Kennedy, NONFACTORY UNIONISM AND LABOR RELATIONS (Berkeley: University of California, Institute of Industrial Relations, 1955).

The factory local is plant-centered. Its leadership tends to be more collective. And its structure extends into the workplace where stewards and others play significant roles in handling grievances and other bargaining related matters. Because factory union bargaining is often conducted on a broader-than-local-union scale, however, higher level officials from the international and intermediate bodies play major roles. (See Exhibit 4.)

These differences between the two types and the many variations within the nonfactory category will be spelled out in the next chapter on the local union. At this point we will only caution:

(1) Nonfactory unionism is by no means limited to the building trades, though most construction unions appear as prototypes. Many diversified unions such as the Teamsters and the Service Employees are made up largely of nonfactory local unions, as are locals of the Food and Commercial Workers, the Theatrical Stage Employees, and some of the Transport Workers. Kennedy's type is strongly imbued with craft union features, but this is not necessary to the type. Thus, not all nonfactory unions are

---

Exhibit 3.   Profile of a Nonfactory Local Union

Local 49, Service Employees International Union, AFL-CIO, Portland, Oregon

Local 49 is a good illustration of why amalgamated locals are also termed miscellaneous or general. Its more than 6,000 members work for many employers, some large and others small. The types of establishments include hospitals and nursing homes, governmental units, manufacturing facilities, and bowling alleys. Its members range from cooks to mechanics and from security guards to clerks.

Local 49 reflects the diversification of Service Employees locals around the country. Unlike factory locals which negotiate a single contract, it must negotiate dozens of different contracts. Consequently its leaders must be broadly versed and flexible.

Exhibit 4.   Profiles of Two Factory Locals

Local 77, Glass, Pottery, Plastics and Allied Workers, AFL-CIO, Delmar, New York

Perhaps typical of the modest-sized, one plant local union of the factory type is Local 77, organized to represent workers at a modern plant opened by Owens-Corning Fiberglass in 1976. The local's 335 members produce building insulation, using electrical furnaces to melt the glass which is processed into the final product. Included are skilled maintenance workers, production technicians, and warehouse shippers.

Local 461, United Cement, Lime and Gypsum Workers, AFL-CIO Macon, Georgia

Chartered in 1966 Local 461 is the second largest local in its international union with slightly over 800 members. All members work at the local plant of the Armstrong Cork Company. Because many CLGW locals are made up of employees at individual cement plants the average local is relatively small. International union staff work closely with the locals, assisting in bargaining, leadership development, publications, and in attacking health and safety problems inherent in most of the union's jurisdiction. In 1984 the CLGW merged with the Boilermakers Union.

craft unions. Most craft unions do, however, fall under the nonfactory classification.

Nor is factory unionism the same as industrial unionism, in the sense of the CIO manufacturing unionism spawned in the 1930s. Many government employee unions, for instance, exist in similar environments and adopt factory union structures, with the agency, municipal department, or hospital being the equivalent of the manufacturing plant. Most nonfactory structures are found among former AFL unions.

(2) The nonfactory category is not a residual category, a catchall for unions that fail to fit the factory classification. Like its "opposite," the factory type, it is one end of a scale. There are a small number of unions which do not clearly fit anywhere on the continuum. The unions of professional athletes, for instance, exist in unusual environments and can only be said to be nonfactory if we view them as the equivalent of local unions, with the national executive director as the business agent.

Dual Government

Alice Cook, writing in the 1960s, thoroughly elaborated on the notion of *dual government* in unions, a concept that had not previously received the full treatment its usefulness warranted.[8]

The union's *internal government* performs functions similar to the governments of other associations with elected leaders (e.g., associations, clubs, PTAs). Membership criteria must be established; dues need to be set and collected. Meetings must be scheduled and held to conduct the business of the organization and to set its policies. Sometimes there is an office to maintain, and there are occasionally matters of internal discipline to be handled.

Internal government is structured like that of most associations, with elected officers and governing boards. The titles of these internal government officers—president, vice-president, recording and financial secretary, trustees, etc.—show no systematic differences between factory and nonfactory unions. The citizens of the internal government are the union's members; the governing docu-

---

[8]"Dual Government in Unions: A Tool for Analysis," *Industrial and Labor Relations Review* 15 (April 1962), pp. 323-49.

ment is the constitution and bylaws. Since the 1959 passage of the Labor Management Reporting and Disclosure Act (LMRDA, also known as the Landrum-Griffin Act, after its sponsors), the conduct of internal union government is expected to comport with minimum standards. No longer can a union, as a few had notoriously done, legally violate its own constitution with impunity, hold elections without notice, suppress opposition in election campaigns, and use the mechanism of trusteeship to shackle dissident locals indefinitely.

The union's *collective bargaining government*, unlike the internal government, arises from the need to conduct an ongoing relationship with another party—the employer(s). Bargaining government is distinct from bargaining structure. Bargaining government deals with the union end of all matters arising out of the labor/management relationship, including negotiations, contract administration, and job referral. Its structure is unlike that of any nonunion organization. It includes the steward system, with its stewards, chief stewards, or committee persons, and grievance committees; local negotiating committees; national negotiating committees; and the many special interest bodies unions establish to formulate proposals, coordinate bargaining, and even approve settlements (e.g., the Skilled Trades council of the UAW; the Corn Council of the Oil, Chemical and Atomic Workers).

At the local level, in a nonfactory union the key position in the bargaining government is that of business agent; in some factory unions, it may be the president; in others, the chair of the shop committee.

Citizenship in the union's bargaining government is gained by virtue of employment in a bargaining unit represented by the union. Those who, in addition, join and pay dues in the union have full rights to vote for bargaining representatives; those who do not are quasi-citizens who receive the benefits but share none of the burdens. The governing document is the contract. The federal law regulating the union's bargaining government is the Labor Management Relations Act (LMRA), which regulates the labor-management-relationship as a whole and indirectly, in most instances, the union's bargaining government. By establishing standards of *fair representation* derived from this statute, the NLRB sets guidelines for the relationship between members and representatives within the union's bargaining government. For instance, bargaining representatives cannot arbitrarily refuse to process grievances by bargaining unit workers who are political opponents or are otherwise in disfavor.

Implications

As a rule, power in the union flows from the bargaining function and attaches to the most authoritative representatives in the bargaining government. The evidence for this generalization is of many types. With few exceptions, member interest, as indicated by attendance at meetings, runs highest in bargaining matters, not in those concerning internal government. Individuals with bargaining responsibility are usually the ones who progress through election to higher office and who occupy the top full-time positions in a local. It is the key bargaining level that is often the locus of power and the recipient of a major share of dues income.

Internal union government is both structurally and functionally standardized, accommodating little to different situations. Bargaining government, however, reflects both the relevant bargaining structure and the structure of the employer's organization. This is particularly noticeable in the factory local, where union bargaining government is matched, through the negotiated grievance procedure, to an often elaborate management hierarchy.

The various overlays of union structure and jurisdiction, each tailored to a given purpose, create a multiple citizenship:

> A given union member can simultaneously be a member and therefore subject to the jurisdiction, of (1) an industrial national union and a craft local union for purposes of internal self-government; (2) a multi-employer city-wide unit for purposes of contract negotiation; and (3) a plant unit for purposes of filing grievances.[9]

Table 10 synthesizes the dual government concept with the information in Table 9 by comparing internal and bargaining governments, both structurally and functionally, in factory and nonfactory settings.

Applications and Qualifications

The dual government notion is a conceptual distinction that can be verified by observation. Sometimes there is not a complete separation. A single official can have responsibilities in both governments, as do presidents in many factory unions. In some in-

---

[9] Jack Barbash, AMERICAN UNIONS: STRUCTURE, GOVERNMENT AND POLITICS (New York: Random House, 1967), p. 20.

Table 10. Dual Union Government

Characteristics	Internal Factory & Nonfactory	Collective bargaining	
		Factory	Nonfactory
Tasks/Activities	Meetings Finances Internal discipline	Negotiations Grievances	Negotiations Grievances Job referral Jurisdiction- maintenance
Leadership	President Vice president Financial secretary Recording secretary Other executive board members	Shop (bargaining or grievance committee) Chief stewards Stewards, sometimes headed by president	Business agent (BA) Assistant BAs Sometimes stewards
Membership/ Citizenship	Union members	Bargaining unit employees	Bargaining unit employees
Governing Document	International constitution Local constitution and bylaws	Collective bargaining agreement (contract)	Collective bargaining agreement (contract)
Regulating statute	Labor-Management Reporting and Disclosure Act (Landrum-Griffin)	National Labor Relations Act (NLRA, or Taft-Hartley)	National Labor Relations Act (NLRA, or Taft-Hartley)
Main source of leadership, authority, or power?	Usually not	Yes, usually	Yes, usually
Comparable to other organizations?	Yes	No	No
Frequently tailored to circumstances?	No	Yes	Yes

stances councils of shop stewards (bargaining government) are constitutionally assigned roles in the internal government.[10]

In some nonfactory locals election to the position of financial secretary (internal) is, automatically, election to the position of business agent. One test of whether an internal or bargaining function is involved is to ask whether the activity is accountable through the constitution or the contract.

[10] For example, see Alice H. Cook, UNION DEMOCRACY: PRACTICE AND IDEAL (New York: Cornell University Press, 1963).

Structural separation is often less complete at levels of government beyond the local. In addition to their executive duties, some international union presidents frequently take the lead in national negotiations. Even within the building trades—long-noted for their local markets and local negotiations—national presidents are assuming increased authority in bargaining.

Internationals distinguished by the presence of both factory and nonfactory locals usually operate somewhat parallel systems geared to the different bargaining needs of the two types of locals.

Matters arising in one government sometimes spill over into the other. Problems of internal discipline that lead to charges and trials often arise over job-related matters, such as a member working for a nonunion contractor or working for less than the union wage scale.

Conclusion

This chapter begins with an examination of union jurisdiction and the varied usages of the term. Jurisdiction entails a description of the environment of a union, a comment on its governance, and a statement of its structural needs. It is the framework for linking the subjects of the chapter.

Elements of jurisdiction and environment lead to an initial typology of unions as factory or nonfactory. The addition of the dual government notion refines the framework by specifying some of the variations in how unions are organized to accomplish different functions. The dual government concept also provides a perspective on power and authority within the labor movement.

To note that certain environmental and jurisdictional traits are associated with certain broad types of union organization and action should not be taken to mean that, given the same environment or jurisdiction, any two unions will adopt the same structure and program. Indeed, unions sometimes respond quite differently to the same environmental stimulus.

Nor is it argued that unions are, or should be, slaves to their environments or that there is a single best structure for each combination of environmental factors. To the contrary, some of the most successful unions are those that take account of environmental influences, identify the potential for change, and then proceed consciously to rearrange the influences. This was the case in the development of the Teamster structure in which small, scattered employers were brought under increasingly broader units for bargaining. But before one can bring about change on this or any scale, it is first necessary to know what currently exists and why.

We have not resolved the question posed by Hoxie—to what extent structural and functional types correspond, i.e., whether particular types of structures are prone to corruption (predatory unionism) and others to social reformism (uplift unionism). Kennedy's typology suggests broad clusters of behavior and ideology associated with factory and nonfactory types. As is usual with unions, the exceptions here would appear to be many, as are the degrees of "fit."

Discussion in this chapter has focused on the local union, where environmental influences are most evident and first felt. From this general framework we can proceed to examine the local in more detail in the next chapter and to examine successively broader levels of union organization in the two chapters following. It is impossible to discuss workers and the workplace or locals and international unions in isolation from one another, for each constantly influences the others. Thus, the separations implied in the following three chapters are somewhat artificial.

Key Words and Phrases

jurisdiction

territorial jurisdiction

trade jurisdiction

industrial jurisdiction

preservation clause

general union

recognition clause

10(k) hearing

work assignment

established bargaining
   relationship

union environment

ease of entry

hierarchy

oligopoly

organization

structure

function

action

process

vestigial structure

government

bargaining structure

coordinated bargaining

pattern bargaining

Robert Hoxie

V. D. Kennedy

factory union

nonfactory union

business agent

Alice Cook

internal government

collective bargaining
   government

fair representation

Review and Discussion Questions

1. Make up a list of meanings for the word "jurisdiction." How many can you think of? Which are broadest, loosest, narrowest? Which are most useful?

2. Pick a union of your choice and describe its environment using the categories in Table 1. Can you locate any influences that are omitted from the table? What problems do you encounter in trying to classify the environment of a single (inter)national union?

3. How is the environment of a building trades union or an industrial union changing? What are the implications for unions?

4. Can you identify an example of a pure factory or nonfactory union? If not, or if the vast majority are not perfect fits, then what is the usefulness of the scheme?

5. Cite a situation where a matter arising in internal government would affect a union's bargaining government. Cite another where the reverse might occur.

6. Early in the 20th century Hoxie wrote that a union strives to organize the entire market within which there is competition for its members' labor. Do you see any exceptions? What does this principle explain concerning variations of union organization and action?

7. Pick a territorial and trade jurisdiction, mix in one element from each heading on Table 1, then design a union structure to meet its members' needs.

Suggestions for Further Reading

Studies of individual unions are often a good source of discussion of jurisdiction and environment. Robert A. Christie's *Empire in Wood*, a study of the Carpenters, focuses on the role of jurisdiction in the growth of that union from the early days of the AFL to the mid-1940s and is perhaps the best single source. For a treatment of how a union (the Retail Clerks) responded to jurisdictional dependency on another (Teamsters), see Marten S. Estey, "The Strategic Alliance as a Factor in Union Growth," in *Industrial and Labor Relations Review* (October 1955). Several of the works cited in footnotes in this chapter are appropriate sources. These include those by Hoxie, Kennedy, Cook, and Barbash. For an older, general discussion of the chapter subject matter, see Philip Taft, *The Structure and Government of Labor Unions*.

For a more complete discussion of bargaining structures and their significance for bargaining power and union behavior, see Thomas A. Kochan, *Collective Bargaining and Industrial Relations* (Homewood, Ill.: Richard D. Irwin, 1980), chapter 4.

Complete bibliographical information for the above titles can be found in the Bibliography.

5

Workplace and Local Union Organization

> The shop steward has to solve the elemental problem of government—
> the relationship of the member to authority.
>
> Joseph Kovner and Herbert Lahne, 1953*

A union organizer, appearing on the scene at a plant or office, will find that the workers are already organized, although not in a union. The existing structure is called the *informal organization* of the workplace. Its manifestations are likely to include:

(1) Informal networks associated with workplace-based activities, such as social cliques, car pools, and employer-sponsored sports and clubs.

(2) Leaders whose opinions are sought by fellow workers on a variety of questions, including complaints about supervision, production standards, and working conditions.

(3) Shop rules and customs, informally enforced by the workers. These codes will cover such matters as what constitutes a reasonable contribution to the output of a work group, what production rate should be maintained, and how to discipline the "rate buster" whose overproduction jeopardizes the rest of the group.[1]

(4) Occasional forms of resistance, such as slowdowns, group protests, and even walkouts. These devices are popularly thought of as purely union-initiated actions.

---

*"Shop Society and the Union," *Industrial and Labor Relations Review* 7, no. 1 (October 1953), p. 7.

[1] To some extent these measures are a response to endemic job insecurity. Among several classic studies see Stanley B. Mathewson, RESTRICTION OF OUTPUT AMONG UNORGANIZED WORKERS (New York: Viking Press, 1931).

In variable situations such as construction, the arena for informal organization is likely to be the trade itself or the contractor's organization. But here the structure is relatively impermanent, varying from job to job. In either case, factory or nonfactory, the absence of a union means that *formal authority* remains with the employer.

The effective organizer identifies the salient features of the informal organization, particularly those of its leaders who are sympathetic to the union. With any success, several of the leaders will become members of the union's organizing committee and, later, officers of the local union. Thus the local union, especially in the factory situation, becomes rooted in the workplace. In this sense one can refer to an *organic relationship* between the local union and the workplace.

Once established, a local union is sustained by the informal organization of the trade or the workplace, which the union utilizes for its own leadership development and communications. But the union also alters or displaces many of the informal ways, substituting more routinized, and even bureaucratic, methods which the union pledges to uphold in accordance with the terms of the contract. How effectively these new forms serve worker aspirations and interests and how closely the tie remains between the local and the workplace will in part determine whether the members view the union as "we," "they," or "it." The outcome is also influenced by a third element in the equation—the international union—whose presence can afford the workers a tremendous advantage but can also impose additional expectations on the local union.

The Standing of the Local Union

By forming or joining a national organization, members of a local have opted to surrender a certain amount of local autonomy in order to realize the benefits of broader combination and coordination. "All for one and one for all" will in theory, and usually in practice, work to everyone's benefit. Situations do arise, however, where a local and the international are at odds. While the international increasingly has the authority, the international that engages heavy handedly in many such encounters may endanger its viability as an effective democratic organization.

Unions have a variety of means for coping with such conflicts. Publications, meetings, contact between locals and internationals through staff representatives, and the election of leaders are methods designed to bring about equity and unity of program and action. There are also formal measures, notably the union constitution, that often allow international officers to control local actions.

Constitutional provisions dividing authority between the local and the international union range along a continuum, from decentralized to centralized. For example, the constitution of the Graphic Arts Union (GAIU) reserved powers not granted the international to the local:

> In respect to all matters governed by the Constitution and laws of the International, each Local is subject to the authority of the International. In respect to all other matters each Local is subject only to its membership.[2]

But, while the GAIU was not one of the more centralized unions, another section of its constitution made clear that the international was the supreme authority on a broad range of subjects:

> The International constitutes the sovereign and supreme organization having full and exclusive jurisdiction.... It possesses full power, in conformity with the Constitution, to make, amend, or repeal general laws and other regulations affecting the government and conduct of the International, its Locals and its members, to decide all jurisdictional and other disputes and controversies arising within it ... and to take any and all other actions as may be necessary and appropriate to accomplish its objectives.[3]

Many union constitutions leave no doubt about the authority of the international, terming locals *subordinate bodies*. Article 36 of the UAW constitution contains a model charter for a local union which reads:

> That said Union forever and under any and all circumstances shall be subordinate to and comply with all the requirements of the Constitution, Bylaws and General Laws or other laws of the International Union ... ; That said Union shall for all time be guided and controlled by all acts and decisions of the International Union. . . .

The international convention of delegates elected by the locals is of course the supreme voice. The ability of a convention, however, to exercise supervision, except to amend constitutions and approve broad policy, is limited. In practice, then, the balance of the inter-

---

[2] Part II, Chapter 1, *GAIU Constitution*, rev. January 1976, p. 26. (The GAIU, following merger, is now titled the Graphic Communications International Union (GCIU).)

[3] Part I, Article II, *GAIU Constitution*, p. 1.

national union's day-to-day authority tends to be exercised by the international officers.

The supremacy of the international is evident in other areas. Contracts negotiated locally are normally approved by the international before taking full effect. Where negotiations are conducted on a nationwide, industrywide, or corporationwide basis, the international usually directs bargaining. In some cases local contracts are in theory negotiated by the international on behalf of the local.

Financial procedures are also indicative. Internationals maintain financial supervision over locals and can place a local in trusteeship for a variety of malpractices. Financial measures to shift control from numerous locals to a single office are designed to standardize practices and preclude ineptness or malfeasance.

These are some indicators of international control over locals, but the underlying causes of a trend toward enlarged national scope and reduced local functions lie elsewhere. As organizations become larger, as many unions have through organizing and mergers, their needs for internal coordination and controls increase, and it becomes increasingly difficult to maintain decentralized structures. The rapidly increasing complexity of the tasks of union leadership and administration ranges from record systems to legal developments. Perhaps the overriding force is that unions feel pressed to develop their organizational capabilities to stay even with the ever-expanding and realigning configurations of corporate structures and technological change.

The portents for local unions are not clear. Will locals become little more than branch offices of national headquarters? Or, will they be vital units of organization and activity, remaining in touch with members and coordinating their efforts with those of the internationals? To strip the local of its functions would be to deny the union a large portion of the environmental sensitivity and structural flexibility that are so necessary. But, to deny the international all control would be to deny the advantages of broader combination and coordination that workers need if they are to deal effectively with massive corporations.

Some Terminology

Although the term "local union" is used in the vast majority of unions, a few use other terminology. The Machinists union (IAM) has local lodges; the Letter Carriers (NALC) has branches; teachers unions sometimes refer to chapters; and other unions refer to divisions.

Generally, locals are affiliated with a national union. The first exception is the *independent local union*. Independent locals are affiliated with no other body and typically represent bargaining unit workers at a single establishment. While some independents are quite aggressive in pursuing union functions, others are barely independent enough of the employer to avoid designation as company unions.

The second exception is the *directly affiliated local union* (DALU). DALUs are attached to the AFL-CIO but do not belong to an international. They are successors of the *federal labor unions*, chartered by the AFL in areas where no union had clear and exclusive jurisdiction. The AFL-CIO encourages DALUs to affiliate with internationals in related jurisdictions. A major event of this type occurred in 1979 when the 10,000-member, directly affiliated New York taxi-drivers local voted to join the Service Employees.

Some unions are notable for the absence of local unions in their structures. Unions of professional athletes, for instance, typically have a player representative from each club who conducts team meetings and serves as a link to the national (leaguewide) body. The team meeting is, however, more of a workplace unit in the bargaining structure than a formal unit of internal union government.

Another union without locals is the Air Line Pilots Association (ALPA):

> All of the approximately 30,000 members belong directly to the International and pay dues to the International. There are Local Councils where pilots are domiciled and a Master Executive Council for each airline pilot group in ALPA, but these are primarily administrative units and not local labor unions in the accepted sense, and without the autonomy normally associated with local unions in the U.S. labor movement.[4]

Both athletes and pilots have relatively permanent bases but travel extensively in their work. The economics of both industries make it unlikely that a local union would be able to accomplish much on its own.

---

[4] Letter to the author from W. W. Anderson, executive assistant to the president, ALPA, October 9, 1979.

Local Union Dimensions

The shape of a local union, the tasks of its leaders, and the roles of its members vary according to size, geographic scope, jurisdictional variety, and the number of different employers, bargaining units, and contracts. A few examples illustrate the range and suggest the implications for local union affairs.

Size. While the average size of a local union in the United States is approximately 300 members, variations in size and structure render this figure virtually meaningless. A contrast within a single union, the United Association of Plumbers and Pipe Fitters ("UA"), illustrates extremes. In 1978 the UA had four members in Local 668, Boulder City, Nevada. Local 669, a nationwide local of sprinkler fitters (fabricators and installers of fire protection systems), listed 6,649 members. The average for the UA's 475 U.S. locals was slightly more than 600.

A handful of "super locals" have more members than most international unions. At the Ford Rouge plant in Dearborn, Michigan, UAW Local 600 had a peak membership of about 80,000 during World War II. Since then several operations have been moved to other locations, but with approximately 38,000 members in 1979, Local 600 remained the largest local in the UAW. The largest Steelworker local in that year was Local 1010, with 18,000 members working at Inland Steel in East Chicago, Indiana.

Not all large locals are of the heavy industrial, factory variety. In fact, the very largest are nonfactory unions.[5] In New York City, Retail, Wholesale, Department Store Union Local 1–S was reported in 1982 to have as members some 60,000 retail workers; Service Employees Local 32B-32J had 55,000 members; and IBEW Local 3 included 37,000. Teamsters Local 743 in Chicago had some 40,000 members. Many other nonfactory locals include well over 10,000 members.

The ascendancy, at least in size, of the nonfactory locals reflects the limitation of most factory local memberships to the employees at a single establishment and the tendency for post-World War II employment to shift toward smaller workplaces. The non-

---

[5] With the one exception noted, membership estimates are for 1979. Terminology is sometimes a problem here. We have not included as a local union AFSCME Local 1000 (formerly the New York State Employees Association), because it resembles a district more than a local union. Local 1000 is reported to include almost a quarter of a million members.

factory union can grow by bringing in workers from more establishments, whereas the factory model would charter new locals for new
units.

Geographical Scope.   The membership of the typical factory
local works under a single roof or in clustered locations. Nonfactory
locals tend to be scattered over a city or a multicounty area, but even
broader territories are not unusual. Take, for example, two Hoisting and Portable locals of the Operating Engineers. Local 12 covers
the southern half of California and of Nevada. The northern parts
of these two states, plus Utah and Hawaii, are within the territorial
jurisdiction of Local 3.

Broad territories are found in seagoing unions whose locals are
organized out of ports, with members working around the world.
Local 669 of the UA has sprinkler-fitter members nationwide. And
considering its numbers (only slightly more than 200 employees of
ATT Communications scattered at several locations throughout Indiana), the statewide territory of Communications Workers Local
5850 must be considered extremely broad.

Occupational Variety.   Cited above were several locals with
diverse jurisdictions, including Teamsters Local 743 and Service
Employees Locals 32B-32J. The different occupational skills and
employment situations in these locals lead to their designation as
heterogeneous, mixed, or simply miscellaneous. They contrast with
the *homogeneous*, or occupationally uniform, locals found in the
building trades, among teachers and fire fighters, and in certain
transportation and service occupations.

Different Employers and Contracts.   The number of different
employers under contract often varies with the size, geography, and
jurisdictional diversity of a local. Also associated with the number
of employers is the prevalence of small establishments, as in unions
of auto mechanics, construction workers, and service workers. But
this is not invariable, because some unions represent many small
units employed in large, often conglomerate-owned establishments
in printing and publishing, department store chains, and grocery
chains.

IBEW Local 3, New York City, is an example of a local with
hundreds of employers under contract. Locals representing many
employers in the same industry often attempt to negotiate a single
contract covering all employers, which are represented by an employers' association. For instance, Service Employees Local 32B-
32J, negotiates for 20,000 apartment house doorkeepers, maintenance workers, elevator operators, and porters working in some

3,000 different buildings. The owners are represented through an association.

Implications for Local Union Organization. The dimensions of a local union can range from a small local whose members work on a single type of product or service for a single employer at a single location to a large local whose members perform all manner of jobs for hundreds of employers at jobsites spread over a vast area. And, as earlier examples illustrate, there exist many combinations in between.

Each situation imposes its own set of tasks on the local union and its leaders. In the first situation, characterized by close working relations, communications can be largely face-to-face. Here, the local is small and does not have full-time officers. Bargaining would appear to be a relatively straightforward affair, with only a single contract to negotiate and few basic differences within the homogeneous membership. In practice, of course, much depends on the employer, as well as the market and the strategy of the union. Bargaining can become complex even in this situation.

In the second case the local relies on full-time officers who travel to scattered job sites to conduct bargaining-related business. These full-time officers, or business agents, are the main contact between the many members and the union. Regular face-to-face contact being unlikely, the union may rely heavily on publications or unit meetings to communicate with the membership. The leadership would need to be well-versed in a broad range of employment situations and occupations. Dealing with varied employers requires a working knowledge of the economics of different types of establishments.

One hybrid union structure close to the factory model is the *amalgamated industrial* local, which typically consists of two or more manufacturing units of different employers that the international deems too small to justify separate locals. Often these units will be in closely related product lines. An example is UAW Local 724, Lansing, Michigan, whose membership at one point consisted of foundry workers employed by five different companies in the area working under five different contracts. A more heterogeneous example is Transport Workers Local 225 in Hackensack, New Jersey, which includes members from five different bus lines, employees of several school systems, and the blue- and white-collar government workers of one township. Locals of this sort generally have some officers elected from each unit and others elected on a localwide basis.

The Factory Local: Workplace and Bargaining Government

The previous chapter sketched the influence of employer structure and bargaining structure on the local union, indicating that functional demands make imprints on the collective bargaining government of both factory and nonfactory unions. Because of their environments factory locals have workplace bargaining governments that are more highly developed than those of their nonfactory counterparts.

In large locals with large corporate employers, one expects to find an array of union representatives, many of them full-time, in the union's in-plant bargaining apparatus. Typically these stewards, committeepeople (UAW), or grievers (Steelworkers) are elected by the workers in their departments, or at the higher levels from multidepartment districts in the plant, and through agreement with the employer often serve full-time on contract-related matters. In smaller locals all or most of the union's bargaining representatives, as well as its internal government officers, work full-time for the employer and are largely uncompensated for their union work. This point-of-production bargaining apparatus is the structure of the local within the workplace. Nationally some 400,000 people serve as stewards or other workplace representatives of their co-workers.

For most members contact with the union is primarily through these bargaining government representatives, and the contact occurs in the workplace itself. It is here that information is exchanged—members make their desires known and get news of other localwide developments and events—and that grievances are filed and usually settled.

The *shop steward*, the union's counterpart of the first-line supervisor, is the first-line bargaining official of the union. The steward's primary responsibility is to enforce the contract and represent members with grievances. While stewards perform other functions, e.g., communications, social service and benefit referral, and sometimes political work, grievances remain their main responsibility. Their effectiveness in resolving grievances is the important measure of their performance. One commentary notes that "Grievances absorb the major energies of union members in the shops and emerge as the determinant of union life in any conflict with other interests."[6]

---

[6] Kovner and Lahne, "Shop Society and the Union," p. 6.

Because of the steward's position in the overlap between work-place and union structure, the steward "really serves two masters—the society of employees from which [he/she] is elected and the union authority."[7] In shops where union strength is lacking stewards may orient toward a third master, the employer. These three reference points—workers, union, employer—and the extent to which union representatives in the workplace orient toward one or more of them are related to a number of employer and employment dimensions, the traditions of the shop, the types of problems which become the source of grievances, and the orientation of workers and leaders toward leadership roles and the possibilities for change.[8] A steward's conflicting loyalties between the shop and union can be a legitimate one, depending on the issues, but the presence of a steward who is so employer-oriented as to neglect worker representation usually indicates deeper problems in the workplace and the union.

Higher level representatives in the bargaining government of a large factory union, such as chief stewards or committee people, are more likely to be full-time. In theory stewards are the initial gate-keepers on problems presented by members, and higher officers become involved only if no resolution is reached at the early stages. In practice much of the chief steward's time is taken up in discussions with other stewards, in second- or third-step meetings with manage-ment, and in investigating grievances. Investigating grievances of-ten involves consultation with the local's president or vice-president (in locals where these officers play a strong role in bargaining) and with the staff representative.

The union staff representative is the international or the inter-mediate unit presence in local union affairs. Assigned several locals to service, this person assists in negotiations, in grievance meetings and arbitrations, and in getting new locals off the ground. The amount of assistance or supervision depends mainly on the abilities of the local leadership and the policies of the union, as well as the representative's own abilities and inclinations. It will also vary con-siderably according to whether the contract is negotiated nationally or by the local leadership. Where bargaining is national many forms of local input go into national demands, and the local itself negoti-ates a "local supplement" to cover local variations. The local's ma-

---

[7] Ibid., p. 6.
[8] James Wallihan, *Workplace Politics and Leadership in a Chicago Printing Trades Union*, Ph.D. Dissertation, Indiana University, 1974.

jor bargaining activity, however, will center on *contract administration*, which concerns the interpretation and enforcement of the collective bargaining agreement and the handling of grievances arising under it. More broadly, the local engages in *grievance representation*, which takes as its starting point the needs of the employees and encompasses, in addition to grievances alleging contract violations, grievances that are more effectively handled through noncontractual means.

The forum for collective leadership and decision making in the bargaining structure of a local union is often the *grievance committee*, sometimes termed the *bargaining committee*. These committees tend to be made up of representatives drawn from all of the stewards to the local president, with the staff representative often joining in.

The negotiated *grievance procedure* illustrates how the union in the workplace organizes to reflect and counter, level by level, the structure of the employer's organization in its conduct of contract administration. Table 11 depicts a simple grievance procedure. The number of steps in the grievance procedure is roughly pegged to the employer's structure, with more steps in larger, more complex and bureaucratic establishments. The table also shows the general hierarchy likely to exist in the local union collective bargaining government.

A distinct part of the union's bargaining government consists of representatives participating in *contract negotiations*, usually held every three years. The local may negotiate all subjects, economic and noneconomic alike, although in many industries it negotiates only local issues, with economic matters left to corporationwide or industrywide bargaining.

In either case local union negotiating committees are selected in a variety of ways. Some constitutions require localwide elections but include *ex officio* (by virtue of office) membership for the presi-

---

Table 11. Simple Grievance Procedure

Step	Union	Management
1	Steward	First-line supervisor
2	Chief Steward	Department head
3	Grievance committee/president	Labor Relations Department
4	Submission to third party arbitration	

dent or the chairperson of the grievance committee. Other constitutions permit appointment by the president or the board, with approval by the membership. Grievance representatives are usually included. In a few instances the grievance committee and the negotiating committee are one and the same.

Negotiating activities reach into the workplace, but not to the extent that contract administration and grievance representation do. To be sure, issues for negotiations arise from the workplace and are discussed there, and committee members are employed there. But negotiations are cyclical and are not tied to the union's day-to-day workplace structure.

Internal Government of the Factory Local

The ultimate policy-making body of the local union is the general membership meeting, chaired by the local union president. Between meetings this function is delegated to an *executive board*, which must authorize certain actions and expenses of the president and other officers. The major executive board positions, and there is variation among unions in the designations, are president, vice-president, financial secretary/treasurer, and recording secretary. The internal government duties of these positions are substantially those suggested by their titles, but unions vary in the bargaining responsibilities assigned to these officers. Secondary board positions are apt to be titled trustees (guardians of the local's property), sergeant-at-arms, guide, and member-at-large.

The Labor Management Reporting and Disclosure Act of 1959 (LMRDA) requires that local union executive officers be elected by secret ballot at least once every three years, the term of office adopted by most unions. The duration of many collective bargaining agreements is also three years. Whether new officers are chosen before or after contract negotiations varies. The LMRDA does not regulate in the same fashion the selection of representatives in the collective bargaining government, unless bargaining officials double as executive officers of local unions. Although a few are appointed, most factory union stewards are elected by members of the unit they represent. Chief stewards are more frequently elected on a localwide basis, but larger plants may be divided into election districts. Terms vary from six months to three years. Bargaining officials are often chosen in the same election as executive officers.

Tied more to internal government than to collective bargaining is a third sphere of local union government, the appointed *com-*

mittee structure. With a chairperson and membership usually appointed by the president, these standing committees cover education, legislation/political action, recreation, union label, community services and a number of other areas. Many locals with skilled workers also have apprenticeship committees. These standing committees are distinct in origin and function from the grievance and negotiating committees that are part of the collective bargaining structure. (See Figure 3.)

Local Politics

Despite the single workplace and industrial identity of the factory local union, the membership is more likely than that of a non-

Figure 3.   A Typical Local Union Internal Government Structure

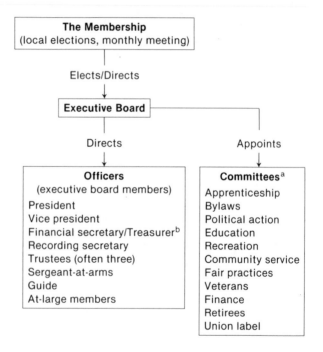

aNonfactory locals of the craft variety will often have an active wage scale committee.
bSome nonfactory union locals, for instance the IBEW and the SEIU, combine the positions of financial secretary and business manager. This combined office thus encompasses both internal and bargaining duties.

factory craft union to fragment into overlapping interest groups. These may be based on employment criteria or other group allegiances. Groups can form along lines of skill, classification, seniority, age, department, race, sex, friendship, and other criteria.

In their classic work on the industrial local union, Sayles and Strauss note that

> A union can be looked at in two ways, as a unified body of members promoting their common welfare through collective action and as a confederation of competing interest groups, each with individual goals.[9]

The issues of local union politics can be classified roughly into collective and divisive ones, the latter pitting the interests of one individual or group against those of another. One challenge of local union leadership is the discovery and implementation of collective solutions to potentially divisive problems. If competing demands of one group of workers against another overwhelm the collective interest vis-à-vis the employer, the union faces fragmentation and operational collapse. The union seeks to implement a variation on the old Lincoln refrain: "A nation divided against itself cannot stand."

While the local union agenda may reflect the desires of apparently conflicting group interests, it can also be heavily determined and sometimes dominated by employment-related concerns that override fractional interests. The employment cycle has a strong impact. When employment in a plant is stable, group interests surface through the grievance procedure. When the economy reaches what is euphemistically termed "full-employment" (about 5 percent unemployed), grievances tend to focus more on classifications, rate differentials, and matters related to "getting ahead." Workers are more willing to file certain grievances when alternative employment prospects are relatively good. Skilled workers are especially mobile.

But when unemployment is high and when layoffs or shutdowns occur, the agenda alters radically. Grievances then involve disputes over who is to be laid off in what order. Now able to pick and choose, some managements attempt to "weed out" workers they retained previously, thus adding to discipline and discharge grievances. The local union must shift gears to keep up morale, inform members of unemployment benefit procedures, and tighten its financial belt. If and when employment picks up in the plant, re-

---

[9] Leonard R. Sayles and George Strauss, THE LOCAL UNION, rev. ed. (New York: Harcourt, Brace and World, 1967), p. 24.

called workers may hesitate to file legitimate grievances while they are still getting back on their feet. Conditions that the union fought for and won in previous years may have to be won anew.

The events that arouse the greatest interest in the factory local are typically local elections, contract proposals, strike votes, contract votes, and proposed dues increases. While these issues create peak interest, they do not sustain meeting attendance throughout the year. Local picnics, dances, and other forms of family entertainment sometimes involve a broad spectrum of members. Other activities, such as education courses and political rallies in the local hall, appeal to a smaller segment of the membership.

The monthly membership meeting is a union institution subject to much attention and lament, the latter due primarily to the low percentage of attendance. Union leaders who measure the interest in the union by attendance resort to all sorts of gimmicks to boost it. Much of this concern misses the mark, since many members participate through what has been termed the "shop society."[10] Failure to attend the monthly meeting does not necessarily signify a lack of interest in the union.

The monthly meeting is an arena for those with an official role or a sustained interest in the affairs of the union. It is a forum for dealing primarily with localwide concerns rather than the individual and small group grievances for which the bargaining government is geared. As it is also a place for those who want to become involved in or to learn more about the union, it is important that the meeting be run in a manner to accommodate these interests.

The meeting also serves, in theory and usually in practice, to allow members a place to question the operations of the local and the actions of its officers. It functions incidentally as an arena in which political aspirants become known, hone their speaking abilities, build reputations, and score points over real and potential rivals for office.

Much of the meeting agenda is typically prescribed in the international constitution or the local by-laws with the reading of correspondence and financial reports, the approval of expenditures, and the usual old and new business, followed by "good and welfare."

Given this routine and the governmental and political functions it serves, the factory local meeting is not likely to attract sustained interest by the majority of members, who would rather spend their free time elsewhere and who deal with union matters in the

---

[10] Kovner and Lahne, "Shop Society and the Union," pp. 3–14.

plant or through scanning the local union newsletter. It is not surprising, then, that members with particularistic concerns attend a single meeting only to write it off as "a lot of rigamarole and politics."

Well-run local meetings are important. But attendance is not the sole or even primary measure of the union's effectiveness. Overemphasis on monthly meetings attendance overlooks other types of union activity in which members can participate—committee work, grievance support efforts in the shop, publications, special bargaining meetings, political rallies, clubs, and other forms of union-sponsored recreation and education. Of all membership activity, that which occurs in the workplace itself is perhaps most critical.

Nonfactory Local Unions

The variety of locals under this heading is immense. Identified in the last chapter were the miscellaneous unions and the craft locals of the building trades and printing trades. Many unions with nonfactory structures consist of workers not officially classed as skilled. These include, among others, hotel and restaurant employees, building service workers, construction laborers, retail clerks and salespeople, and attendants. Figure 4 illustrates the combination of two dimensions often found among nonfactory environments and unions.

The reader should note that Figure 4 does not include industrial workers, such as skilled tradespeople, who might fall under one of the cells in the column headed "primarily stable." The em-

Figure 4. Nonfactory Union Varieties and Examples

Occupation	Employment Situation	
	Primarily variable	Primarily stable
Skilled, apprenticeable	Carpenters, Electricians, Musicians, (hiring hall or referral) 1	Printing trades (amalgamated) 2
Semiskilled or nonskilled, nonapprenticeable	3 Laborers, stage hands (hiring hall)	4 Store clerks, hotel and restaurant employees (miscellaneous)

phasis on "primarily" is important because many employment situations are mixed in that a large complement of relatively permanent employees may be supplemented with a supply of casual labor, often obtained through union referral, at peak periods. This situation exists, for example, in the entertainment, printing, and tourism-related industries.

Of what significance are the Figure 4 dimensions for structure and leadership in the nonfactory local union? Recall that the organic tie to the workplace was stressed in the earlier discussion of the origins and structure of factory unions. In variable or mobile employment situations no such permanent bond can exist. Consequently the union's structure is centered at the union hall, and its workplace organization is barely visible.

In the right-hand column headed "stable," most workers, whether skilled or unskilled, will see the same coworkers on a more or less daily basis. In the "variable" column they will not. Similarly, in the top row headed "skilled/apprenticeable" there will be a consciousness of trade or craft, if not necessarily of work location, with stable groups of coworkers. Thus some regularized form of workplace organization by the union is most feasible in stable work force situations. Elsewhere trade or craft consciousness to some extent substitutes for the lack of stability, as in the building trades, or reinforces stability, as in the printing industry. The strongest workplace organization in nonfactory situations, then, would be expected in the stable, apprenticeable situations such as the printing industry (Cell 2).

Indeed this is generally the case. The skilled printing unions, for instance, have long been noted for the prominence of the chapel, the formal organization of the workplace that preceded the formation of local and national printing unions. In their constitutions many printing trades unions recognize the existence and functions of the chapel and its head, the chapel chairman.

Another relevant characteristic of employment stability is its impact on grievances and, hence, on the tasks of the union and its prime bargaining representative, the business agent. Where workers are hired entirely through the employer and not as a result of carrying a union card or union referral, they share some characteristics of factory employment in that workers have a stake in a job with the particular employer. This contrasts with the hiring hall, referral, or casual situation in which this stake is less apparent. Filing a formal grievance under these conditions is hardly relevant, especially since the job may only last another week or two. Consequently grievance procedures in high turnover situations are simple and focus on the business agent, unlike the formal multistep procedures found in the large factory situation.

A grievance takes on more meaning in the stable situation. But where there are a few workers at each location, the nonfactory union does not replicate the elaborate structure found in factory situations. While the steward may play a strong initial role in presenting the grievance, further appeals are usually turned over to the business agent.

Pursuing the logic of Figure 4 further, it can be seen that the opposite of the skilled/stable situation is the unskilled/variable combination (Cell 3). In this group, represented by construction laborers, catering employees, and similar occupations, one generally finds almost no workplace organization or stable leadership and a strong reliance on the union hall and the business agent.

In between are the skilled/variable situations, typified by the apprenticeable building trades (Cell 1), in which a relatively homogeneous craft perspective may begin in the family and is enhanced by uniform training, pay rates, and occupational prospects. To some extent this compensates for the absence of a stable work location and workplace structure. While workplace organization here usually consists solely of an appointed job steward acting as a lookout for the business agent, the identity with the union and the craft as well as the opportunity to obtain other employment make the absence of stability less critical.

Also between the two extremes are the semiskilled/stable groupings (Cell 4), typified by the store units that make up locals of the Food and Commercial Workers. There is still a reasonable expectation that workers of the same major grocery chain will see the same coworkers from week to week. Thus the workplace for retail clerks provides a point of identity and stability. Again, because the units are relatively small, workplace representation usually consists of a single shop steward who acts as the first point of contact with members and serves as the eyes and ears of the business agent.

Where stable employment locations or scattered groupings of workers in similar occupations exist, some unions attempt to stimulate unit organizations to serve as a sublocal union focus of activities. Thus a local representing all manner of units might hold separate meetings for hospital workers, drivers, and building service workers. Others, like grocery clerks Local 770 of the UFCW in Los Angeles, have held mass local union meetings.

Many of the larger miscellaneous or amalgamated locals have developed in such a way that they perform functions similar to those of intermediate bodies in other unions. By facilitating member participation in subunits, they attempt to counter the centrifugal tendencies inherent in large unions of diverse jurisdiction. This has also been described as "breaking the local down into convenient-sized and relatively homogeneous groups, without destroying the overall unity of the local. . . ."[11]

Unlike the typical factory local, which negotiates a single contract with a single employer, nonfactory locals negotiate either with many employers bargaining through a multi-employer association or with many employers with whom it negotiates separate agreements. It may also coordinate its efforts with those of other unions, even to the point of negotiating jointly with them. Multiple contracts, even where they are not staggered evenly over the years, makes negotiating more of a year-round activity for many nonfactory locals. It also puts a premium on leaders, notably business agents, who are familiar with different settings and able to negotiate effectively in each.

At Center Stage: The Business Agent

Even where the business agent lacks any role in the union's internal government, he or she is the most prominent official at the union hall and, hence, in the local. While many of the business agent's bargaining responsibilities are not unlike those performed by bargaining officials in a factory local, others are more unique to nonfactory locals:

(1) *Many nonfactory unions, especially in the building trades, maintain health and welfare funds and pension funds.*

The business agent will typically serve as a trustee or administrator for such funds in which the union and employers share equally in management. In almost all factory situations, control over the use of pension funds rests entirely with employers.

(2) *Many nonfactory locals take responsibility for organizing new units.*

In the factory union, organizing is normally the responsibility of the staff of the national or intermediate body. Where business agents and their assistants or local organizers establish initial and sustained contact with members in new units, there can be a decided advantage in local union elections.

---

[11] Herbert J. Lahne and Joseph Kovner, "Local Union Structure: Formality and Reality," *Industrial and Labor Relations Review* 9, no. 1 (October 1955), p. 27.

(3) *The position of the BA in the communications structure of the local union has a clear impact.*

Units with little or no contact with one another are all in touch with the business agent on a regular or intermittent basis.

In addition, where there is a lack of substantial workplace organization, the business agent is the clear link with the union hall. The fact that the business agent is in touch with many employers in the local market area brings a broader economic perspective that enhances the business agent's position.[12]

The astute business agent who does not alienate any large segment of the local's membership probably enjoys a substantially greater tenure in office than does the factory union president who is subject to the often volatile nature of local union politics. Despite the fact that local meetings are chaired by the president and not the business agent, it is the business agent's report that is usually the most prominent item on the agenda. The bargaining government of these locals largely dominates the internal government, as evidenced by the fact that the business agent's is the full-time position.

Several variants should be noted:

(1) *Some locals elect all their business agents.*

The Sheet Metal Workers, for instance, elect a business manager and often one or more business representatives, depending on the size and finances of the local. Other unions elect a "directing business agent," who then appoints assistants and organizers. Where assistants are appointed there is obviously a greater potential for patronage power, and the appointing official in turn takes greater responsibility for decisions, for better or worse.

(2) *Some unions elect full-time secretary/treasurers who are responsible for office administration, finances, and record keeping.*

The presence of other full-time elected officials can serve to check the one-person dominance of the business agent.

(3) *Several locals have merged the top positions in the internal and bargaining governments by combining the offices of business agent and president, usually under the latter title.*

Combining the two positions streamlines the organization and may serve to limit internal conflicts. Many printing trades locals in different internationals have taken this step.

(4) *The role of the business agent in the local should not be*

---

[12] An excellent description of the business agent role in the nonfactory union is the booklet by Van Dusen Kennedy and Wilma Rule Krauss, *The Business Agent and His Union*, rev. ed. (Berkeley: University of California, Institute of Industrial Relations, 1964).

*confused with positions of the same title or with staff representatives
in intermediate bodies.*

While intermediate bodies, such as joint boards and district
councils, perform many functions similar to nonfactory locals, they
are a level higher in the international union structure. (See Chapter
7.)

(5) *Business agents in local market unions that are heavily dependent on favorable state and municipal legislation and enforcement activity often spend considerable time lobbying and meeting
with representatives of other unions with similar needs.*

Building codes have been of long-standing importance to the
building trades unions, as have the terms of government construction contracts. Municipal ordinances, codes, and licensing arrangements also impact on food service establishments, laundries, taxi
and local delivery drivers, building services, and retail establishments—all areas in which affected unions have a stake. State and
municipal workers' unions are perhaps even more dependent on
legislation. For these and other reasons certain nonfactory unions
form councils that take on significant coordination and communications functions. Examples are the local Building and Construction Trades Councils and the Allied Printing Trades Councils. In
some localities public employees' councils are emerging.

(6) *Whether a union can afford a full-time representative depends, obviously, on the level of its dues income and its general financial condition.*

Some nonfactory craft locals with as few as 50 members have
full-time officers; for most, a minimum of 200 is probably more re-
alistic. Factory locals, on the other hand, are likely to approach
1,000 members before paying a single full-time official from union
funds. The dispersed nature of employment and the special needs of
the trade tend to make a full-time representative more essential for
nonfactory locals. (See Figure 5.) This was recognized in the 19th
century when unions engaged walking delegates, the ancestors of
today's business agents.

Conclusion

Nonfactory locals seem to enjoy a particular advantage in the
realm of organizing, so critical to their survival. Where organizing
is largely the responsibility of the local, as it is in the building and
printing trades unions, the Service Employees, the Teamsters, and
to a large extent in the retail unons, experience, training, and incen-

Figure 5. Dual Government of a Nonfactory Local Union

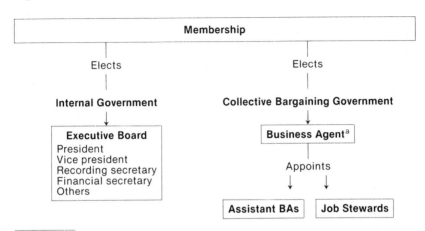

a As noted in text, the business agent is sometimes selected by virtue of election to the office of financial secretary. Assistant business agents are sometimes elected.

tives are easier to develop. Leaders can enhance their own positions within internationals by organizing new units and developing large locals. Staff salaries and promotions can be pegged to organizing results. More members are likely to have been involved in organizing campaigns themselves. And the sheer variety of units may develop in leaders a flexibility that benefits organizing campaigns.

As it applies to some individual cases, the comparison between factory and nonfactory locals is overdrawn. But it points to a major consideration for international unions, the subject of the next two chapters. How can union structure be geared to provide the incentives and experience necessary to deal with complex and rapidly changing environments and the varied skills required for union effectiveness?

Members of a factory local typically are less likely to perceive the necessity of organizing and its connection with their own situation. The leaders, emerging from a single location and judged by their effectiveness in dealing with the needs of members at that location, usually have no particular experience in or knowledge of organizing. If they were to organize another plant, it would probably be chartered as a separate local, with no "political" advantage to the organizers. On top of this, many factory unions tend to organize primarily within their familiar industrial jurisdictions and are hence less able to relate to other types of employment.

The new *staff representative* typically emerges from this background. Often a former local president, the new "rep" will be unfamiliar with organizing and unacquainted with conditions in other plants within the same industry. Assigned to assist several locals in bargaining and internal affairs, the staff representative is also asked to organize new locals, a task for which he or she may be singularly unprepared. It is perhaps surprising then that many new staff reps do develop the necessary flexibility and talent to manage at least modest successes and occasionally even spectacular ones.

Key Words and Phrases

informal organization
formal authority
organic relationship
subordinate bodies
independent local union
directly affiliated local
   union (DALU)
amalgamated industrial local
   union
shop steward

contract administration
grievance representation
grievance committee
bargaining committee
grievance procedure
executive board
committee structure
"mature phase"
shop society

Review and Discussion Questions

1. What changes are likely to occur in a workplace when it becomes unionized?

2. Interview a knowledgeable factory or nonfactory unionist or union leader. What is the extent of union structure in the workplace of his or her local? Is there a representative of the union present? If so, how is he or she selected and what are the duties of the position?

3. How does the complexity, or lack of it, of factory or nonfactory unionism reflect or depart from the employer's organization structure?

4. In addition to those tentatively identified, what other advantages or limitations do you think might be associated with two different types of union structure?

5. What, if any, is the basis for the statement that nonfactory unions must organize to survive? Does this apply more to nonfactory than to factory unions?

6. What do you think is the proper "place" of the local union? What are the consequences of laissez faire versus centralization policies of internationals with respect to locals? Does your answer apply equally to all unions?

7. Attend a union meeting. What parts of the agenda receive the greatest attention? The greatest discussion? Who participates? What concerns are evident from the leadership? From the rank-and-file?

8. Compare a factory and nonfactory local union. Draw a chart listing each position to be found in the bargaining and internal governments, and any overlaps, at different levels. You might interview union leaders about the "governmental" responsibilities of different positions.

9. On Monday Chester approached Brenda, his steward, and asked her what happened at the monthly union meeting held over the weekend. Brenda replied: "If you want to know what happened, go to the meeting yourself. Don't expect me to be your chief delegate and reporting service." Speculate about what might be behind this exchange. Was Brenda's response appropriate? Why or why not?

Suggestions For Further Reading

The works cited in footnotes, especially Sayles and Strauss, *The Local Union*, and the articles by Kovner and Lahne, remain readable and excellent perspectives on the workings of factory unions and their relationship to the membership in the workplace. An excellent in-depth treatment of the development of a single factory local is Peter Friedlander, *The Emergence of a UAW Local, 1936–1939*. Kennedy and Krauss, *The Business Agent*, is very brief but covers the main aspects of the business agent's role in the nonfactory local. A large number of local union histories have appeared in recent years. An older study of several locals is Joel Seidman, et al., *The Worker Views His Union*. See also Jack Barbash, *Labor's Grass Roots*. For in-depth reading on union constitutions, see Leo Bromwich, *Union Constitutions*.

For a thorough treatment of contract administration and grievance representation at the local union and workplace level, see Bob Repas, *Contract Administration: A Guide for Stewards and Local Officers*.

Informal organization in the unionized workplace is examined in Leonard Sayles, *Behavior of Industrial Work Groups*, and James Kuhn, *Bargaining in Grievance Settlement*.

For works on the building trades, a standby somewhat dated by the developments of the 1970s is George Strauss, *Unions in the Building Trades*. Scott Greer, *Last Man In*, focuses on structure, the business agent role, and participation at the local level.

An excellent study of participation, focusing on women within the local union, is Wertheimer and Nelson, *Trade Union Women: A Study of Their Participation in New York City Locals*.

For a review of the literature, see George Strauss, "Union Government in the U.S.: Research Past and Future," *Industrial Relations* (May 1977).

Complete bibliographical information for the above titles can be found in the Bibliography.

6

Internal Government and Administration of the International Union

Organized labor is not just the union you join, it is an organization which you must mingle in, contribute time and valuable thinking to. Build your union as you would build your home. For without it, you're without a real home.

From an essay by 16-year-old
David Simmons, son of a Textile
Workers union leader shot to
death during a 1951 strike at
Bemis, Tennessee

Though remaining logically separate, the internal government and the collective bargaining government are structurally less distinct at the international union level than at the local level. Very few international union officials have duties limited entirely to one sphere or the other.

This chapter surveys internal governance and administrative organization in the international, although at several points it also addresses bargaining matters. The next chapter focuses on the influence of employer structure and the bargaining environment on union structure and examines some developments in union structure.

International Union Origins

No single explanation accounts in any detail for the rise of all national unions. Most of the early national unions, formed during the period from the 1850s to the end of the century, were federations of pre-existing locals. Much like the original 13 colonies, these locals realized the need for broader coordination. They at first took limited, but then conclusive, steps to surrender some of their authority and create a more centralized government. And, much as the remaining states were established by the nation, today international unions more often grow by chartering new locals.

Several conditions, in different combinations, led locals to form national units. The expansion of product markets, made possible by improvements in transportation that some argue led to the separation of employees from employers and the formation of the earliest craft unions, in turn created the need for wider coordination. Goods produced cheaply in one locale could now undercut goods produced under better wages and conditions in another. Later in the 19th century, the spread of the factory system, the emergence of employer associations seeking to combat workers' organizations, and the introduction of new technology fundamentally changed the employment relationship and heightened the tactical need to coordinate across local union lines.

Where employment relations remained relatively localized, as among Molders, Printers, and Transit Workers, the need for national coordination, though still present, was not as compelling. Consequently the local unions, while formally subordinate bodies, tended to retain more of the dues dollar and more power. National unions in national and international product markets, such as steel and auto, assumed more authority, particularly over collective bargaining matters. Even in these cases, constitutional authority was tempered by the techniques of persuasion, required in an organization where officers must stand for election.

Formal Government of the International Union

The international union is the broadest unit of individual union citizenship (membership). An individual can be a member of the local and the international, but only an organization can be a member (affiliate) of the AFL-CIO or another multi-union organization. The international, regardless of how or when it was formed, is the source of sovereign powers within the labor movement.

Since 1959 federal law has prohibited certain practices within unions. For the most part, however, the law expects only that a union adhere to those rules of internal governance that it enacts in its constitution, the written expression of authority relationships.

Most union constitutions cover jurisdiction; qualifications for membership; the method of selection, duties, authority and compensation of international officers; sources and handling of funds; the administration of union benefit programs; internal discipline and appeals; procedures for calling and conducting conventions; and provisions for amending the document itself. Major attention is also devoted to the powers, scope, and governance of subordinate organizations, mainly the locals. Most constitutions stipulate that local records, funds, and property belong to the international and that the international may place locals in trusteeship (administration or supervision by the international) for a variety of causes.

Compared to their prominence in union activity, administrative organization and collective bargaining receive little attention in constitutions. The *civil service*, the appointed clerical, technical, and maintenance people who staff international and regional offices, is presumed to fall under the direction of the elected officers, principally the president and the secretary treasurer, as modified only by contracts negotiated with *staff unions* (termed unions-within-unions). Collective bargaining is sometimes addressed indirectly through reference to the international's authority to approve strikes and the payment of strike benefits. A few former CIO unions go beyond this, devoting sections of their constitutions to multilocal bargaining situations. Some craft union constitutions identify bargaining goals and standards. But the international's role is generally more a matter of practice than of constitutional elaboration.

The Convention

The supreme governing body of the international union is the convention. The local unions elect convention delegates, the number varying with the size of the local.

No large organization can be closely supervised by a large body which meets infrequently. Conventions make general policy and program decisions. They amend constitutions, adjust dues formulas, hear appeals from the judicial decisions of subordinate bodies, and approve broad statements of policy, often formulated by the international officers, their staffs, and convention committees. In most unions conventions elect officers and establish their salaries and expenses.

At most conventions the top officers and other influentials set the tone and direct events. Their position at the hub of union communications and their influence with many local officers, as well as their experience in convention management, make major surprises unlikely. International officers and staff usually prepare the passage of major policy changes by preconvention discussion and promotion with local leaders, followed by consolidation on and about the convention floor. The tendency for conventions to be orchestrated by the top leadership does not mean that its plans never go awry, as those who have had proposed dues increases rejected can attest. Barring major internal rifts, however, the president and the executive board will control both the pace and the results of the deliberations.

Conventions serve other purposes. As publicity events they call attention to union programs. As rituals they perform a solidifying and therapeutic function. As social occasions they serve to renew acquaintances among unionists who may see one another only at conventions. And for some they are a business-with-pleasure vacation, sometimes including the delegate's spouse and family. Often implicit is a reward for past service and an inducement to make continued contributions to the union.

The convention is also a learning experience and an arena for union politics. What happens in the halls and hospitality suites is often more important than what occurs on the floor. Union experiences are compared, strategies discussed, deals made, and careers advanced. In these respects union conventions are not unlike those held by other organizations.

In their early years most unions held annual conventions. Currently, a convention every two, three, or four years is more common. The lower frequency probably reflects the stabilization of affairs after the founding years, the consolidation of control by top officers, the declining need for basic policy making at conventions, the size and complexity of the union, and the substantial costs of holding conventions. The limits and infrequency of conventions increase the significance of the international executive board in union governance.

International Officers

Making up the international, or general, *executive board* are the president, the secretary treasurer, and from one to nearly 40 elected vice-presidents or directors of geographical units. The distribution of power between the president and the remainder of the board varies among unions, as do the specific duties assigned board members.

The President. The constitutional authority of presidents ranges from "weak" to "strong" depending on the range of matters covered and the degree of authority exercised. The strong presidency is exemplified in the Electrical Workers. As noted in the last chapter, the IBEW president determines the jurisdiction of locals. Article 17 of the IBEW constitution empowers the locals to make their own rules and bylaws as long as they do not conflict with the constitution. The president is then granted considerable leeway to interpret the constitution, to approve or reject local by-laws, and to oversee other local union actions.

Weak-president constitutions usually assign this power of interpretation and approval to the executive board, but this alone does not signify a weak president. With rare exceptions, even constitutionally weak presidents are at least "first among equals" on their boards. A strong personality, political popularity, and a number of organizational considerations can enhance this influence. While most presidents have great authority in operating decisions, many cannot gain approval of major policy changes without extensive persuasion of board members and the leaders of key membership units.

A broad range of styles is evident among union presidents. Some pay little attention to day-to-day administration, leaving this to an executive vice-president, the secretary treasurer, or an appointed chief-of-staff, while they travel the jurisdiction directing major negotiations, conferring, making speeches, and lining up political support for the union's program. Others keep lower profiles, maintaining a firm grip on administration.

The Secretary Treasurer. Second in command and often likely to succeed to the presidency, whether by election or interim selection by the executive board, is the international secretary treasurer. In some unions this officer works side-by-side with the president and has major assignments and visibility. In others this person has primarily "inside" responsibilities over *secretary treasurer's departments*, units handling accounting, purchasing, finance, and membership records.

The Executive Board/Vice-Presidents. Unions differ, too, in the number and duties of executive board members, sometimes synonymous with vice-presidents, and whether they are headquarters or field officers. In the majority, board members are elected at-large, a procedure that would appear to reduce the likelihood of successful opposition to the top leadership. In the two dozen or so internationals with more than 25,000 members whose executive board members are elected from geographic units, a few well-publicized cases led to the belief that significant electoral opposition to incumbents is greatly increased.[1]

Subdivided, as opposed to at-large, election units may indeed make executive board members less dependent for reelection on the support of top officers. Much depends, however, on factors such as the nature of the industry and its bargaining patterns and whether international executive board members draw the bulk of their salary by virtue of election alone or depend instead on compensation for specific assignments by the president or the board.

Recruitment. Three categories of people based at international union headquarters are distinguishable by their recruitment patterns or "career ladders." Most elected officers—primarily those who make up the executive board—have progressed from local union office through other positions in the union structure to their present offices. Their path is clearly a political one. A second group is made up of appointed staff who began their careers with election to local union and perhaps higher offices, but then advanced by appointment to international staff positions. Examples are international "reps," organizers or "field reps." A third category is the union's civil service, those staffers who enter from outside the union rather than progressing "through the ranks." This group includes technical, clerical, and maintenance staff.

Most unions prefer to recruit technical staff from their ranks, when individuals with the necessary expertise can be located. Where the need is for research economists, attorneys, financial experts, editors, and health and safety experts, however, unions usually look to the outside. In most cases unions are able to locate outside people who have technical expertise and share union goals.

Two types of leaders depart from the typical "up from the ranks" pattern. In one pattern the officer begins as a union staffer, or joins the staff before being elected to major positions, then enters the electoral arena at a relatively late point. The late Jerry Wurf, president of the American Federation of State, County and Municipal Employees, is an example of a top officer who spent the better part of his career in appointed positions prior to entering the electoral arena.

---

[1] Sara Gamm, "The Election Base of National Union Executive Boards," *Industrial and Labor Relations Review* 32, no. 3 (April 1979), p. 308.

A variant is the emergence in top office of attorneys with little shop experience. Murray Finley and Jacob Sheinkman of the Clothing and Textile Workers are cases in point. This union has recently designated a number of its civil servants as vice-presidents. Although these cases have touched off speculation in the press about a new trend toward professionalization in union leadership, they remain exceptions.

A different pattern is found in some building trades unions. Edward Carlough, president of the Sheet Metal Workers, and Maurice Hutcheson, former president of the Carpenters, for instance, were both groomed by their fathers and succeeded them in office. This pattern is to some extent in line with customs in the construction industry, where fathers often pass along to their sons the trade, its skills, tools, and lore.

Once in office the continued incumbency of presidents of most large internationals is fairly secure. This security is based largely on the inherent advantages of incumbency, including control over staff assignments and the central position of the role in the union communication structure. Turnover is more often a result of retirement or death. But occasionally an incumbent is defeated in an election by another top officer, often the secretary treasurer, who also shares many of the advantages of incumbency.[2]

The path to a vice-presidency varies. In some cases incumbents retire voluntarily in mid-term, giving the executive board the opportunity to name a replacement who is later endorsed for election. As suggested earlier, it is believed that board slates and endorsements carry greater weight in unions where election is at-large than in those where voting is by geographical constituency.

In other cases elections are relatively wide open, with several candidates vying for endorsement and votes from subordinate bodies and rank-and-file members. Rank-and-file members are apt to know very little about second-level leaders from other areas, and therefore in referendum elections members rely on endorsements from leaders whom they do know. Slating and endorsements are perhaps even more critical where election is by convention delegates.

---

[2] This was observed of presidential turnover situations during the 1960s in the Steelworkers and the Electrical Workers (IUE). Occasional hard fought campaigns by "outsiders" (those not in a headquarters position) against incumbents or incumbent-sponsored candidates are seen, but these candidacies begin with two strikes against them. Given the resources available to incumbents, success for their opponents usually requires overwhelming membership dissatisfaction.

All of this suggests that there are many paths to top office, with considerable variation among unions, and that influence tends to come from the top, with ground swells of opposition the exception.

The International Union at Work

Headquarters Locations. Washington, D.C. has become the preferred location for international union offices. Gone are the days of *voluntarism*—the view that government should maintain a hands-off policy with respect to labor—espoused by the early AFL. When voluntarism was an integral part of union policy, there was no compelling reason for a union to locate in the capital.

Nowadays organized labor is increasingly affected by legislation and actions of various federal government branches. These matters are a primary focus of the AFL-CIO. Hence internationals, too, find it convenient to cluster near the seat of government, the Federation, and one another.

In 1978, 39 AFL-CIO affiliates (36 percent) maintained headquarters in the capital. That these 36 percent accounted for 60 percent of the affiliated membership shows the tendency for the larger unions to locate in Washington. Eighteen percent of independent unions, representing 52 percent of the independent union membership, maintain Washington headquarters.[3]

Larger unions locate in the capital because of the scale of their operations and the dispersion of their members. Large unions can best afford to participate in the full spectrum of union efforts, maintaining legislative offices and a variety of other activities. Smaller unions, which lack major resources and whose membership often is concentrated in one or two regions far from the capital, locate near their jurisdictions and operate on a smaller scale. An example is the United Furniture Workers, which in 1979 followed its 30,000 membership to the south, and relocated its headquarters from New York City to Nashville, Tennessee.[4]

Another exception to the pattern of major unions locating in the capital is those industrial unions that remain near the traditional centers of their industries—the UAW in Detroit, the Steelworkers in Pittsburgh, the Clothing and Textile Workers in New York, and the Rubber Workers in Akron, Ohio.

---

[3] Data are from the Department of Labor, Bureau of Labor Statistics, *Directory of National Unions and Employee Associations*, Bulletin 2079 (Washington, D.C.: Government Printing Office, 1980), p. 77.

[4] In 1981 the United Paperworkers also moved from New York to Nashville.

Administration

Gathered at international headquarters are elected officers, officials appointed from the ranks, and civil servants. How these people are organized to get the union's work done varies with the union's size, financial resources, jurisdictional complexity, and the policies and styles of its leaders, past and present.

The number and titles of international union departments usually reflect the scope of headquarters functions. Some departments, such as publications, health and safety, and legislation, provide a specific service to all locals. Others serve particular employment groupings in the membership. The Machinists, for example, have coordinators for airlines, railroads, and auto mechanics. The IBEW establishes divisions for utilities, telephone, and manufacturing locals. The UAW has corporate departments, headed by vice-presidents, which coordinate bargaining matters with each of the "big three" auto manufacturers. Many unions with predominantly private-sector memberships have recently established government-employee departments. Table 12 indicates the departments found most frequently.

The UAW is noted for its elaborate breakout of departments. At one count it had 27 bargaining departments, 17 technical and administrative departments, and 7 departments designed for special blocs of members.[5] At the other extreme are many smaller unions that merge several functions within a single department. Typical combinations are research and education, public relations and publications, legislation and political education. In these unions individual officers and staff will often wear many hats. Where they exist, specialized departments may be one-person operations.

Union Publications. Almost all unions, regardless of their size, publish regular newspapers, magazines, or journals. The *International Operating Engineer*, the *Airline Pilot*, the *International Teamster*, and the *Sheet Metal Worker* appear in magazine format. Newsprint publications include *Steel Labor*, *White Collar* (OPEIU), the *Utility Workers Light*, the *American Teacher*, and the *Public Employee* (AFSCME). Some publications consist largely of local union news, listings of death benefits paid, officers' columns, executive board minutes, financial reports, and coverage

[5] Jack Barbash, AMERICAN UNIONS: STRUCTURE, GOVERNMENT AND POLITICS (New York: Random House, 1967), p. 88.

Table 12. International Union Departments*

Departments	Examples of Where Found
Bargaining Departments	
Organizing	Many unions
Industry and trade divisions	Many, especially those with diverse jurisdictions
Corporate departments	Several, e.g., General Motors, Ford, and Chrysler, Departments of UAW
Arbitration	Steelworkers, others
Representation and Service Departments	
Legislative, Political Education	Most larger unions, many others
Public Relations	Most larger unions, many others
Publications	Most larger unions, many others
Research	Most larger unions, many others
Education	Most larger unions, many others
Apprenticeship	Larger unions, where relevant
Community Service	Some large industrial unions
Fair Practices/Civil Rights/Women's	Some large industrial unions
Safety and Health	Most larger unions, many others
Retirees	Mineworkers, UAW, other
International Affairs	Several, especially larger unions
Union Label	Many
Legal	Many, although smaller unions often rely on outside counsel
Internal Administration (often "Secretary-Treasurer's Departments")	
Accounting	Most larger unions
Membership Records	Most larger unions
Finance/Investments	Most larger unions
Pensions	Most larger unions
Insurance, other benefits	Most larger unions
Data Processing	Most larger unions
Mailing	Most larger unions
Maintenance	Most larger unions
Personnel	Most larger unions

*Note that the functional divisions in the listing are somewhat arbitrary. The activities of a legal, research, legislative or fair practices department, for instance, often relate directly to collective bargaining, as do pension, finance, or data processing.

of the activities of top international union officers (replete with photos). Others, like *Labor Unity* (Clothing and Textile Workers) and *Solidarity* (UAW), contain a variety of staff-written features. Regardless of formula, most international union publications devote substantial space to the union's legislative and bargaining programs.

Many unions put out additional special-purpose publications, such as department newsletters, education and organizing materials, legislative and political action memos, union histories, and organization descriptions. The Service Employees, Machinists, Teachers, and Government Employees are among those with newsletters designed for local union leaders. Editions aimed at different industry segments are not unusual.

Union publications are printed in a union shop, either in-house or commercially, and carry a *union label* (called a "bug") designating the name and number of the printing union involved.

Research and Education. Research and education functions are assuming greater prominence as unions attempt to cope with complex organizational needs requiring information and training. Research is often geared to bargaining needs, from investigating the financial status and background of an employer whose workers are organizing prospects to developing backup material for negotiations. Education often takes the form of what is termed *unionizing the organized* through developing understanding of the union's goals and procedures. Another emphasis is leadership training in the increasingly complex skills required of staff and local union officers.

Data Processing. Keeping track of membership records, dues payments, accounts and inventories, and sending mailings are now among the many tasks performed by computers in large organizations. With their often large and diverse memberships and varied dues formulas, unions, like all large organizations, need information systems equal to the task. Hence computers are a standard feature of many headquarters operations.

The computer is also prominent in political action and bargaining. Membership lists are correlated with voting district information in order to facilitate timely and accurate mailings, an effort in which some internationals cooperate with the AFL-CIO.

More recently, unions have put the computer to use in research and bargaining. This entails entering the terms of contracts and other types of data on the computer so that they can be analyzed and results provided to participants in the bargaining process. A local or national union negotiating team, for instance, might need to know the range of settlements in an industry in order to bargain the best deal for its members. Confronted with a low average wage estimate from the employer, the committee might have no information with which to counter the assertion. If the relevant data are in the computer, however, punching a few keys or making a call to the national office can produce the needed information in a usable form. This is one of the simpler uses of the computer, but it illustrates the possibilities.[6]

Planning. Unions have been generally slow to adopt systematic planning, budgeting, and administrative procedures adequate to cope with their many needs. Lack of funds and staff comparable to those of major corporations prevents unions from taking full advantage of the most modern technology. But the comparison with business can also be used as a rationale for rejecting efforts to operate in a more systematic manner. "If we make use of management techniques," some claim, "then we'll be no different from the other side—the corporations." As large organizations, however, unions cannot escape the need to put planning and organizational efficiency to use in benefitting their members. Some have done so with alacrity, others reluctantly, and yet others have resisted new techniques.[7]

A large part of the task is one of selecting methods and technologies appropriate to the goals, *scale*, and resources of the union. Planning, budgeting, and organization-design can be scaled to the needs of any organization or group, regardless of size. Purchasing a million dollar computer may be beyond the means of many unions, but the inexpensive models now available open up time- and effort-saving possibilities for unions.

Union Finance

Antiunion employers and consultants assert that the union operates "just like the employer"—it is a business out to make a profit, not an organization out to achieve justice for workers. This propaganda equates union leaders ("bosses") with corporate executives out to "fatten their coffers" at the expense of the unwary worker. To maximize revenue the union puts into the field a sales force (union organizers) who will go to just about any length to sell their product (membership cards).

---

[6] A broader range of applications is discussed by several contributors to an early volume on the subject by Abraham J. Siegel, ed., THE IMPACT OF COMPUTERS ON COLLECTIVE BARGAINING (Cambridge, Mass.: MIT Press, 1969). Developments since then have demonstrated many more uses.

[7] For a discussion of this problem see Derek C. Bok and John T. Dunlop, LABOR AND THE AMERICAN COMMUNITY (New York: Simon Schuster, 1970), Chapter 5, which focuses on the development of a planning process in the Laborers' International Union and the problems of achieving economies of scale in union operations.

The jurisdictional diversity of many unions is thus held to be, not an effort to broaden the scale of organization to improve the lives of more workers and protect the wages, benefits, and conditions of its current membership, but an effort to get more dues wherever the revenue is to be found.

Unions cannot sustain their efforts without dues. Indeed, while the greatest portion of union activity is uncompensated effort by millions of members, paid full- and part-time officers coordinate much of this effort and provide supporting services. In the bargaining government of most local unions, a portion of grievance and negotiating activity is performed on the employer's time. Other expenses incurred in defending interests of members are of a nonsalary nature. Office maintenance, publications, arbitration, and travel expenses are some of the activities supported by dues money.

Union Dues. A look at the collection and distribution of union income reveals a lot about how the labor movement is organized and financed. With few exceptions, dues are collected at the local union level. In factory and single-employer nonfactory situations, dues are typically *checked off* (deducted from wages) by agreement with the employer, who remits the money to the local.[8] In casual and mobile employment situations (such as the building trades), dues are usually paid by each member at the union hall, on the job, or by mail.

Dues constitute the largest portion of union income, although initiation fees and other assessments make up a significant percentage of income for some craft unions. Other income accrues from investments and, sometimes, rents.

When dues are received by the local union, the financial officer (financial secretary or treasurer) deposits the money and writes checks for *per capita assessments* to each of the various bodies with which the local affiliates. These payments (also known as "per caps," per capita taxes, or PCAs) are computed as a fixed amount per member per month. The largest per capita payment by locals, determined by the union constitution, goes to support the international and its intermediate bodies. Smaller per caps go to the state and local central bodies, trade councils, and other units the local might join.

The international's secretary-treasurer makes certain per capita payments on behalf of the international itself. For AFL-CIO af-

---

[8] In some unions checkoff payments go to the international, which then remits to the local its portion.

filiates, these go to the Federation and any of its trade departments to which the international union belongs. As of July 1985 the AFL-CIO per capita was 31 cents per member per month.

The per capita assessment is thus the major means for financially supporting and linking the many levels of the labor movement.

Dues Structures. The amount of union dues and their distribution among different levels is referred to as dues structure. As a rule both the local and the international, acting in convention, participate in formulating dues structures. International constitutions establish per capita assessments and often set a minimum dues level, which locals can exceed if they so wish. Dues will be higher where they include premium payments for participation in sickness-and-death benefit programs administered by the international.

In 1974 it was not unusual for dues to fall in the $6 to $10 per month range, with a respective $2 to $4 going to the international.[9] But the inflation of the later 1970s caught up with unions, and most have since greatly increased their dues. Many have changed from a fixed rate to a formula setting dues at some percentage of income. Two hours pay per month is perhaps a typical equivalent under such systems, with absolute dues levels being higher in craft than in industrial and service unions.

The manner in which revenues are allocated among different levels of the union reflects the industry, its bargaining structure, and the structure of the union. While the major share of dues going outside the local is normally to the international,[10] the percentage of dues going to this per capita varies.

A recent development is the *political checkoff*, a negotiated provision for deducting money from the wages of those who authorize regular contributions to union political action. This system has survived court challenges by organized foes of unionism, in part because companies are allowed to make such deductions for management and nonunion employees.

Union Assets. The media image of unions suggests holdings of great wealth. In fact the total assets of all unions combined would not place the entire labor movement in the same range as one top corporation. Leo Troy has estimated that as of 1969 the combined

---

[9] See Charles W. Hickman, "Labor Organization Fees and Dues," *Monthly Labor Review* 100, no. 5 (May 1977), pp. 21–22.

[10] State AFL-CIO per capita affiliation fees, for instance, rarely exceed 50 cents per month.

assets of U.S. unions, including the member-financed benefit funds of some unions, totalled some $2.6 billion. While this appears as a sizable sum, it represents less than $150 per member.

Fifteen years later comparable figures were not available. One can surmise that the intervening inflation as well as real asset growth would contribute to 1984 figures that were at least double, if not quadruple, the 1969 total. As an example, the UAW alone, though strapped for operating funds, had built a strike fund by 1984 of over half a billion dollars. In the event of a major national strike, however, this seemingly vast sum would last only a few weeks.

The distribution of these assets among different levels of union organization is shown in Table 13, which indicates that, during the 1960s, the major share of assets was distributed about evenly between locals and internationals (headquarters units), with about 5 percent held by other bodies. One might expect that the internationals' share has increased relative to that of locals, but there are no known data to support this conclusion. The fact is that despite the sovereignty of the international a major share of union assets is retained in the locals.

Assets Management. Examination of how unions handle their assets suggests they are not as businesslike as their opponents suggest. Assets are highly liquid, in cash as opposed to investments. Where unions invest, they shy away from long-term, speculative, potentially high-return prospects. This practice is defended on several grounds: that the rationale for the assets—defense against employers—requires quick access to substantial reserves in order to

---

Table 13. Total Assets of U.S. Unions, by Type of Organization, 1962–69

(in millions)

Year	Local Unions	Central Unions[a]	Headquarters Units[b]	Total
1962	$ 867	$ 94	$ 810	$1,771
1966	1,095	121	990	2,206
1969	1,272	139	1,236	2,647

[a]Central unions are defined to include district, state, and local associations, the AFL-CIO, and its departments.
[b]Headquarters units are defined to include regional, national, and international unions.
Source: Leo Troy, "American Unions and Their Wealth," *Industrial Relations* 14, no. 2 (May 1975), p. 136.

maintain the credibility of the union's strike weapon; that investment of union funds in high-yield, speculative investments might result in disaster and would run counter to the interest of the membership; and that as a rule of thumb a union should have sufficient *reserves* to allow it to survive two years with no income whatsoever.

A study of financial reports from 500 local unions in the New England area from 1970–72 confirms the general conservatism of union financial practices.[11] Building trades locals, in general, were found to have the greatest reserves and to be the most solvent. Many industrial locals and unions with aggressive organizing programs had reserves sufficient only for a few weeks' expenses.

How the Money Is Spent. Unions provide to their members annual reports detailing income and expenses, as required by the Labor Management Reporting and Disclosure Act (Landrum-Griffin Act) of 1959. Local unions publish these statements in their newspapers and newsletters or report them at meetings. Internationals often devote a section of their newspapers annually or semi-annually to financial reports, as well as publishing them in convention proceedings and filing them with the Department of Labor.

From these data it is clear that salaries, rents, and administrative expenses absorb a significant portion of income in both internationals and locals. The New England study classified locals by industry and reported expenditures as shown in Table 14.

Table 14. Local Union Expenditures

(percent of total receipts)

Industry	Administrative	Education	Per Capita Payments	Professional Fees
Construction	40.7	0.4	28.2	1.0
Durables	30.9	3.4	42.5	2.2
Nondurables	11.5	2.0	58.1	0.1
Utilities	31.8	0.6	29.7	1.8
Services	36.3	1.3	29.9	2.0
Teamsters	39.5	0.3	21.3	2.0

Source: Allison, "Financial Analysis of the Local Union," *Industrial Relations* 14, no. 2 (May 1975), p. 153.

---

[11] Elizabeth K. Allison, "Financial Analysis of the Local Union," *Industrial Relations* 14, no. 2 (May 1975), pp. 145–155.

While these data do not give details of local union spending, they suggest three things: First, the variation in the small percentages spent for education indicates that industrial local unions (as indicated by durables and nondurables) are more education-oriented than others; second, the high percentage allocated to per capita payments by industrial unions confirms the difference between national and local market unionism—that is, unions bargaining on an industrywide or national scale will locate more resources in headquarters; and third, the percentages attributable to professional fees do not confirm the view that "lawyers have taken over the local union." These figures do not, of course, include the expenses of any salaried lawyers or those retained by international unions.

Officer Salaries. The 1981 salaries of the presidents of most major international unions fell in the $50,000–$80,000 range, comparable to salaries of corporate middle managers. *Business Week* reported a salary average of $76,000 for top labor leaders in that year, noting that this was only a 77 percent increase over the previous decade, compared with a 100 percent increase for rank-and-file workers.[12]

The departures from these averages are noteworthy. At the top is the International Brotherhood of Teamsters, which at its 1981 convention raised the salary of then-president Roy Williams to $225,000 and that of General Secretary-Treasurer Ray Scholessling to $200,000. International vice-presidents and trustees were raised to $55,000.[13]

As early as 1976 there were reportedly 21 Teamster officers drawing over $100,000 in salary and expenses, but generally this was through *pyramiding* different local and international positions (sometimes including positions in unions other than the Teamsters). In this manner Harold Friedman of Cleveland, Ohio, in-law of current president Jackie Presser, combined his $233,000 salary as president of Bakery, Confectionery and Tobacco Workers Local 19 with income from the Teamsters for a 1980 total of $429,000. At the other extreme was the $22,000 earned by Dennis Glavin, president of the United Electrical Workers Union, an amount pegged to the pay of the union's highest paid rank-and-file members.[14]

---

[12] "Rank-and-File Austerity Filters Upward," *Business Week*, no. 2738 (May 10, 1982), p. 118.

[13] *The International Teamster* (July 1981), p. 24.

[14] *Business Week*, no. 2738 (May 10, 1982), p. 118.

In 1981, the 10 highest paid union officers headed nonfactory unions. These included both the presidents and secretary treasurers of the Teamsters and the Laborers.

Comparisons with top corporate officials are perhaps unavoidable, despite the difference in duties and circumstances. A clear salary gap remains: A comparison of 1974 compensation for the five highest paid union and management officials shows the union officials with a total of $605,000, less than one-seventh the $4.3 million received by the top five corporation heads.[15]

Where they are large enough to afford them, local unions often peg the salaries of full-time officers to the earnings of the people they represent or compute them by some formula based on negotiated wage increases. Local presidents and other officers of small factory locals are typically unsalaried, although they are often allowed by the negotiated agreement a given number of hours per week for collective bargaining representation, and are compensated by the union for time off the job due to union business (often termed "lost time"). While practices vary, a factory local with more than 1,000 members is apt to have at least one full-time officer.

Because of the dispersal of their units and the hall-centered nature of their activities, nonfactory locals must rely more heavily on full-time officers who can move freely about the jurisdiction. To support these activities a higher dues level is required. It is not unusual to find a local of 50 or 100 members with a full-time business agent.

A study of 2,000 Ohio local unions over the period 1962–67 found that 92 percent of all officers in the sample were compensated less than $5,000 per year (in 1960s dollars, of course). Perhaps significantly, the study reported a 35 percent turnover rate among officers in this bracket during the period studied; turnover among those earning more than $10,000 was 24 percent.[16] A higher salary is no guarantee of continuation in office, but the higher the compensation the lower the turnover.

No sketch of union compensation is complete without mention of the vast majority of officers and stewards who work for no finan-

---

[15] Ray Marshall and Brian Rungeling, THE ROLE OF UNIONS IN THE AMERICAN ECONOMY (New York: Joint Council on Economic Education, 1976).

[16] Leon Applebaum and Harry R. Blaine, "Compensation and Turnover of Union Officers," *Industrial Relations* 14, no. 2 (May 1975), pp. 156–67.

cial reward except, perhaps, a remission of dues. This is the volunteer base of the union without which it cannot achieve its goals.

Financial Controls. Establishing foolproof controls against the misuse of funds is impossible, as the many banks and other corporations subject to embezzlement, misappropriation, bribes, and kickback schemes can attest. Considering the tens of thousands of often inexperienced local union officers responsible for union funds, unions have achieved a solid record of avoiding major abuses. Part of this record can no doubt be attributed to accounting and audit procedures installed at all levels and backed by the authority of the internationals, which can place locals in trusteeship for financial malpractice. It can also be traced to procedures for monthly financial reports to the membership and to the notion that union finances are the members' business. Basically, however, it is the honesty and effectiveness of most officers and their pride in the union that makes this record possible. If union activists sometimes appear defensive about this record, it may be because antiunion elements are so quick to seize upon the exceptions and publicize the slightest hint of scandal.

Conclusion

Parts of the development and the internal government of a union resemble that of the nation. Some dimensions of its administrative operations are similar to those of other large organizations. While union finance and salary practices reflect in part those of other bodies, they have features derived from the uniquely union responsibilities of the organization.

In the area of collective bargaining government, the resemblance to other organizations dissolves. Not only is this sphere uniquely union, it is the dimension that is most adaptive to changes in the environment. The next chapter examines the influence of employer structure and the bargaining environment on union structure, as well as some developments in union structure.

Review and Discussion Questions

1. What are the sources of power within the union for each unit— local union, international officers, general president, others? What determines whether a unit will be relatively strong or weak in its exchanges with other bodies in the union?

2. Imagine an international union in which each local is entirely autonomous. What problems or advantages would result?

3. Imagine an international union in which each local was a branch office of national headquarters. What patterns of structure and behavior would be different from those described in this or previous chapters?

4. In a few cases what have been termed "civil servants" have been elected to international union office. Is this the wave of the future? Is it a healthy or unhealthy development, or neither?

5. How should union salaries be determined? In a given union what criteria might be used in setting salaries?

6. What might account for the higher turnover in locals where officers' salaries are lower than in locals where officers' receive higher salaries?

7. Make a list of political, financial, administrative, and other factors that should be considered in establishing dues structures within an international union. Consider need and ability and willingness of the members to pay. What, if any, "appropriate" dues structure emerges?

8. Do you see any conflicts between the values of democracy and efficiency in conducting union affairs? What are they and what, if any, resolutions of the conflicts can you suggest?

Key Words and Phrases

federation	union label
trusteeship	union bug
civil service	unionizing the organized
international convention	check off
international executive board	per capita assessment
general executive board	dues structure
international president	political check off
international secretary/	union assets
treasurers department	salary pyramiding
international departments	turnover

Suggestions for Further Reading

Several treatments of individual international unions are: James E. Cebula, *Glory and Despair: A History of the Molders Union*; Joseph E. Finley, *White Collar Union*, narrates the development of the Office and Professional Employees; Thomas R. Brooks, *Communications Workers of America: The Story of a Union*, does the same for the CWA; Lloyd Ulman,

The Rise of the National Trade Union, traces the stages and forces culminating in the development of the international union.

The most complete study of government within the national union is William Leiserson, *American Trade Union Democracy*. Related to its subject is Bromwich, *Union Constitutions*, noted at the end of Chapter 5.

Complete bibliographical information for the above titles can be found in the Bibliography.

7

The International Union: Organizational and Bargaining Imperatives

Union power is the power of government, namely rule-making adminis-tration, and the specific subject matter of union rule-making is rela-tions of members to their jobs and to each other. Some rules, especially among craft unions, are exclusively union-made, but in modern collec-tive bargaining most job rules are the result of contracts between unions and employers. Most of the business of a union is to promote the inter-ests of its members by the creation and administration of rules favorable to them.

Joseph Kovner and Herbert Lahne (1953)*

Unions respond to two imperatives: First, like other organiza-tions, they must develop structures and practices that are opera-tionally effective and make relatively economical use of staff and other resources; second, as representatives of their members in the employment relationship, they must adjust their structures to ad-dress those of the employers with whom they deal, seeking to bring these employers into favorable bargaining orbits.

Because their structures are most heavily influenced by this bargaining imperative, unions can be described as bargaining-sensitive organizations. But purely organizational considerations retain some influence of their own, independent of the union's need to bargain.

This duality is seen in the operations of the intermediate body in union organization, the first subject of this chapter. The chapter then looks further at the structural determinants of union bargain-

*"Shop Society and the Union," *Industrial and Labor Relations Review* 7, no. 1 (Octo-ber 1953), p. 7.

ing power and at instances of internal consolidation and merger among unions, which are responses to both organizational and bargaining needs.

Intermediate Bodies

International unions would find it difficult to service and coordinate directly the efforts of hundreds of local unions. As a result they develop units that fall between the international and the local and serve to group locals by area or by employment type for more effective coordination. *Thus an intermediate body is a combination of local unions within the same international.* Though more inclusive definitions would permit it, intermediate bodies should not be confused with multi-union or interunion bodies, such as Printing Trades Councils, Building Trades Councils, or Central Labor Councils, that represent locals from different international unions.[1] Not so clear-cut, but also excluded from our definition, are some of the special interest units in the bargaining government that represent sublocal membership groupings and often work in conjunction with, or are indistinguishable from, an international union department.[2] Examples are the Skilled Trades Councils of the UAW and the white collar and women's units of many unions.

The major functions of the more significant intermediate bodies are servicing the bargaining needs of local unions—assisting in negotiations, participating in grievance meetings, and in some unions, organizing new locals. Secondary functions, in terms of time consumed, involve assisting officers to conduct the affairs of internal government and administration in the local, including strengthening organizational links between the international and the locals. Legislative affairs and education are often included in intermediate body functions. Affiliation is more often voluntary in the less prominent intermediate bodies, and they usually do not perform bargaining or service tasks.

Intermediate bodies may be governed by delegates representing the covered locals. Or they may be truly administrative arms of

---

[1] One major analysis includes such multi-union bodies in the definition of intermediate bodies, but recognizes this difference when it excludes them from consideration. See Herbert J. Lahne, "The Intermediate Union Body in Collective Bargaining," *Industrial and Labor Relations Review* 6 (January 1953), p. 163 f.

[2] Jack Barbash, in a discussion of intermediate bodies, includes these special-purpose bodies. AMERICAN UNIONS: STRUCTURE, GOVERNMENT, AND POLITICS (New York: Random House, 1967), Chapter 5.

the international, in which case the term "body" can be misleading. In several cases they have no governmental existence except to define the unit from which international executive board members are elected.

These units are also classifiable according to their relations with the locals. Some are virtually superlocals, assuming nearly all the authority elsewhere exercised by a local union. Others maintain some distance and play more limited support roles.

Classified according to the elements just noted, two major types of intermediate bodies with significant bargaining service functions can be identified:

Quasi-Local Union Bodies. These units appear most often in local market situations where they encompass several local unions in a metropolitan or multicounty area. Many are of the type that absorb local functions rather than supplement them. Perhaps the clearest examples are the district councils with which most building trades locals of the Carpenters and the Painters are required to affiliate. In these unions the locals are virtually vestigial structures, having few significant functions. Full-time business agents from the district council handle organizing, negotiations, contract enforcement, and policing the jurisdiction.

Quite similar are the joint boards of the Amalgamated Clothing and Textile Workers Union. Each joint board is run by a manager who appoints business agents to service locals. The locals in the geographical area maintain their own treasuries and make per capita payments to support the joint board. They also elect delegates who meet monthly to set joint board policy. The functions of the joint board revolve around bargaining, but they include such tasks as maintaining financial records, conducting education programs, and coordinating publicity efforts.

District lodges in the Machinist's union and councils in the State, County and Municipal Employees (AFSCME) operate in similar fashion, though with variations in terminology. In the IAM these units are headed by a *directing business agent* and in AFSCME by a council president. In AFSCME the major councils are the power bases in the national union and their presidents usually double as international union vice-presidents.

Regional Servicing and Administrative Units. The most prominent units of this type are found in the major factory-type unions. Examples are the regions of the UAW, the Machinists and the Communications Workers, and the districts of the Steelworkers, the American Federation of Government Employees, the Rubber

Workers, the Electronic Workers, and the Oil, Chemical and Atomic Workers. As noted in the last chapter, some of these units are the election districts for international executive board members. In others election is at large and assignment to a region is made by the executive board. The primary responsibilities of these units concern collective bargaining, while additional tasks relate to administration and internal government. Each of these bodies employs staff representatives (sometimes termed international representatives) to assist the locals, but the locals retain control over a wide range of activities.

Other Intermediate Bodies. There are numerous other bodies which do not receive significant amounts of per capita support from locals or appropriation from internationals, chiefly because they do not perform major bargaining or service functions. Some are consultative bodies; others, like the state councils of the IAM, serve to direct legislative concerns, conduct education programs, and provide platforms for both local and international officers.

Bargaining Alignments in Intermediate Structures. Bargaining needs often cross geographical boundaries. Consequently many unions have overlaid additional forms to address needs arising out of common employer and common industry situations. This logic was expressed by Lahne:

> One thing which stands out is that in unions which have multiple locals in the same branch of industry in the same area, and in which each local is a potential competitor of every other local either for the work or for a share of the employer's wage bill, there must be and there is a strong intermediate body to handle matters of collective bargaining.[3]

It is a simple extension of this logic to see its application at a national or international level.

A few unions organize locals into intermediate bodies entirely along employment lines. In addition to the geographical district lodges noted above, the Machinists have two other types of districts. The *industrial district* is made up of locals with a common employer or sharing a large plant, such as Boeing in Seattle. The other is the *railroad and airline district lodge* representing workers employed by one or more carriers at terminals across the country. In addition to service functions, this type of district coordinates bargaining efforts.

---

[3] Lahne, "The Intermediate Union Body," above, note 1.

The American Federation of Government Employees (AFGE) realized its geographical districts were not sufficient to deal with large federal agencies that coordinate their labor relations nationally. Consequently, in the late 1970s, the AFGE took steps to create structures that would "match up" with such agencies as the Veterans' Administration. To date, these bodies have not become full-blown intermediate units, but simply bargaining coordination mechanisms.

We have noted the complex structure of the UAW, which raises some problems in classification. While some of the UAW units are essentially international union departments, others are delegate bodies that coordinate bargaining for entire locals sharing a common employer. The UAW's Dana Council, for example, coordinates bargaining for all UAW locals at plants of the Dana Corporation, a major parts supplier. Whether we call this an intermediate body is arbitrary; it is certainly worthy of note.

Contrasted with the complexity of the UAW is the simplicity of the Steelworkers, which until the 1960s coordinated the common employment interests among locals entirely through the international office and the geographical districts. In the late 1960s the union established a number of Industry Conferences and assigned to some of them major bargaining responsibilities. Indeed, few unions of any jurisdictional complexity have avoided subdivision for bargaining purposes.

The advantage of having even a district subunit between the locals and the international can be seen in the way it allows for simplified communications. Where there is a need to coordinate bargaining with a common employer, several districts may contain plants of that employer. The international can work through the district rather than having to organize and direct each of the locals individually. The administration of multilocal contracts can also be handled more uniformly when it is subdivided rather than fully fragmented.

The purely organizational imperative for the formation of intermediate bodies is seen in the advantages of pooling resources and expertise to provide services to locals that the locals, acting separately, could not provide for themselves and that the international cannot efficiently provide. The bargaining advantage begins with the broader contacts and exposure to employer practices that are possible for staff whose contacts span several, as opposed to a single, establishment. It is further extended where the district and its staff provide built-in coordination by virtue of dealing with several establishments in the same industry or of the same employer. These advantages are balanced, of course, by the unfamiliarity with detail that "goes with the territory."

There is no generalization that describes the consequences of intermediate bodies concerning the distribution of power in the international. The intermediate unit is an arm of control by the international over the locals, a channel for local influence on top officers, and a platform from which challenges to these leaders can be mounted. It also serves as an intermediate step in leadership progression—most local leaders are not catapulted directly into top international positions, but gain experience and exposure along the way.

Because few unions can gear their structures exclusively to geographical, trade, or industrial dimensions, they develop overlapping subdivisions suited to each. Typically these subdivisions take the form of intermediate bodies, or what we call quasi-intermediate bodies, that aggregate certain interests for internal political reasons or for bargaining effectiveness. The result is often a complex grid system that must be reevaluated and adjusted in response to changed circumstances.

The "Rep"

Working out of intermediate body offices are union representatives who carry titles ranging from business agent to staff representative or international representative. Regardless of title, these reps are the key links between the locals and the broader units in the international. They are expected to perform, on behalf of several locals, the bargaining and servicing functions of the intermediate body and to serve as a liaison with various international union departments. Even where the international sends in specialists, such as organizers, to assist in particular work or where the major agreements are bargained nationally, the servicing representative's job is a demanding one. This person is expected to be a generalist who is at the same time expert in each phase of local union activities and able to deal with a variety of different management representatives and situations.

We noted in Chapter Five that these representatives in factory unions are usually former local union presidents who indicated some ability to handle their local situations, which rarely include organizing. Placed in a job requiring organizing and a broader range of tasks in several locals, many adapt well. Given the expectations of locals and the demands on the servicing representatives' time, it is not surprising that some, effective or not, become scapegoats for failures and disappointments.

Internationals made up primarily of nonfactory locals usually do not rely on international representatives to handle multipurpose servicing for locals through intermediate bodies. International representatives in these unions are usually assigned specific tasks such as organizing, judicial appeals, and handling jurisdictional matters, and are subject to reassignment on a task-by-task basis. This is particularly the case in the construction unions, where large regional intermediate bodies lack the prominence found in factory unions.

In nonfactory settings there tends to be either a nonfactory local structure or its equivalent in the form of a quasi-local intermediate body, such as a district council, that absorbs local functions. This parallels the role of the business agent in the local, who performs a broad range of bargaining and service tasks for several *units*, and the rep who does the same for several *locals* as an employee of the international or of an intermediate body.

The Structure of Union Bargaining Power

The power of capital within labor-management relations is based on the ability to provide or withhold a livelihood. The strength of labor is based on the fact that workers are the source of value. Without them there can be no product, no service. But to realize this potential they must act in concert; they must be organized. The measure of this power is the ability, by withdrawing their labor, to inflict damage on the employer sufficient to bring it to acceptable terms. It is the ability to strike effectively.

The ability to strike effectively and thereby to realize economic improvements depends on two sets of conditions.[4] The first set determines whether the employer has the ability to pay higher compensation. These conditions are met where the employer can either pass on higher labor costs through price increases or can absorb these costs through productivity improvements. Employers can pass on higher costs where they have monopolies in the product market,

---

[4] This discussion follows that in Charles Craypo, THE ECONOMICS OF COLLECTIVE BARGAINING (Washington, D.C., The Bureau of National Affairs, Inc., forthcoming).

where the industry is regulated, or where they operate in *spatial monopolies*, geographical areas that are insulated from competition by producers in other areas.

The second set of conditions determines whether the union has the ability to make the employer provide economic improvements. These are conditions of organization and bargaining structure aimed at improving the tactical effectiveness of the strike—the ability to force concessions. This set has three elements:

(1) The union must organize all who provide the product or service, wherever one worker can potentially undercut the others. This is termed the *relevant work force.*

(2) If different unions represent part of the relevant work force, they must *eliminate competitive unionism* by coordinating their bargaining efforts.

(3) The bargaining structure must be *consolidated* and sufficiently *centralized* to ensure either that a single agreement covers all or that all employers are subject to identical economic terms.

A couple of examples suggest the application of these conditions. A union representing only one plant of a ten-plant chain producing an identical product will be unlikely to have a major impact on compensation if the employer can shift production to unorganized plants. But if the product is ice, if ice is indispensable and if the unionized plant is the only one that can provide ice to a key area, then the union, through bargaining, may substantially increase compensation for the workers at this plant.

Similarly, if the product or service cannot be transported beyond a local area, as in most types of construction, then a union representing all who provide this product or service in the area can bargain economic improvements. If the union, however, represents only a minority of the relevant work force, employers who grant substantial increases will be at a disadvantage with their competitors.

In the example of the ten-plant chain, if each of the plants produces for the national market and each is organized by a different union, the unions must coordinate their efforts or the employer will be able to play them off against one another. *Coordinated bargaining* entails establishing similar or simultaneous contract expirations, setting common goals, and settling on essentially identical terms.

Finally, the union(s) must ensure that a single agreement covers the relevant work force or that the economic terms of separate agreements are identical. The result is to *remove wages from competition* so that no employer can gain a price advantage over its competiton by paying lower wages. This is achieved through centralization of bargaining structure sufficient to standardize the terms.

Unions strive to fulfill these conditions. Their successes in national product markets occur where negotiating units are broad and centralized or where strong patterns are followed and employers cannot easily drop out of the established bargaining orbit.

The Impact on Union Government

The need to adapt to the environment in order to achieve bargaining power has several consequences for the distribution of authority within unions and for union democracy.

We have already noted the complex mechanisms that many unions construct to consolidate bargaining input from membership groupings. The overlays of councils and departments in the UAW, the Teamsters, and the Machinists are directed largely to aligning internal structure to bargaining needs.

We also observed the tendency in local unions for power to attach to those with greatest bargaining responsibilities—the business agent in the nonfactory local, for instance, is the dominant individual. The same tendency extends to the international union level, where those officers at levels who conduct bargaining are the most prominent.

A corollary is that dues income is generally allocated in proportion to bargaining responsibilities. In local markets where the local union handles most bargaining, the local will retain a larger share of the dues dollar.

The prevailing trend is for unions to respond to bargaining needs by internal centralization. In national markets with few producers, auto and steel for instance, the internationals took the lead in concentrating bargaining structures. Top officers assumed increased authority and responsibility. The increased complexity of many problems led to greater reliance on staff expertise. The role of the locals was limited mainly to prenegotiations input, to negotiating local supplemental agreements, and to the early steps of the grievance procedure. Because the agreement is national, contract interpretation must be more centralized, and major grievances are usually settled by national union representatives meeting with corporate headquarters representatives.

Even where the opposite situation exists—where many employers in labor intensive industries compete—similar results can ensue. The imperative here again is for the union to bring the relevant work force under identical economic terms. But to do so it must first bring the numerous employers into a single association for purposes of bargaining. Absent this consolidation in such industries, a non-union employer, or one that negotiated better economic terms for itself, would be in a position to underprice its competitors. Such situations once existed in the clothing, bituminous coal, and over-the-road trucking industries. In each case the union was able to stabilize the industry by negotiating a contract with an association representing scores of employers. And in each case this was accompanied by some centralization of power within the union.

Even unions in some of the traditionally local market industries are experiencing shifts in bargaining authority from the locals to the international. In several building trades unions, for example, this shift can be attributed to some combination of the following:

(1) The national scope of efforts by construction users, primarily large corporations, to lower their costs, with a resulting increase in *national maintenance agreements* stabilizing the terms of plant construction-and-expansions work between unions and contractors.

(2) The increased role of the internationals in negotiating national *project agreements* covering nuclear and other major construction efforts. Typically local unions are allowed to refer workers to these projects, but the terms under which they work are those negotiated by the international.

(3) The fact that several contractors operate on national and international scales, requiring a more consolidated union response.

Meanwhile other local market unions such as police and fire fighter organizations are relatively unaffected and have not seen major shifts from locals to internationals.

Conglomerates and Multinationals

The relatively recent extension of conglomerate and multinational corporations, neither of which is entirely new, into new spheres of activity poses a threat to union bargaining effectiveness. Conglomerates operate in more than a single industry. Multinationals, in their most developed form, integrate their raw material supply lines, production, and marketing across national boundaries. With the arrival of the "world car," for instance, vehicles produced by "domestic" auto corporations are assembled from components obtained from several nations. These same corporations enter joint marketing and even production ventures with "foreign" multinationals.

The ability of the multinational to shop among nations for the best deal and locate its plants accordingly can make a mockery of negotiated and legislated labor standards. The relevant work force becomes greatly extended. Even if it is unionized, coordination is difficult because it is apt to be represented by British, German, Japanese, or heavily restricted South African or Brazilian unions. Thus far there have been only preliminary efforts by U.S. unions to coordinate with these overseas unions.

With conglomerates, the boundaries of the firm and the industry no longer match. With immense financial resources spread among diverse ventures, many conglomerates have an increased ability to withstand a strike in one segment while proceeding with the activities of the others, which subsidize the parent and increase its ability to resist. And as subsidiaries are acquired and traded away by distant, often invisible, holding companies, unions are faced with a "here today, gone tomorrow" dilemma. Organization that was appropriate at one time, as was the one-industry unionism established in the 1930s, becomes misaligned. The relevant work force must encompass the scope of the employer's operation, going beyond the product lines suggested earlier.

As Alexander has put it,

> To allow union and bargaining structural change to develop so that tactical strike power diminishes is a path toward ineffectualness, and a threat to the very existence of unionism. To maintain an effectual bargaining position, union structure has changed over time, and bargaining structure generally has become more centralized and of broader scope. And these structural adjustments can be viewed as a response, though sometimes a halting and delayed one, to basic and continuing change in the structure of productive activity within which the union must function.[5]

---

[5] Kenneth O. Alexander, "Union Structure and Bargaining Structure," *Labor Law Journal* 24, no. 3 (March 1973), p. 167.

Where a union cannot organize effectively it cannot bargain, and where it cannot bargain effectively it cannot organize. Each is a necessary condition of the other.

In line with our earlier discussion of bargaining imperatives, the indicated union response would seem to be further consolidation to match the new employer configurations, be they multinational, conglomerate, or both. This would seem to remove participation and policy control further from the rank-and-file and from local union officers. This is not to say that, once established, centralized bargaining structures and the corresponding centralization of authority within unions is irreversible. Changes in the environment, such as declining demand for the product, or in unionization of the relevant work force, as occurred in coal, indicate as much. But the issue of what, if any, is the acceptable, necessary, or even possible balance between centralization of authority for bargaining and internal democracy remains.

Updating Union Structure: A Local Union Merger Program

The interplay of bargaining and more purely organizational imperatives as they lead to changes in union structure is illustrated in this and the following section, which deal with structural consolidation at two levels in the labor movement.

The following story concerns a nonfactory union in the service industry, its organizational and bargaining problems, and how, in one city, it overhauled and updated its structure. This case goes to the heart of union structure and the tasks of one of its key figures, the business agent, and by extension the staff representative in industrial unions. It also illustrates changes in bargaining government and servicing structures, how unions struggle to keep pace with changing industry and employer structures, and the local-international union links within the structure of the labor movement. The story is true.[6]

As of 1980 a single local union, Local 6, represented all 60,000 members of the Hotel Employees and Restaurant Employees International Union (HERE) in New York City and some of its environs. Six years earlier no fewer than 14 different locals of HERE represented the same jurisdiction. One was the original Local 6, with

---

[6] Based largely on a report in *Nation's Labor* 9, no. 10 (October 1979), pp. 10–16, with permission.

about 30,000 members. Most of the 13 other locals were considerably smaller. Each was organized along craft lines—cooks, waiters, bartenders, counter people, maids, and so on. Sometimes these craft locals were further limited by the type of establishment that employed their members—clubs, restaurants, hotels, sports arenas, chain restaurants, and luncheonettes. Some locals held jurisdictions that had not thrived since prohibition days. Others had declined in recent decades due to the spread of fast-food chains, which are notoriously difficult to organize.

In one way or another most of these locals were in trouble. Declining work led to declining membership and declining treasuries. This, in turn, seriously impaired the ability of the union to represent its shrinking membership or to reverse its fortunes by organizing new members and new establishments. The bargaining situation was a puzzling patchwork of small, dissimilar agreements.

Because of the craft pattern of organization and the nonfactory structure of the union, in one restaurant alone 15 employees had four different business agents representing them. One business agent would represent one craft group, under its separate contract. Another would come in to handle the problems of a different craft. Thus, several different locals of the same international had dealings with the same employer. A consolidated structure would allow a business agent to make a single trip to take care of problems affecting all members at an establishment.

The New York situation was perhaps an extreme one. Declining membership, duplication of effort, lack of accountability, and the proliferation of local fiefdoms were among the many manifestations of the problem.

Local disorganization of this sort does not have to be repeated too many times in different jurisdictions before the international suffers a massive organizational hemorrhage. The HERE suffered from the outdated structure and jurisdictional lines of many of its nearly 500 locals representing nearly 400,000 members. The union adopted an aggressive survival program, of which New York City is the major showcase. Between 1974 and 1979 the 14 separate locals became, on paper at least, one organization. A series of mergers first brought the smaller locals into progressively large blocs. The final consolidation was a 1979 merger of this recently pyramided local structure with Local 6 and two others.

The merged local is now organized more along industrial, rather than craft, lines. It is aligned into three divisions according to the type of establishment in which its members are employed—club, restaurant, and hotel.

A merger of this magnitude takes many years to complete. One hurdle is convincing elected local officers accustomed to "running their own shows" that there is a greater good and someone has to give. Initially an excess of officers may be retained as a condition of merger. Also, time is required to renegotiate contracts, consolidate benefit plans, and organize new staff assignments. But the long-run gains from better representation, elimination of duplication in administrative costs and staff time, and more effective organizing efforts should result over the coming years as the merger is consolidated.

The HERE is not the only international union facing similar problems.[7] Nor is it the only international to take steps to overhaul its structure and operations. Consolidation does not automatically lead to improvements, to more effective unionism, or to better representation. But where the structure of union activity is not geared to the realities of the environment—especially where small scale employer organization is replaced by multinational and conglomerate ownership—or where the sheer number and diversity of small establishments make fragmented unionism ineffective, consolidation is often a necessary step.

Problems similar to those of the former constituent locals of HERE Local 6 exist at a different level, that of the international. Similar solutions are being advanced at this level—namely mergers of struggling, often small, internationals into larger ones.

International Union Mergers

Unions have split, reorganized, reaffiliated and merged throughout the history of the labor movement. If reduction of competition and increased bargaining power are two rationales for merger, organizational problems are another. Many unions are simply too small to support the staff and programs necessary to deal with their environments, particularly those in which employers are merging into larger and more powerful conglomerates and multina-

---

[7] The Bricklayers, Masons and Plasterers union in the 1960s, by one report, had 30 to 40 locals in the metropolitan Boston area, some dating back to horse-and-buggy days. John T. Dunlop, "What's Ahead in Union Government," in Joel Seidman, ed., TRADE UNION GOVERNMENT AND COLLECTIVE BARGAINING (New York: Praeger, 1970), p. 201.

tionals. Also, inflation and unemployment have eaten away at union resources, compounding the problem.

When a small union is absorbed by a union many times its size, the process is more one of *acquisition* than *merger*. Typically the larger union will make no adjustments in its name or structure other than sometimes to name the president of the "acquired" union to a vice-presidency or to create a small division named after the new jurisdiction. The smaller union usually represents a shrinking jurisdiction and is faced with a "merge or fold up" alternative.

This was the case when the 100,000-plus Printing Pressmen in 1973 acquired the 8,000-member Stereotypers, and the occasion was used to update the name to the International Printing and Graphic Communications Union; when the 25,000-member United Shoe Workers joined the Clothing and Textile Workers; when the Boot and Shoe Workers joined the Retail Clerks, which later merged with the Meatcutters to become the UFCW; when the Sleeping Car Porters, down to 1,000 members, joined the Railway, Airline and Steamship Clerks; and in 1979 when the 11,000-member Lathers affiliated with the Carpenters. In each case there existed an apparent jurisdictional relationship between the two unions.

The logic of union mergers can be classified as *vertical, horizontal*, or *strictly for scale*. Each expresses a particular form of jurisdictional, organizational, or bargaining advantage, often designed to reduce rivalry and enhance unity.

Vertical Mergers. A vertical merger is the combination of two unions, one of whose members supplies the raw material or work of the other, sometimes for the same employer. The two groups work in adjacent stages of the work process, and each can benefit from joining with the other. The merger not only reduces rivalry where their work meets but lets them present a common front to employers.

Printing production, for example, contains a number of adjacent steps, suggesting part of the rationale for a proposed merger between the Newspaper Guild and the Typographical Union and to some extent the rationale for the combination of Photoengravers, Lithographers and Bookbinders that brought about the Graphic Arts International Union, which then merged in 1983 with the Printing & Graphic Communications Union to form the Graphic Communications International Union (GCIU).

Horizontal Mergers. Horizontal mergers occur where the work of two unions is independent but where the two share or compete for membership in the same broad setting or jurisidiction. In one situation there is contiguous work, and, often, a common employer and jurisdictional rivalry; in the other, a separate but similar type of jurisdiction indicates that the two unions have something in common. The first we term a *jurisdictional merger*, the second, a *consolidating merger*.

Jurisdictional mergers include those of the State, County, and Municipal Employees (AFSCME) with the New York Civil Service Employees Association (both of whom included state employees in their jurisdiction) and the 1979 merger of the Retail Clerks and the Meatcutters to form the United Food and Commercial Workers. These latter two unions fought for years over competing claims for work in retail groceries. The merger of several postal craft unions into the American Postal Workers Union is a case similar in its logic to the merger of New York craft locals of the HERE, described earlier.

Consolidating mergers are different in degree from jurisdictional mergers in that the unions may share the same general line of work but have no major jurisdictional problems with one another. This appeared to be the case for discussions, since suspended, between the Insurance Workers and the Office and Professional Employees, who organize in different segments of the broad white-collar field, and between the Molders and the Allied Industrial Workers. (In 1983 the Insurance Workers merged with the Food and Commercial Workers.)

Strictly-for-Scale Mergers. While the advantages of size, consolidation of effort, and *economy of scale* are a major consideration in all mergers, there are instances where this appears as virtually the only logic. The merger of the Bakery and Confectionary Workers with the Tobacco Workers in 1978 appears to have had little industrial, jurisdictional, or bargaining logic behind it and to have been based largely on scale considerations. Some tobacco companies, however, have purchased bakeries, and products of both are marketed in similar ways.

Between 1956 and 1976, 95 different unions were involved in mergers, with most having under 50,000 members.[8] The number of unions affiliated with the AFL-CIO dropped from 137 in 1956 to 96 by late 1983.

Consummating union mergers is a complicated business.

---

[8] Charles J. Janus, "Union Mergers in the 1970s," *Monthly Labor Review* 101, no. 10 (October 1978), p. 14.

Union leaders are presumably adept at bargaining, but the demands of merger negotiations are unique, extending beyond the experience gained in collective bargaining negotiations. There is no fixed deadline, no possibility of calling a strike, and little clout to a refusal to settle. At the same time strong leadership egos are on the line, for unless retirements are imminent, someone has to occupy the top positions and someone the second-level spots in the merged union. Difficult financial, legal, personnel, and facilities questions are also involved. Because of the difficulty in creating instant unity, many agreements call for a gradual elimination of duplicate facilities and consolidation of organizational units. Some near-mergers have broken up because intermediate and local level leaders have opposed them; others, because the details could not be negotiated, despite the apparent logic of the combination.

Trends

If economic recession, inflation, and vanishing work lead unions to seek mergers, the overriding need is to operate on a scale necessary to accomplish the tasks of collective bargaining and organizing. As businesses consolidate and shift operations, it becomes increasingly difficult for unions to keep pace, especially when they are small and fragmented. Power in the labor movement becomes increasingly centralized, with the trend even affecting many of the traditionally most decentralized unions.

As unions become larger and more centralized, they must face problems inherent in all large-scale organizations—how to retain flexibility and allow for innovation. In addition they encounter the problem of how to retain democratic control by the membership—a dilemma not found in business enterprises. As unions continue to merge in order to realize greater efficiencies of scale and bargaining advantage, particular attention will have to be devoted to overcoming these accompanying problems.

Mergers are not the only answer, but they are one way in which many unions are addressing their problems.

A Postscript: Canadian Membership

While this is a book about unions in the United States, it is appropriate to comment on the Canadian segments of unions with U.S. headquarters. As noted at the outset of the book, the term *international* generally designates that a union's membership extends to Canada.

The significance of Canadian membership is at least twofold. First, it reflects the need for solidarity across national boundaries. Many major employers operate on both sides of the border, and this makes logical some type of combined effort. Second, workers also face common predicaments stemming from identical employers operating on a worldwide basis, so there is no logical reason why combined organizatonal efforts should be limited to Canada and the United States.

Cross-national efforts are often weakened by the centrifugal forces of nationalism. The fact that most Canadian segments of U.S.-based unions are in a minority status has led to resentment and occasional conflicts. Canadians are often underrepresented in the top leadership, and the election of a Canadian vice-president is the most typical union accommodation. The rise of nationalism in Canada and the feeling that U.S.-based unions extract from Canadian members more dues money than is returned in services have led some Canadian locals to disaffiliate and to realign with Canadian unions and federations. This has been a particular problem for U.S.-based unions in the forest-products industry where at one point 40,000 workers disaffiliated. On the other hand, Canadian members often carry significant weight in international union elections and conventions, and they can represent a tie-breaking potential if they vote in a bloc.

Some unions with a significant Canadian membership have gone well beyond token responses in their efforts to accommodate U.S. and Canadian differences. The International Woodworkers of America, with a slight majority of its 115,000 members in Canada, appears to have accommodated both interests. One adaptation to nationalistic sentiment is reflected in recent developments in the Broadcast Engineers and Technicians (NABET). Organized as a union of the National Broadcasting Company engineers in 1933, NABET was joined in 1952 by technical employees of the Canadian Broadcasting Company. In the early 1970s a number of the Canadian locals, spearheaded by French-speaking units, pushed for separation. At the 1974 convention, the two parted on generally amicable terms. They retain loose ties in name and coordinate through a Multinational Executive Council (composed of the two Executive Councils), which has only advisory powers. In addition, portions of each organization's conventions meet jointly. Within this loose umbrella organization, the branches are autonomous, each with its own constitution and finances.

This background explains the apparently contradictory statements in the NABET constitution that "This Constitution shall not apply to the Union's organization and membership in Canada" followed by a statement that the union "shall be multinational in scope."

In 1984 the Steelworkers union, following a bitter campaign involving nationalist invective, elected a Canadian, Lynn Williams, as international president.

The long experience of ties between Canadian and U.S. workers through membership in the same international unions points in two directions. It is an example of the kind of cross-national effort that workers and unions must develop on an even broader scale if they are to deal effectively with multinational corporations. But at the same time it suggests the difficulties of maintaining equity, real and perceived, in contributions and benefits. Workers share common predicaments regardless of language and nationality, but the desire to maintain national integrity and to some measure of autonomy is a fact of life that must be addressed as unions attempt to become more multinational in scope.

Conclusion

Union structures reflect two general types of functional demands, or imperatives. The first, governmental and administrative effectiveness, is a need faced by all large organizations to some degree. The second, however, is unique to unions. It is the need to maximize bargaining effectiveness with employers.

The resulting forms include intermediate bodies which perform both administrative and bargaining tasks, the balance depending on the union. Intermediate bodies permit both a diffusion and a consolidation of power in most unions. The principal contact with the locals is through those we have called staff representatives, although the terminology varies by union.

Other internal structures reflect the need to communicate with and mobilize members on the basis of employment and political criteria. The result is an often-complex gridwork of cross-cutting coverages.

Membership losses, the desire to increase bargaining power, and the need to adjust to new alignments of employer organization and power seem increasingly to lead to mergers among locals and among internationals. Bargaining logic leads also to the internationalization of union organization; thus far the major example has been the merging in some industries of U.S. and Canadian unionists into the same organizations.

The next chapter describes the major ways in which functional needs lead different unions to combine across union lines and across international boundaries.

Key Words and Phrases

intermediate body
quasi-local union bodies
district
region
joint board
servicing
international representative
relevant work force
coordinated bargainaing
removing wages from
  competition
national maintenance
  agreement
national project
  agreement

product market
labor market
conglomerate
multinational corporation
acquisition
union merger
vertical merger
horizontal merger
jurisdictional merger
consolidating merger
strictly-for-scale merger
economy of scale

Review and Discussion Questions

1. Do you agree or disagree with the statement, "Only a unified, monopolistic, centralized union with a strong president can deal with monopolistic corporations"? Why?

2. To what extent can intermediate bodies resolve the organizational problems of international unions?

3. Research a union of your own choosing. What types of intermediate bodies does it have and what are their purposes? What influence do these bodies have in centralizing or decentralizing power within the union?

4. What role do the different levels of union organization play in collective bargaining? How does the union's bargaining structure reflect or deal with its environment?

5. From your knowledge of organizations, gained from this book or

elsewhere, what problems in addition to those mentioned do you think have to be ironed out in merger negotiations?

6. What would be the ideal merger? Why? You might discuss this with reference to the characteristics of two unions, real or of your own creation.

7. Construct a chart tracking the conditions for union bargaining power, given different situations, to what you believe to be the most appropriate bargaining and union structures.

Suggestions for Further Reading

Hoffa and the Teamsters, by Ralph and Estelle James, is a fascinating analysis of how bargaining and union structures were overhauled in the jurisdiction of one international union. *Trade Union Government and Collective Bargaining*, Joel Seidman, ed., has several contributions relating to internal government and bargaining structure. For an analyses of industry structure and technology as it bears on different unions, see *Labor Studies Journal* (Winter 1979).For a useful compilation of different views on that subject, see Banks and Stieber, editors, *Multinational Unions and Labor Relations in Industralized Countries*.

Dated but still relevant to the subject of this chapter are some of the titles on the Comparative Union Government Series, published in 1962. The series includes studies of the Retail Clerks, the Carpenters, AFSCME, the Machinists, the Teamsters, the OCAW, the Brotherhood of Railroad Trainmen, the UAW, and the Steelworkers.

On union mergers see Gideon Chitayat, *Trade Union Mergers and Labor Conglomerates*, and Gary N. Chaison, "A Note on Union Merger Trends, 1900–1978," *Industrial and Labor Relations Review* (October 1980).

Complete bibliographical information for the above titles can be found in the Bibliography.

8

Multi-Union Structures

The strongest bond of human sympathy, outside of the family relation, should be one uniting all working people, of all nations and tongues and kindreds.

Abraham Lincoln, to a committee of the
New York Workingmen's Association,
March 21, 1864

An injury to one is an injury to all.

Motto of the Industrial Workers of the World

The axiom of power that "in unity there is strength" is especially appropriate for workers' organizations. Concerted activity is more potent than the efforts of individuals and isolated units. The whole has greater power than the sum power of its separate parts.

As workers combine in unions, they find that local and international union structures do not address all their employment needs. Some situations require coordination among different unions, giving rise to *multi-union*, sometimes termed *interunion*, structures in the labor movement. Multi-union structures cross union lines, encompassing representatives of more than a single international.

The best known multi-union bodies are those associated with the national AFL-CIO:[1] There are state federations; local central bodies; and in industry sectors, national and local trade and industrial bodies. Less well-known are coordinated bargaining agencies; limited structures for cross-national coordination; and the many informal arenas, including politics and education programs, in which representatives of different unions gather.

---

[1] National federations such as the AFL-CIO, the Canadian Labor Congress (CLC), and the British Trades Union Congress (TUC) are often designated "trade union centers."

The AFL-CIO

The core functions of the AFL-CIO (the "Federation") are political representation, public relations, and interunion coordination and dispute resolution. But in recent years the Federation has broadened its activities by encouraging mergers and other forms of consolidation, expanding education programs, and increasing its support role in organizing and collective bargaining.

Behind this new emphasis are at least two trends that make better coordination essential. The first is the trend toward concentration of ownership, especially across product lines through conglomerates. Second is the growing impact of government on unions and collective bargaining. Both developments increase the need for a strong mechanism to coordinate strategy at the national level, a function for which the Federation is designed.

The AFL-CIO has been described as the "United Nations of the labor movement" and by John L. Lewis as a "rope of sand." George Meany once described it with a business metaphor:

> It's like the Fifth Avenue Association in New York. The Fifth Avenue Association embraces all the merchants on Fifth Avenue who desire to belong to the Fifth Avenue Association. But each one runs its own business.[2]

Each of these characterizations alludes to the differences among autonomous internationals that must be overcome for the Federation to act with authority on behalf of all. The power of the leadership rests on a delicate balance based in part on attention to the special needs of each bloc of affiliates and in part on finding areas of consensus.

Formation. The AFL-CIO is a complex organization composed of units with diverse origins. Many state and local central bodies existed prior to the 1881 founding of the Federation of Organized Trades and Labor Unions (FOTLU), from which the AFL emerged. Other elements—committees, departments, regional structures—developed in later years. Many have clear AFL antecedents while some can be traced to the CIO.

The formation of the independent CIO in the 1930s changed the composition of the U.S. labor movement and altered the configuration of its internal politics. No longer could the AFL leadership

---

[2] Interview in *AFL-CIO News*, September 17, 1977.

rest comfortably on its largely craft-union base and its exclusionist philosophy.

Over the next two decades several changes occurred within each federation. The organization of new members proceeded rapidly, but rival unionism led to destructive raids on established bargaining units and expensive competition for new ones. The post-World War II wave of anti-union sentiment in Congress led to the 1947 passage of the Taft-Hartley amendments to the National Labor Relations Act, virtually all of which were unfavorable to labor. Labor leaders began to speculate whether a unified labor movement could have blunted this effort.

Two developments in the late 1940s and early 1950s critically weakened the CIO. First, labor was touched by a wave of political repression that continued to grow. A total of 11 unions either withdrew or were expelled from the CIO in 1949–50, their leaders accused of adhering to the program of the Communist Party. A second development was the hostility between leaders of the two largest CIO unions, the Auto Workers and the Steelworkers. By the early 1950s the CIO was on shaky footing, both organizationally and financially.

In 1952 CIO leadership passed to Walter Reuther of the Auto Workers after the death of Philip Murray of the Steelworkers. At about the same time as the change in CIO leadership, AFL head William Green died and George Meany, formerly secretary-treasurer, became president. Where Murray and Green had been antagonists since the 1930s split, Meany and Reuther were relatively unencumbered by this past. In 1955, the two federations formally merged, with Meany assuming the presidency. Reuther became head of the *Industrial Union Department* (IUD). The IUD was a newly formed arm representing most of the former CIO affiliates and former AFL unions with industrial membership.

AFL-CIO Affiliation: Process and Politics

International unions enter and, occasionally, exit the Federation for many reasons. Many unions have survived outside the AFL-CIO. But affiliation affords several benefits, some immediate and others prospective. Immediate benefits include the many services provided affiliates, collectively and individually, such as research, education, publications, lobbying, and public relations. Most affiliates would add that they gain a sense of legitimacy from being part of the "official family" of organized labor. Prospective benefits such as publicity, lobbying, and boycott support depend on the political and bargaining needs of the union, on the number of unions sharing the jurisdiction, and on the willingness of other affiliates to provide concrete support. These benefits can be substantial.

There have been two major exits since the merger. The 1957 expulsion of the Teamsters resulted from the inability of Meany and other Federation leaders to prevent James Hoffa from assuming the presidency of that union. More broadly, the incident arose from the controversy over union corruption that culminated in the McClellan Committee hearings and the passage of the Labor Management Reporting and Disclosure Act (LMRDA). The 1968 withdrawal of the UAW, largely the result of personal and policy disputes between Reuther and Meany, was quite different. Reuther opposed Meany's international affairs posture and felt that Meany's philosophy was steering the Federation away from progressive policies. It was not until 1981, after Meany's retirement and subsequent death, that the UAW reaffiliated.

Other unions that have been in or out of the AFL, the CIO, or the combined federation at one time or another include the Mine Workers, the United Electrical Workers, the Machinists, and the west coast Longshoremen (ILWU). The Teamsters and the National Education Association are the million member-plus unions which remain independent of the AFL-CIO.

The AFL-CIO constitution grants to the Executive Council the authority to issue affiliation charters. The Council, made up of 33 vice-presidents plus the top two officers, may then delegate this authority to the president. But the constitution also states that where the jurisdiction of a new applicant would conflict with that of an existing affiliate, the written consent of the affiliate is required. Despite ambiguities over what constitutes a jurisdictional conflict, this provides affiliates with a form of veto power over new applications. For instance, the application of the 60,000-member Telecommunications International Union, a federation of telephone workers whose jurisdiction overlaps those of the IBEW and the Communications Workers, was rejected in this manner.

Finances. Affiliates make several types of per capita payments to sustain the AFL-CIO. In addition to the regular 31 cents per month for each member in the United States for basic affiliation,[3]

---

[3] Most will contribute to the Canadian Labor Congress (CLC) based on the number of their members in that nation.

internationals may make additional per capita payments to trade and industrial departments based on membership in the "jurisdiction" of each.

Local unions pay per capita assessments to state and local AFL-CIO central bodies and to local trade and industrial councils with which they affiliate. Some international constitutions require locals to affiliate with central bodies but many ignore these provisions, creating a problem to be discussed later in this chapter. It is a poorly kept secret that some internationals and locals understate their membership for purposes of making per capita payments, which probably explains why the AFL-CIO often reports substantially fewer affiliated members than does the Labor Department.

In 1981 the Federation took in $32 million, 90 percent of it in per capita payments, and had a net worth of about $23 million.[4] Impressive for an individual, the AFL-CIO's "wealth" is considerably less than that of some internationals.

Structures and Functions of the AFL-CIO

The complex purposes of the AFL-CIO result in a structure that at first glance seems a confusing collection of fragmented units, with no apparent unifying logic. However, an examination of these units and their functions reveals that while the Federation is not streamlined, there are coherent patterns. Thus the more significant bodies fall under one of the following categories:

(1) *Governance* is concerned with the electoral and representational process at the national level.

(2) *Staff departments* organized for administrative support. These include multipurpose field offices established within geographical regions.

(3) Departments organized along broad *trade or industrial lines.*

(4) *State and local central bodies* representing affiliated local unions, usually in units of civil government jurisdiction such as a state or county.

---

[4] Secretary-Treasurer's Report, in PROCEEDINGS OF THE FOURTEENTH CONSTITUTIONAL CONVENTION OF THE AFL-CIO, 1981, ed. John Barry (Washington, D.C.: AFL-CIO, 1982), II:15. [Volumes of the PROCEEDINGS are initially published in paperback as two volumes; when bound in hardcover, both volumes appear in a single volume, but the original pagination is retained—Ed. note.]

Governing Structure. The biennial convention is the supreme governing body of the Federation. It elects officers, affirms broad policy, and resolves outstanding disputes. (See Chart 1.) But like international union conventions, much of its function is ceremonial, and authority between conventions is exercised by the *Executive Council*, the two top officers, and the staff.

Delegates to the AFL-CIO convention are selected by the internationals, usually at their conventions, with top officers designated as delegates *ex officio*. Other delegates to the Federation's biennial convention represent central bodies and trade/industrial departments.

The Executive Council consists of the president and the secretary-treasurer, plus 33 vice-presidents who by custom are usually presidents of influential affiliates. The council replaces its own members upon death, retirement, defeat in an election, or resignation. These appointments are routinely confirmed by election at the next AFL-CIO convention.

The Executive Council, and often an even smaller informal group within it, along with the two top officers is the real directing force in the affairs of the Federation. The *General Board* plays a governing role only on matters referred to it by the officers. Very little of importance has been referred to it. The most powerful affiliates are already represented on the Executive Council.

Staff Departments. These departments carry on the day-to-day headquarters and some field operations. Some departments, like Accounting, Data Processing, Library, Purchasing, and Reproduction and Mailings, have the same roles as in most large organizations. They provide administrative and technical services. Others—Civil Rights, International Affairs, and Occupational Safety, Health and Social Security,[5] for example—are assigned substantive areas. Economic Research, Education, and Information have somewhat more comprehensive backup responsibilities and often work closely with Legislation and Political Education, which are assigned core Federation functions. Field operations are carried out by Department of Organization and Field Services (DOFS) staff assigned to one of eight AFL-CIO regions.

DOFS is the most extensive of the staff units and receives about 20 percent of the Federation's operating budget. Field representatives operate within their regions to integrate the work of AFL-CIO

---

[5] The result of a 1983 consolidation of the Department of Social Security with the Department of Occupational Safety and Health.

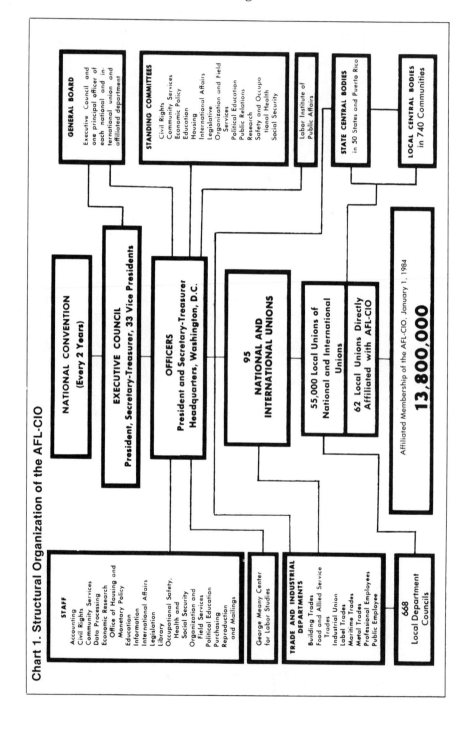

Chart 1. Structural Organization of the AFL-CIO

NATIONAL CONVENTION
(Every 2 Years)

EXECUTIVE COUNCIL
President, Secretary-Treasurer, 33 Vice Presidents

OFFICERS
President and Secretary-Treasurer
Headquarters, Washington, D.C.

95
NATIONAL AND INTERNATIONAL UNIONS

55,000 Local Unions of
National and International Unions

62 Local Unions Directly Affiliated with AFL-CIO

Affiliated Membership of the AFL-CIO, January 1, 1984

13,800,000

GENERAL BOARD
Executive Council and one principal officer of each national and international union and affiliated department

STANDING COMMITTEES
Civil Rights
Community Services
Economic Policy
Education
Housing
International Affairs
Legislative
Organization and Field Services
Political Education
Public Relations
Research
Safety and Occupational Health
Social Security

Labor Institute of Public Affairs

STATE CENTRAL BODIES
in 50 States and Puerto Rico

LOCAL CENTRAL BODIES
in 740 Communities

STAFF
Accounting
Civil Rights
Community Services
Data Processing
Economic Research
Office of Housing and Monetary Policy
Education
Information
International Affairs
Legislation
Library
Occupational Safety, Health and Social Security
Organization and Field Services
Political Education
Purchasing
Reproduction and Mailings

George Meany Center for Labor Studies

TRADE AND INDUSTRIAL DEPARTMENTS
Building Trades
Food and Allied Service Trades
Industrial Union
Label Trades
Maritime Trades
Metal Trades
Professional Employees
Public Employee

668
Local Department Councils

departments and central bodies. DOFS staff cooperate with the Legislative Department and the national Committee on Political Education (COPE) to streamline the efforts of internationals and central bodies to register voters, conduct political education, and turn out voters. These efforts often include the temporary assignment of staff to assist state federations.

The other major area of DOFS activity is to assist in organizing and to foster cooperative organizing campaigns in industries and areas where internationl unions are active or potentially active. The DOFS regions also provide organizational assistance and consultation to central bodies to develop more effective programs and increase local union affiliations. Occasionally they will assist in mergers of small local central bodies to bring about larger units with greater capabilities.

The departments of *legislation* and *political education* are responsible for the Federation's political functions. These departments provide not only legislative research and lobbying capability, but play a key role in designing strategy and mobilizing voters for the election of candidates favorable to labor. The task of involving unionists in the electoral and political process is assigned to COPE, the Committee on Political Education. Achieving COPE goals requires extensive coordination throughout the labor movement, but especially with the central bodies and the Department of Organization and Field Services. The next chapter deals with the substance and the machinery of labor's political activity.

The *Community Services Department* is at the center of a network of almost 400 full-time labor liaison representatives in local communities who assist in the delivery of the services of voluntary and public agencies to union members and their families as well as to others. These labor representatives serve on boards and committees, train local union counselors to assist members, assist in United Way fundraising efforts, and in numerous other ways link the labor movement to the community. The department has been active in programs dealing with drug and alcohol abuse, labor and the arts, and the varied activities of the United Labor Agencies (ULAs).

The *Education Department* prepares and distributes a variety of training materials and labor education resources for use by affiliates. It maintains an extensive labor film library for inexpensive rentals, makes available a catalog of these holdings, publishes a newsletter called *Education Update*, monitors education legislation in Congress and the activities of education agencies, and represents the Federation with other institutions through representatives who sit on all manner of boards and commissions. Its scope encompasses both labor and general education.

The *Economic Research Department* specializes in the analysis of economic matters of concern to the Federation—employment, taxation, and collective bargaining patterns. Staffers develop much original material and assist in its policy applications by serving on government advisory boards, publishing in a variety of media, speaking, and participating in educational forums.

The *Information Department* publishes, in addition to other materials, *AFL-CIO News*, a weekly newspaper of brief items and features on political, organizational, and bargaining issues and events of concern to affiliates. While the Information department handles general publicity and public relations for the Federation, individual departments often publish newsletters in their areas. We have noted the Education Department's *Education Update*. Organization and Field Services distributes two periodicals of particular use to organizers—the RUB Sheet (*Report on Union Busters*) and STIR (*Statistical and Tactical Information Report*).

In 1981 the Federation established the Labor Institute for Public Affairs, a nonprofit corporation governed by the members of the Executive Council, in order to disseminate labor viewpoints to members and to the general public. By 1983 LIPA distributed television shows to cable stations, independents, and network affiliates and was investigating other ways to make use of the latest communications technology.

The George Meany Center for Labor Studies, a nonprofit corporation governed by a board of trustees made up of labor and nonlabor members, conducts intensive education programs for union leaders on its campus just outside the capital in Silver Spring, Maryland. Thousands of full-time union officers and other representatives have participated in Center programs covering everything from contract negotiations, grievance arbitration, and organizing techniques to publicity, arts, computer literacy, and political issues. Through Antioch University, the Center operates a college degree program, making it possible for full-time officers and staff to obtain Labor Studies degrees without interrupting their union work.

Several of the functional staff departments have counterpart relationships with *standing committees* (see Chart 1). Members are appointed by the AFL-CIO president. These committees vary in their level of activity, usually serving as advisory bodies for the respective departments, where such matchups exist. Article XII of the AFL-CIO constitution, titled Committee and Staff Departments, suggests that each committee maintains its own department separate from the corresponding staff department. But, aside from stating that each committee shall be provided with adequate staff, the article is devoted to committee functions, described in such terms as "to assist the Executive Council," "be concerned with," "shall undertake to recommend programs in. . . ." The major reference to staff departments is that they "shall be established where appropriate under the direction of the President to function in the fields of activity described above. . . ." In almost every case where a corresponding department exists, it is the department, with its full-time staff, which is the hub of activity. Upgrading a committee to a department assigns new importance to a function.

Some committees are almost vestigial, having been created to serve a need in years past and then retained in title when the concern abated. Such is the Committee on Ethical Practices, formed during the 1950s concern with internal union affairs.

Trade and Industrial Departments. This third dimension of Federation structure consists of units representing internationals with common jurisdictional interests. It is a structural dimension that is being revitalized as unions address changes in their environments.

Trade and industrial departments are supported by per capita assessments paid by international unions based on the number of their members falling within the department's jurisdiction. A single international may affiliate with two or more trade and industrial departments. The IBEW, for example, has segments of its varied membership affiliated with the Building and Construction Trades, Industrial Union, Maritime Trades, Metal Trades, Professional Employees, and Union Label and Service Trades departments. More typically, an international will pay department per capita to one or two such units.

The national trade and industrial departments charter and support local area councils. While local building trades councils are the most widespread, food and beverage, metal trades, and union label trades councils thrive in many localities.

The 15 international unions affiliated with the *Building and Construction Trades Department (BCTD)* share employment situations at both national and local levels. Consequently the BCTD maintains an active staff, publishes a variety of literature, conducts conferences, and promotes combined organizing drives. The department is particularly active in the legislative arena. Despite some defeats in its efforts to implement new legislation (such as the situs picketing bill to remove restrictions on unions in the construction industry), it has thus far succeeded in blocking efforts by nonunion contractors and other employer interests to destroy prevailing wage (Davis-Bacon) legislation. The department and its affiliates are also a major force in the internal politics of the Federation.

Many local building trades councils meet on a regular basis, exchanging information on political and bargaining needs and jurisdictional problems. This interaction is vital to unions that are affected so directly by the actions of state and local governments—in the letting of contracts, the establishment and enforcement of building codes, and other routine events in the industry. Local building trades councils are often joined, informally at least, by representatives of the nonaffiliated Teamsters whose transport jurisdiction is vital to construction, as it is to so many other industries.

While quite active, especially in efforts to promote coordinated bargaining among unions facing common employers, the *Industrial Union Department (IUD)* never attained the major standing that many expected. Nevertheless the IUD maintains a sizable staff promoting coordinated bargaining, joint organizing campaigns, and boycott efforts against nonunion employers and labor law violators. It also maintains research, health and safety, and public relations programs, and works with other Federation lobbyists in Congress.

The *Food and Allied Service Trades Department*, reestablished in 1976 after a lapse of 15 years, is currently a center of innovation. Initially headed by a part-time president of one of its major affiliates, the presidency was later made a full-time position.

The Food and Allied Service Trades Department is active in a jurisdiction where employer concentration is increasing rapidly and where technological change is an ongoing problem. It has responded with a research program, the active encouragement of local councils, and the promotion of mergers among affiliates. The major affiliate, following several mergers, is the Food and Commercial Workers (UFCW).

This new effort coordinates the activities of a number of unions active in the processing, distributing, and serving of food, with all but the processing being performed primarily by nonfactory unions in local markets. The department thus integrates many of the concerns of the retail, entertainment, restaurant, and hotel trades.

The *Union Label and Service Trades Department* is unique in that it is made up of almost all the AFL-CIO affiliates, led by those with a stake in promoting consumer adherence to the union label, the badge of union-made goods and services. The department is active not only in promoting the label, but in coordinating boycotts of nonunion products and establishments.

Other departments are similarly organized around the common interests of affiliates.

Central Labor Bodies. The fourth and last major organizational segment of the federation is made up of the state and local central bodies. The 50 *state federations* (plus one in Puerto Rico) and some 740 local central bodies are chartered by the Executive Council and operate under the AFL-CIO constitution. But the power and finances of these bodies are based on the locals within their areas that choose to affiliate with them.

The rub is the phrase "choose to affiliate." Despite a constitutional stipulation that international unions must "instruct" their locals to join the central bodies in their areas, the 24,000 locals affiliated with their state federations in 1982 represented only 55 percent of the AFL-CIO membership. Estimates of local central body affiliation are similar.

Florida, a right-to-work state, is a case in point. Florida has an aggresive state federation, as reflected in a report that a cooperative organizing program it sponsored resulted in over 50 percent union victories and boosted membership in AFL-CIO unions in the state to 353,000. Yet only 120,000 of these members had per capita taxes paid to the state federation by their locals in 1982.

Other states face comparable affiliation problems. Overloaded central body leaders lack the financial resources to fulfill their visions. Many states with sparse union membership have to establish higher per capita rates to sustain even modest programs, thus making it expensive for locals to affiliate. These central bodies are caught in a vicious circle.

Affiliation with central bodies tends to follow the employment cycle, dropping when employment (and hence local union treasuries) is down.[6] But much of the problem is due, not to the inability of locals to pay, but to the parochial attitude of some local leaders who are unwilling to contribute to or benefit from the broader labor movement.

Where the problem becomes severe, central bodies are barely able to perform their core functions—political representation at the state and local level and voter mobilization, coordinated through

---

[6] Executive Council Report, in PROCEEDINGS OF THE TWELFTH CONSTITUTIONAL CONVENTION OF THE AFL-CIO, 1977, ed. John Barry (Washington, D.C.: AFL-CIO, 1978), II:67.

COPE, for elections at all levels. Nevertheless a few central bodies perform these core functions and also support effective union label, education, publicity, and community service programs, as well as managing to assist in organizing campaigns, strikes, and boycotts.

State federation lobbying efforts in state legislatures are essential to the well-being of workers. Unemployment and workers' compensation and some tax legislation is enacted at the state level. In addition, enabling legislation for state and local government employee unionization, occupational health and safety enforcement, and environmental and public utility rate structures affecting workers and their families are often state-controlled. More will be said in the next chapter about the significance of federalism for union political action.

Local central bodies are the successors of the early city centrals that performed both political and occasional bargaining functions for unions in their areas.[7] While they no longer perform bargaining tasks, their structures remain geared to political efforts at their respective levels of government.[8]

Herein lies an advantage, but also another problem. The central body potentially excels in a task—political action—that is vital to workers and unions, but the task is perceived as secondary to collective bargaining by many and even unnecessary by some. This, combined with the reliance on voluntary affiliation, makes it easy for locals to find excuses not to affiliate. In addition, several other structures in theory perform political and other functions overlapping those of the central bodies. These structures include international unions, some intermediate bodies, and local unions, as well as local trades councils in some areas. The central body structure remains a problem spot in the AFL-CIO.

Linkages: How Affiliates Relate to the Federation

Having described the broad outlines of the AFL-CIO and its ties to various levels of union structure, it is now useful to view the relationship from the perspective of the international and its subordinate bodies. Exhibit 5 depicts how the International Union of Operating Engineers (IUOE) links up with the Federation.

---

[7] They are often called central labor councils or central labor unions.

[8] Stephen Cook and Miles Stanley, *Making It Go: A Handbook for Local Central Bodies*, Information Series 8 (Morgantown, W.Va.: Institute for Labor Studies, West Virginia University, 1970), 1.

**Exhibit 5. How One Union Links Up With AFL-CIO Bodies:
The International Union of Operating Engineers**

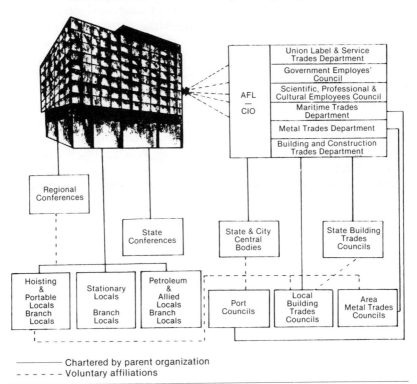

——————— Chartered by parent organization
- - - - - - Voluntary affiliations

The left half of the chart portrays the IUOE and its subunits, the right half those of the Federation.

The top portion of the chart shows, through lines running from headquarters to several departments and councils, the national level affiliations. The IUOE's department and council affiliations are based on the number of members working in the respective jurisdictions for whom the international pays per capita assessments.

As an affiliate the IUOE is, of course, represented in AFL-CIO conventions. Its president is one of the 33 federation vice-presidents sitting on the Executive Council.

As in most internationals, the regional and state conferences of the IUOE are internal units with no direct links to Federation structure.

The locals affiliate with state and local AFL-CIO central bodies on a voluntary basis (bottom of chart, left to right). They also affiliate with local councils (port, building trades, and metal trades) associated with national trade and industrial departments, as their jurisdiction dictates. Thus a hoisting and portable local in a land-locked city with members working primarily in the construction industry may affiliate with state and local building trades councils. A similar local in a port city may affiliate with a port council, based on the percentage of its members in maritime-related work. As the solid line indicates, this port council is chartered by the Maritime Trades Department of national AFL-CIO. The port councils coordinate political efforts, especially those related to government action affecting shipping. They may also assist in exchanging bargaining information. The chart fails to depict ties with unions in other countries, a link that is discussed later in the chapter.

Other Multi-Union Organizations

Several support groups, with membership and chapter structures, have AFL-CIO attachments. The A. Philip Randolph Institute (APRI) grew out of the Negro American Labor Council, founded by Randolph, who was also organizer of the Brotherhood of Sleeping Car Porters, to eliminate race discrimination in the labor movement. APRI operates within the AFL-CIO "orbit" with a small staff and local chapters in many areas. Similar, but of more recent origin, is the Labor Council for Latin American Advancement (LCLAA). Emerging from the leadership ranks of several affiliates was the Coalition of Black Trade Unionists which by 1983 reported membership in 67 international unions organized into 26 chapters.

An autonomous organization encompassing members of independents and AFL-CIO affiliates is the Coalition of Labor Union Women (CLUW). Formed in the mid-1970s, CLUW has informal national ties with the AFL-CIO, notably through its president, Joyce Miller, who sits on the AFL-CIO Executive Council. The organization represents the interests of women as workers and as union members.

Joint organizing campaigns between two or more unions are another form of multi-union organization. While not widespread, some have achieved notable successes and have extended into the representation phase. In Chicago, for instance, a local of the Service

Employees and a local of the Teamsters combined to form the Hospital Employees Labor Program (HELP). In California a coalition of three independents—the American Association of University Professors (AAUP), the State Employees' Association (CSEA) and the National Education Association (NEA)—known as the California Faculty Association (CFA) represents some 19,000 faculty members in the state university system.

Less formal ties among unions are sometimes forged in the political arena, in education programs, in boycott efforts, and in less formal arenas which further informal contacts among unionists and increase solidarity.

The Internal Disputes Plan

The 1952 no-raid pact between the AFL and the CIO was a first step toward creating a framework for resolving jurisdictional disputes among unions. Disputes occur in organizing and bargaining when one union claims work or representation rights also claimed by another union.

What is now Article XX of the AFL-CIO constitution was developed in 1962 to extend the dispute resolution procedures initiated by the earlier pact. Article XX states that "no affiliate shall organize or attempt to represent employees as to whom an established collective bargaining relationship exists with any other affiliate." Such a relationship exists when a union is recognized by an employer for over a year as the bargaining representative or when it is certified by the NLRB.

Alleged violations are handled through a disputes procedure. The claim is submitted to a panel of mediators selected from affiliates by the AFL-CIO president. If mediation efforts fail, the case is heard by a member of a standing panel of impartial umpires selected from outside the Federation. The umpire's ruling takes effect unless an appeal is made to the full AFL-CIO executive council.

Where all appeals are exhausted and the guilty party still refuses to comply with the ruling, several sanctions can be invoked. The *noncomplying union* cannot file a complaint against any other union and is not entitled to aid from any affiliate or to the services of the Federation. The Federation then publishes through its media the name of the noncomplying party.

In practice the few noncomplying unions—there were three listed in 1979—are seldom entirely cut off by the Federation. The provisions of Article XX have, however, resolved the vast majority of complaints. Of the 2,129 complaints filed between 1962 and mid-1981, 57 percent were settled in mediation. Of the 910 cases submitted to umpires, violations were found in 60 percent. Only 37 cases were submitted to the executive council, which set aside or modified the rulings in 18 cases. During this period there were 169 complaints that a union failed to comply with the ruling after appeals were exhausted.[9]

Leadership in the AFL-CIO

Describing leadership in a federation as diverse in composition and complex in structure as the AFL-CIO is no simple task. We will sketch only the more prominent aspects.

The overriding element shaping the leadership task in the federation is the interplay of *centrifugal* and *unifying* tendencies among affiliates. The centrifugal forces separate affiliates on the basis of differences, real and perceived. Often they reflect narrow and short-run interests or historic sources of division. Jurisdictional and craft rivalry, for example, are most bitter among crafts that are closest to one another. Open craft versus industrial union rivalry has declined since World War II but remains a source of potential cleavage within the AFL-CIO. Other differences among affiliates are situational, as when one union fails to support another's boycott because the first union's members work on the product at a different stage of production. If unleashed, these centrifugal forces could push affiliates along divergent paths to fragmentation.

In contrast, the unifying forces arise from the common interests of workers and unions and lead to unity around shared principles. They are summed up in "An injury to one is an injury to all," a truth a union involved in internecine strife may find difficult to see.

The interplay of these two forces expresses the potential for leadership of several types. One type is the "balancing act" in which leaders try to express in equal measure the perspectives of all, occasionally playing affiliates off against one another. A variant of this approach is the strategy of avoiding positions on issues over which there is apparent conflict among affiliates. A third approach, increasingly preferred in recent years, is to build on the unifying forces, emphasizing issues of strong common interest.

---

[9] AFL-CIO, PROCEEDINGS OF THE FOURTEENTH CONSTITUTIONAL CONVENTION, II:60-1.

Policy made in the Executive Council originates from several sources, including staff, affiliates and other bodies, and top Federation leadership itself. Its adoption is based both on the initial acceptability of the policy and on the abilities of leadership to garner agreement.

Another dimension of leadership in the federation is personal, not institutional. Over the years George Meany, Federation president for a quarter century, developed vast personal influence. Some of it derived indirectly from his perceived influence in government and in the labor movement and yet other parts more directly by virtue of personality. Much of Meany's power, however, was based in a coalition of union presidents seated on the Executive Council. This bloc represented diverse views but was unified around a foreign policy and a basic approach to the U.S. political system, party politics, and goals and methods for the labor movement. Initially this group consisted largely of building trades and maritime union leaders but over Meany's long tenure came to include many industrial unionists.

In late 1979 Lane Kirkland inherited much of the institutional power of the AFL-CIO presidency, the goodwill of most affiliates, a backlog of pressures for change from affiliates not in the "Meany coalition," but not the personal influence developed by Meany over the decades. That the new leadership acknowledged these pressures seemed evident by several changes of emphasis effected in 1980-81. The addition of two women to the Executive Council, the discussion of new political strategies such as expanded participation in primary elections, the sponsorship of Solidarity Day (the September 1981 march on Washington of over 400,000 people), and the move to consider support for a presidential candidate prior to party nomination—all seemed to reflect at least a change in style.

Much of this shift can be viewed as organized labor's response to a number of endemic problems—notably the problems of organizing and bargaining midst the wave of concessions granted employers by several unions in the 1970s and 1980s and the electoral defeat of 1980.

Multinational Labor Organization

The rise in the number and influence of multinational corporations (MNCs) has presented national unions and national federations with a serious problem of cross-national coordination. Not only do many MNCs promote competition among nations to lower labor standards as an inducement for MNCs to locate, but plants in one country are threats to the bargaining strength of workers in another. For instance, auto workers in one nation are increasingly part of the relevant work force for those in another. If an MNC can successfully condition its location of a plant in one country on a guarantee of lower wages, tax advantages, government pledges to refrain from regulating working conditions, and other such terms, it can affect the ability of workers in another country to obtain better terms.

Unions have consequently begun to coordinate their activities through a variety of mechanisms. The principal federation of Western bloc unions is the *International Confederation of Free Trade Unions (ICFTU)*, rivaled in the Eastern bloc by the *World Federation of Trade Unions (WFTU)*. The AFL-CIO pulled out of the ICFTU in 1969. It rejoined in 1981. Several AFL-CIO unions maintain affiliations with the *international trade secretariats*.

The trade secretariats are the global equivalents of the AFL-CIO's trade and industrial departments, coordinating the activities of affiliates in related trades and industries. Of some 18 secretariats, the better known are the International Metalworkers Federation (IMF), whose affiliate unions have a worldwide membership of 14 million; the International Chemical Workers Federation (ICF); and, technically not a secretariat but a federation of associations, the International Federation of Air Line Pilots' Associations (IFALPA).

The IMF is active in exchanging information and promoting education on a variety of common problems, such as occupational safety and health, governmental repression of national labor movements, technological change, economic threats, and wages and working standards. While much of this is directed toward more tightly coordinated bargaining efforts among affiliates in different nations, there have thus far been few successful efforts. But there have been instances of sympathy strikes and other forms of assistance by one union on behalf of another overseas. In order to promote closer coordination, the IMF has also spawned World Auto Councils.[10]

IFALPA, the pilots federation, held the world's first multinational, multicompany shutdown in 1972 in an effort to pressure gov-

---

[10] See Burton B. Bendiner, "A Labor Response to Multinationals: Coordination of Bargaining Goals," *Monthly Labor Review* 101, no. 7 (July 1978), pp. 9–13, for a discussion of the World Auto Councils.

ernments to take steps to prevent hijackings. Many of IFALPA's other activities, like those of its U.S. affiliate, the Air Line Pilots' Association, are similarly related to safety.

As world economies become more integrated, these cross-national efforts can be expected to increase. But in attempting to strengthen ties, unions face several barriers. These include not only language, customs, economic and governmental differences, and other traits of nationalism, but often a preference for the bargaining structures that worked well in the past under the old conditions.

Compare Exhibit 6 to Exhibit 5 on page 165. Exhibit 6 depicts the way another union, the Machinists, links up with multiunion structures, including the international trade secretariats. The international union has direct links to two secretariats, the metal workers and the transport workers federations. Based on those members in the railway industry, the international also affiliates with the Railway Labor Executives Association and the Canadian equivalent, the Canadian Railway Labor Association.

IAM's other affiliations are similar to those of the Operating Engineers in Exhibit 5. There are national union ties to the national trade and industrial departments and local lodge ties to state and local central bodies. As with IUOE, the intermediate bodies (district lodges and state and provincial councils) have no federation ties of their own.

In addition to the multinational union bodies with which the AFL-CIO or its member unions affiliate, the Federation participates in two other types of international labor activity. In 1980 it returned to an earlier policy of participating in the U.S. delegation to the *International Labor Organization* (ILO), a United Nations agency organized on a tripartite basis (government, labor, and business). At the behest of the AFL-CIO, in 1977 the U.S. government had officially withdrawn over policy differences with the Eastern bloc delegations.

The AFL-CIO has historically conducted its own foreign policy. The federation's policy extends into the realm of action, where it conducts numerous programs designed to train foreign unionists to protect what it perceives as its interests, which it defines as protecting "free trade unionism" and opposing communism in third world and other nations.

Three arms of AFL-CIO foreign policy are the African-American Labor Center, the Asian-American Free Labor Institute, and the *American Institute for Free Labor Development* (AIFLD). AIFLD funds field representatives in the Caribbean and Latin

Exhibit 6. **Links to Multi-Union Bodies, National and Worldwide: The International Association of Machinists**

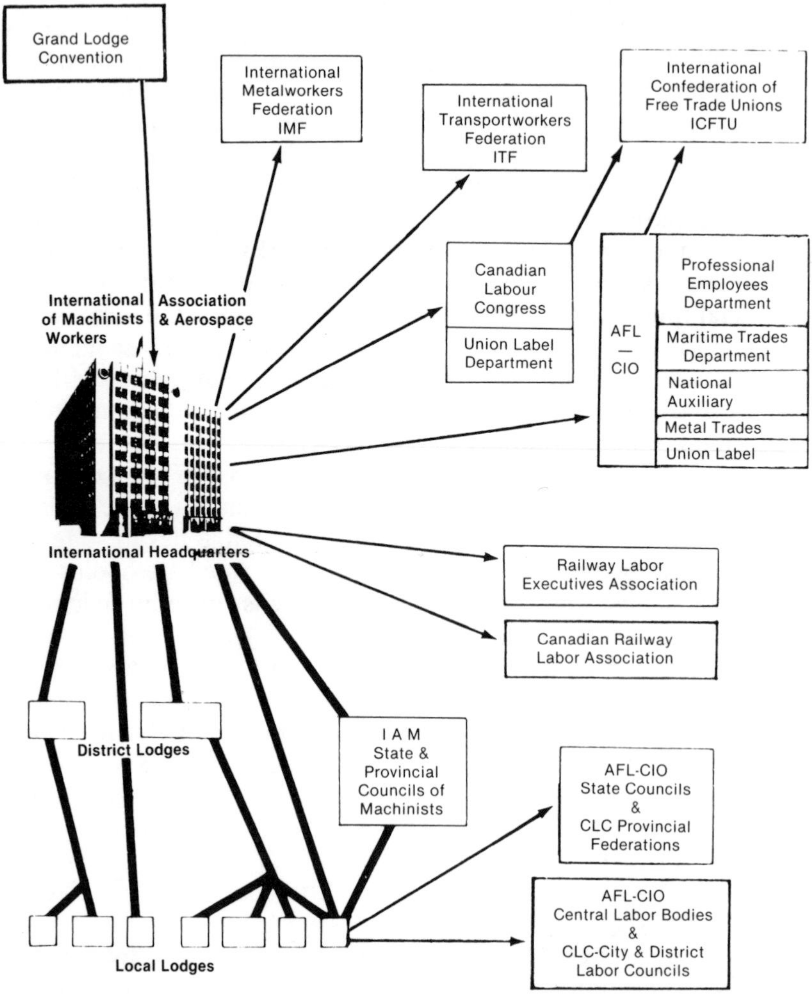

America, and it conducts a variety of technical assistance and training programs for foreign unionists, both in their own countries and at specially held classes in the United States.

Formed in 1962 as a nonprofit corporation, AIFLD was heavily financed through the U.S. Agency for International Development (AID) and included in its governing body several representatives of corporations with extensive Latin American holdings. This support, the fact that AIFLD worked closely with U.S. agencies in the field, and the fact that some of its backers opposed popular movements in Latin America led to considerable controversy. Its activities continue, with private funds and AID contracts for agrarian development and social projects a focus.

Multi-Union Bargaining Agencies

Union structure, as noted earlier, is often adapted creatively to address the unique features of employer organization and employment situation. Most of the multi-union structures discussed thus far perform primarily nonbargaining functions. Although some unions engage in coordinated bargaining, this is usually an effort to work out common approaches, not to sign a single agreement. The separate *bargaining units* remain intact.

One multi-union structure that does act as bargaining agent is the trades council. The council itself is the certified bargaining agent and negotiates agreements with one or more employers. But the workers in the bargaining unit retain membership in their separate unions. This is the predominant pattern among the *metal trades councils* found in naval shipyards and other federal installations. There are currently about 50 such councils in federal activities, holding exclusive rights to represent some 63,000 workers.[11]

The Metal Trades Council of Texas City, Texas, affords an example of how this arrangement operates in the profit sector.[12] Located in the Gulf area of the state noted for its heavy concentration of petro-chemical plants, this Metal Trades Council (MTC) was formed in the mid-1940s under the auspices of the local building trades council.

The Texas City MTC now represents members of 11 different unions employed by five corporations—Union Carbide, Monsanto, GAF, Texas City Refining, and Gulf Chemical and Metallurgical Corporation—altogether some 3,000 workers. The Council negotiates a separate contract with each employer; but each affiliated union handles grievances on behalf of those in its craft.

---

[11] AFL-CIO, PROCEEDINGS OF THE FOURTEENTH CONSTITUTIONAL CONVENTION, II:314.

[12] Based on an interview with Paul Teague, Operating Engineers' Local 347 and business manager of the Texas City Metal Trades Council, August 13, 1979.

The contracts between the MTC and each employer include a checkoff provision by which the employer deducts and forwards dues not to the Council, but to the members' own union. Each union then pays 50¢ per month per capita to support the Council. Per capita is based on the number of employees in each union's craft jurisdiction, whether they are members or not. With this incentive, the Council and its affiliates have achieved about 97 percent membership among those eligible in this right-to-work state. The MTC is headed by a business manager from one of the affiliates. It is governed by a board made up of six delegates per local union.

Maintaining this pluralistic structure requires much informal negotiation among the different unions. By custom and agreement among the affiliates, the Council negotiates equal wage and benefit improvements for journeymen of each craft. Jurisdictional understandings are reached and for the most part abided by. Ratification of each of the five agreements is by secret ballot, with a majority of the total membership in the plant required for approval.

While the Texas City MTC model might not work everywhere, its adherents feel it is ideally suited to conditions in the industry, providing labor with all the advantages of a *wall-to-wall unit*[13] while preserving individual craft membership and identity. As such, it is a mixed form, somewhere between craft and industrial unionism. It clearly provides for organization on a multi-union basis, avoiding much of the interunion conflict that might result were each of the eleven craft unions to bargain individually. Despite occasional difficulties arising from craft pride and jealousies, the Texas City structure has proved viable over the years.

Conclusion

Questions crucial to labor's future revolve around multi-union organizations. The interlocking of the elements of the environment increases the need for interunion cooperation, which is the strong point of these bodies. They play a key role in keeping the structure of the labor movement relevant to a rapidly changing corporate and technological environment.

The AFL-CIO supports coordinated bargaining, union mergers, organizational streamlining, and education for the increas-

---

[13] A comprehensive, as opposed to craft, bargaining unit in which all classifications and crafts are represented by the same union.

ingly complex tasks of union leadership. One vision sees, by the end of the century, a more powerful federation coordinating the efforts of ten to twenty mega-unions resulting from successive mergers.

This vision must contend with the dangers of size, centralization, and distance. While it is unlikely that the Federation will assume the internationals' responsibilities for bargaining, it may play a more prominent supporting role. And the fact that the effectiveness of bargaining and the state of the economy are influenced by decisions made in boardrooms and passed on through Washington will add to the importance of the Federation's legislative and political role.

How do a Federation and its mega-union affiliates remain responsive and responsible to its members? How can it avoid bureaucratic rigidities? Is there a danger that the local union of the future will resemble the branch office of a large insurance company?

Some would dismiss such concerns. Bok and Dunlop, the latter a former Secretary of Labor, seem to distrust the rank-and-file worker and the local union leader. They argue that a leadership two or three steps removed from the membership can take a longer, more "statesmanlike" view.[14] Others argue that such a distant leadership cannot possibly be attuned to the desires of workers, producing a critical need to maintain relevance at the top.

A related problem concerns the Federation's effectiveness at its core function—representation of workers in the national political arena. If the growth of employer power in Congress and elsewhere in Washington and the states continues to outpace labor's ability to protect its members' interests, the strategy of putting labor's eggs in the basket of conventional politics may become discredited.

Although it does not necessarily begin there, bargaining success is tied to success on the political front. The range of labor's political pursuits is the subject of the next chapter.

Review and Discussion Questions

1. "Competition is a way of life under capitalism. What's good for business should be good for unions. Therefore the labor movement would be better off if there were still competition between the AFL and the CIO and, furthermore, between the different internationals and each of their locals." Do you agree or disagree? Why?

---

[14] Derek C. Bok and John T. Dunlop, LABOR AND THE AMERICAN COMMUNITY (New York: Simon and Schuster, 1970), p. 199.

2. Construct a chart showing the different organizational units of the labor movement at each level from local through federation. Indicate the primary and secondary functions of each. Identify each case where there appears to be more than one unit at the same level with the same primary or secondary functions. Does one reinforce or detract from the efforts of the other?

4. "The structure of the AFL-CIO may not be 'neat' but it makes sense." Do you agree or disagree? What do you see as the primary advantages and disadvantages of this structure?

5. What are the needs for, and problems in achieving, viable multinational unionism? What are the prospects, short and long run?

Key Words and Phrases

multi-union organization	established work relationship
interunion organization	noncompliance
Walter Reuther	centrifugal tendencies
George Meany	unifying forces
Executive Council	International Confederation of
ex officio	Free Trade Unions (ICFTU)
General Board	World Federation of Trade
staff departments	Unions (WFTU)
Department of Organization and	International trade secretariats
Field Services	International Labor
AFL-CIO regions	Organization (ILO)
standing committees	American Institute for Free
trade/industrial councils	Labor Development (AIFLD)
central labor bodies	metal trades councils
state federations	mega-union
internal disputes plan	wall-to-wall unit
Article XX	

Suggestions for Further Reading

Several of the items cited in the text of this chapter are excellent primary or secondary sources on multi-union organization. These include *AFL-CIO News*, which every library should receive. For special publications and newsletters, contact the appropriate staff, trade, or industrial department or other unit.

The major source on the merger of the AFL and the CIO, authored by a figure intimately involved in the process, is Arthur Goldberg, *AFL-CIO: Labor United*. A somewhat dated, but still useful, description of multinational union structure and function is David C. Hershfield, *The Multinational Union Challenges the Multinational Company*.

Complete bibliographical information for the above titles can be found in the Bibliography.

9

Labor in the Political Arena

The problem in America is not that the top 100 corporation presidents
are violating the laws, though God knows they are. The problem is
they're making the laws.

Nicholas Johnson,
Federal Communications Commission, 1972

It is better to vote for something you want and not get it, than to vote for
something you don't want and get it.

Eugene V. Debs,
from URW Labor Scrapbook

This chapter traces the contours of labor's political agenda and
describes methods of political influence favored by different unions.
The prevailing method for most of the labor movement centers on
electoral and lobbying activity. Within this broad framework, variations can be explained by such factors as a union's industry and
market environment as well as by the structure of the union itself.

Labor's Bifocal View

Organized labor views the world of politics through bifocal
lenses. Through one lens it sees immediate needs to protect and advance the interests of workers and their unions. Accordingly, it acts
as a political interest group, or pressure group, on their behalf.
Through the other lens it sees the broader needs of the working class
and the great majority of the society. In response to this second focus, many unions engage in political activities whose impact on
union members is indistinguishable from its impact on most citizens. These efforts bring labor into coalitions of mutual interest

178

with other groups; such coalitions are a vital source of political allies.

The second focus, historically an important part of labor's vision, not only enhances labor's ability to act in its own interests, but enables it to take on many of the tasks associated with traditional political parties—voter registration, volunteer mobilization, canvassing, and election day get-out-the-vote efforts.

The self-interested, relatively conservative justification for union political involvement is expressed in the often-heard phrases that "What is won at the bargaining table can be lost in Congress" and "The contract has to be backed up at the ballot box." But broader, less self-regarding motivations are equally important. These include the notions that a strong labor movement is essential to a democratic society and that labor is the major force representing the interests of those who are relatively powerless.

Much of labor's political involvement is the necessary activity of an economic institution whose members' interests cannot be addressed entirely through collective bargaining. Collective bargaining is the currently preferred mode of determining wages, benefits, and other terms of employment. It works—up to a point and under certain conditions. These conditions, however, do not apply equally to all, and they are increasingly subject to change by government action.

In the long run, unions can best help their members only by protecting the interests of all workers. Despite some "warts," labor has a more long-standing and effective record on behalf of progressive measures accruing to the benefit of the society than any other major institutional grouping in the nation.

The Making of Labor's Political Agenda

The question "What is the union doing in politics?" is sometimes posed as the assertion "Unions should stay out of politics." These expressions often betray the assumption that union political activity is a recent phenomenon.

Historically, workers ofter saw as self-evident the need for political activity. Even before what we now know as unions existed, workers in the colonies saw the threat to their freedom posed by the British crown, and they formed the backbone of such revolutionary groups as the Sons of Liberty. With independence they faced new struggles with employers and representatives of the upper classes who dominated federal and state governments.

As the voting franchise spread, the first labor parties in the world were formed, beginning with the 1828 organization of the Workingmen's Party in Philadelphia. While it is questionable whether these political parties were formed and directed primarily by workers, it is clear that they and many of the unions of the day gave voice to popular demands in platforms calling for free public education, abolition of imprisonment for debt, reform of the militia system and the factory laws, and support for the 10-hour workday.

Finance capital grew and industrialization advanced during the mid-19th century. Unionism spread to such industries as railroading, steel making, and mining. Labor continued to back political activity, especially during times of economic downturn. Significant were the National Labor Union and the Knights of Labor, both predominantly worker organizations, and such issue-oriented electoral organizations as the Greenback-Labor Party and the Henry George campaign, and later the Populists and the Socialists.

The spread of worker organization during the latter half of the 1800s saw workers increasingly pitted against the political power, and often the military might, of employers served by state militias or by private employer armies such as the Pinkertons. It was a relatively obvious conclusion for many workers that the power of employers was enhanced by their control of government and that cutting off the use of government as an employer weapon was a necessary first step toward redressing their grievances.

The AFL and Beyond

The first enduring break in the pattern of comprehensive union political efforts was the posture of the American Federation of Labor under Samuel Gompers. This posture is probably responsible for the belief that labor traditionally avoided politics. Even in the case of the AFL, this notion is largely mistaken.

The AFL-Gompers philosophy is expressed in two phrases—*voluntarism* and *nonpartisanship*. Voluntarism is the doctrine that government should keep hands off matters of labor-management relations and that workers should rely on their unions and the mechanism of collective bargaining, not legal enactment, to promote their interests. Nonpartisanship meant simply that labor would form attachments to no political party but would instead work with candidates and officeholders from either major party who were sympathetic to labor. In brief, labor should "reward its friends and punish its enemies" at the polls.

To the extent that the AFL was made up of autonomous unions of skilled workers, this philosophy had a certain appeal. Skilled workers had greater bargaining power and hence less need of government protection. Nevertheless the record shows that this philosophy was often honored more in rhetoric than observance. The AFL was itself on record in support of positions affecting the substance of bargaining. It advocated the 8-hour workday and various forms of protective legislation, including laws restricting the use of women and children in the workplace. Like its opposition to immigration, the latter position served to protect the members of affiliates from competition in the labor market.

Affiliates and central bodies often ignored voluntarist philosophy at the local and state levels, advocating a variety of political reforms, social insurance and welfare programs, and legislation regulating labor-management relations.[1] Nevertheless, the activity of the national federation, though it included compiling voting records and endorsing certain candidates, never involved substantial sums of money.

Following the period of AFL domination at the national level, the labor movement returned to its earlier posture of major involvement in political activity, though in a greatly altered form. The quantum leap occurred in the 1930s depression years and was symbolized by the $469,000 contributed to the 1936 Roosevelt campaign by the United Mine Workers under John L. Lewis—an amount five times greater than that spent for political purposes by the AFL during the preceding 30-year period.

At no time in its history has the labor movement been entirely united in its view of the appropriate mode of political activity for workers and their unions. At various points major blocs have supported: staying out of politics and relying on economic weapons (in either conventional or revolutionary fashion); bipartisanship; linking up with one or another major party; broad third party movements; forming a labor party; establishing socialism; and combining different approaches. But since the 1930s and particularly since the AFL-CIO merger, the prevailing and, for the Federation, offi-

---

[1] See Gary Fink, "The Rejection of Voluntarism," *Industrial and Labor Relations Review* 26, no. 2 (January 1973), pp. 805–19.

cial mode has been to rely on political education and electoral action within the current party-system framework, usually in close association with the Democratic Party. This preference has placed a premium on labor's ability to act both as a pressure group and, insofar as it is supported by a stable base of voters whom it mobilizes for elections and other political work, as a quasi-political party. Unlike the West European labor movements with the their broad-based political parties, the AFL-CIO (despite its advocacy of general interest positions) remains to a large extent what has been called the political arm of market unionism.

Sorting Labor's Issue Agenda

The notion, introduced earlier, that labor sees politics through bifocals, suggests a separation between self-interest and social-interest, between particularistic and general concerns, and perhaps between immediate and long-run impacts. The real world is, of course, rarely this simple. But the bifocal concept is a base upon which to build an analysis of the different types of issues in which the labor movement, or some of its constituent unions, becomes involved.

A more elaborate classification follows this logic: Unions and workers have political concerns arising from

(1) Their needs to organize employees and to exist as autonomous institutions representing their members in bargaining with employers (*institutional matters*);
(2) A stake in preserving and expanding employment opportunities (*jobs and employment issues*);
(3) The desire to protect and enhance the compensation and working conditions of those they represent. To do this they must, as a rule, protect the status of all workers (*class issues*);
(4) Their stake in protecting the interests of their members and others as consumers and citizens and in realizing their vision of a society in which these interests are best protected (*societal issues*).

The four categories form a hierarchy in which each is a necessary condition for the others. Thus a union that cannot survive as an organization cannot effectively protect the jobs and conditions of its members. And one that cannot defend the interests of its own members is unlikely to be effective in advancing class and societal issues. At the same time labor's success in advancing societal and class issues can further enhance its viability as an institution and its success in advancing its members interests.

This classification suggests the basis for many labor positions. There are, of course, issues that do not fall neatly into a single category, but bridge two or more. Following are examples of issues from the agendas of one or more unions, or labor as a whole:

(1) *Institutional Issues.* Most issues in this category involve labor-management relations legislation or laws regulating the internal affairs of labor organizations. For instance, labor would like to eliminate section 14(b) of the Labor Management Relations Act which grants states the right to ban union security provisions in negotiated agreements. Other examples come from the government employment sector. Unions representing state and local government employees want favorable state bargaining laws. Federal employee unions push for the removal of restrictions on their ability to bargain for their members. All of these issues reflect efforts to enhance the organizational integrity and bargaining ability of unions.

(2) *Employment ("Jobs") Issues.* Among the hundreds of issues on which unions took positions over the past decade were the following: clothing imports, log exports, "American bottoms" (ships), nuclear power, and the Humphrey-Hawkins bill. Some of these issues concerned a broad spectrum of unions and workers. The Humphrey-Hawkins bill, for example, was designed to increase general employment levels. The impact of others was targeted on particular sectors, industries, or corporations. All dealt with employment.

Building trades unions often emphasize particularistic job issues, measures favoring highway construction, nuclear power, or casino gambling, for example, that provide construction work for their members. But such employment concerns are not limited to the construction industry. The shift of clothing fabrication overseas has drastically reduced employment in the "needle trades." The export of raw logs affects employment in the forest products unions. And the declining use of U.S. flagships has prompted maritime unions to call for more shipping in "American bottoms."

The impact of employment issues on unions may vary. Virtually all unions perceive a stake in measures promoting economic growth. But they may split on questions such as nuclear power. Several unions with no direct employment stake are active, or have leaders who are active, in coalitions opposed to nuclear power. Others, such as the United Mine Workers, have a direct stake in alternative energy sources. Still others have jurisdictions spanning at least two sides of an issue. The Operating Engineers, for example, stand to benefit from employment opportunities added by nuclear plant construction. But this union also represents thousands of members working in the western coalfields. The Sheet Metal Workers and the Plumbers and Pipefitters both promote solar energy systems. The former cites the advantages of solar air systems, while the latter understandably prefers fluid systems.

High unemployment contributes to situations in which union and worker interest in job preservation sometimes conflicts with the longer-run interest of the society in such matters as conservation. When wood-products unions oppose the reservation of lands for wildlife and primitive areas their members are accused of not seeing beyond their stomachs. In a full-employment economy a worker might be able to support conservation without a resulting loss of livelihood.

Employment issues have a way of becoming class issues pitting workers against major corporations. At one level the desire for more jobs and better conditions often runs up against employers' desires for profits without payrolls, substituting capital for labor, machines for workers. Another level of divergent class interests is seen in the recent Chrysler "bailout" debate. The immediate question involved a single corporation and the jobs of thousands of UAW members. But the broader impact engaged the concerns of corporate leaders about the future of capitalism, which some saw being eroded by government support for foundering corporations. Many corporate representatives who had applauded the early 1970s bailout of Lockheed later decided this was a bad precedent. That this became a class issue dividing workers and the corporate elite was illustrated in a *Wall Street Journal* column applauding the fact that "many corporate executives are at last becoming conscious of their interests as a class."[2]

(3) *Class Issues.* This category covers a variety of legislative and political efforts. Some, like the Chrysler issue, involve decisions about the nature of the economic system. Other measures protect and advance the income, employment standards, and working conditions of the majority of working people or some segment thereof, not necessarily limited to union members. Some impact immedi-

[2]David Vogel, "Manager's Journal," *Wall Street Journal*, January 14, 1980.

ately on a particular category such as young, female, minority, handicapped, or low income workers, but the broader effect is likely to be protection for all.

Examples are many: union efforts to promote occupational safety and health legislation, equal employment opportunity measures, opposition to the use of lie detectors in employment matters, unemployment compensation, and workers compensation are but a few instances. In each case the most immediate beneficiaries are organized workers because organization itself enables them to take better advantage of the laws. Not only can unions educate members about rights and procedures under existing legislation, but they can use collective bargaining and grievance procedures to enforce adherence to many requirements.

(4) *Societal Issues.* Issues in this classification apply to the great majority of the population, not only as workers, but as citizens and consumers. Thus labor, especially at the international union and federation level, is generally unified around support for educational opportunities, consumer and environmental protection, equalizing the impact of the tax system, making it easier for people to exercise their rights as citizens (registering, voting, for example). As with class issues, societal issues afford opportunities for joining in coalitions with other like-minded organizations.

The current approach of the leadership of the U.S. labor movement is to work within the prevailing capitalist framework to advance the interests of workers. This entails support for collective bargaining as the preferred mechanism for establishing employment terms. It requires political action to protect the bargaining mechanism and the union as an institution, as well as to secure the rights and benefits that collective bargaining does not or cannot attain.

Thus it is possible to see a progression in the issue classification just presented. From institutional, through employment and class, to societal issues, the focus broadens from bargaining concerns to nonbargaining matters, from the particular to the general, from union members, to all workers, to all people. And moving down the same list, one can see that as labor shifts from special to general interest matters, its potential for popular support increases. As this potential broadens so too does the potential for union involvement in political coalitions.

Political Assets

Power resources are distributed unequally among classes and groups. Natural political resources are in reality a power advantage—the initial endowment of a group entering the process. The effectiveness with which a group uses this endowment, mixes it with other resources, and organizes largely determines its success in achieving political objectives.

A comparison between the labor movement and the corporations illustrates a contrast in resource advantages. Workers and unions are relatively poor in wealth, especially on a per capita basis. They find their initial advantage in numbers, large numbers of people. Business, especially the larger corporations, is relatively weak in numbers but strong in wealth. To be sure, labor does raise and spend money in politics, but this money originates in small contributions from millions of individuals. Despite its ability to offer contributions to political candidates, labor's real strength is the number of volunteers it can activate. Business on the other hand, with its initial dollar advantage, is able to purchase a large proportion of the political services it needs to influence votes.

Labor then, relies on numbers to amass what money it can. Business relies more on money to amass numbers. The immediate goal of each, to the extent it plays by the rules of conventional electoral politics, is ballots cast on behalf of sympathetic candidates.

Success in this effort, regardless of differences in natural advantage, requires considerable inputs of analysis, planning, and organization. Having popular issues and emotion on one's side helps, as does access to, or control of, media.

All this assumes a measure of access to a functioning political system. Where the system is ineffective or where major groups are denied the opportunity to participate, there is often a resort to other weapons. Where frustration arising from powerlessness does not result in passivity, it may lead to violence—small group terrorism, massive confrontation, revolution, or sustained military action. Malcolm X, the noted black leader of the 1960s, once posed the option as "the Ballot or the Bullet," suggesting that those who are denied an effective ballot sometimes feel forced to resort to other means.

In simplified fashion, this notion of political resources can be expressed as "the five Bs of political power." (See Exhibit 7.)

Despite their avowed adherence to the conventional means of influence, labor leaders and employers in the mid-1970s began to

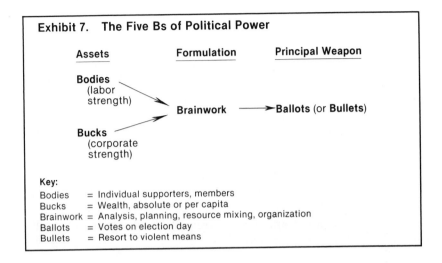

Exhibit 7. The Five Bs of Political Power

Assets	Formulation	Principal Weapon

Bodies (labor strength) → Brainwork → Ballots (or Bullets)

Bucks (corporate strength) →

Key:
Bodies = Individual supporters, members
Bucks = Wealth, absolute or per capita
Brainwork = Analysis, planning, resource mixing, organization
Ballots = Votes on election day
Bullets = Resort to violent means

increasingly and openly acknowledge a growing consciousness of opposed employer class and working class interests. Business interests, long represented by such groups as the Chamber of Commerce and the National Association of Manufacturers, were increasingly coordinated and vocalized by a group known as the Business Roundtable, a body made up of the chief executive officers of top industrial and financial corporations. Formed during the 1960s and active in a variety of efforts that pitted it against labor, the Roundtable took the lead in opposing labor law reform, situs picketing legislation, and government aid to the Chrysler Corporation. Such developments led Douglas Fraser, then president of the UAW, to observe that "leaders of the business community, with few exceptions, have chosen to wage a one-sided class war."[3]

To the extent that labor carries on this intensified struggle using conventional political weapons, it must rely on its ability to mobilize primary resources—people and dollars.

Political Money

A series of revisions in the law regulating the sources and uses of campaign funds have affected labor and business groups, with the full impact not yet determined. A brief review of these developments is in order here.

---

[3] Letter of resignation to members of the Labor-Management Group, July 17, 1978.

A distinction exists between union dues money (regular treasury funds) and funds voluntarily contributed for political purposes, also known as "free money." The 1971 Federal Election Campaign Act and subsequent amendments and court rulings established guidelines for union and corporate political fund raising and spending. Regulated are such matters as:[4]

(1) Who may raise how much, from what sources, for political purposes.
(2) The segregation of treasury funds from voluntary donations, and the legitimate uses of each.
(3) Under what circumstances unions may solicit nonmembers and corporations nonexecutives and stockholders.
(4) The amount and form of contributions to political candidates and campaigns.

As of 1984 the law permitted union treasury funds (dues money) to be used to communicate on any subject, including politics, with union members and their families. These funds, and corporate treasury funds, can also be used to raise voluntary contributions and can be used in nonpartisan registration and get-out-the-vote efforts. Dues money may not be contributed to candidates for federal office or used to urge the public-at-large to support such candidates.[5]

The new federal law and Federal Election Commission guidelines led to a proliferation of Political Action Committees (PACs) as repositories and dispensers of voluntary contributions. Most of these PACs are corporation sponsored.

While most corporate and union PACs target separate constituencies, some corporations attempt to solicit hourly employees. But as one observer noted, "The PACs that try to cast their net too widely soon find that it doesn't pay to be too democratic. The financial return just isn't worth it." An employer advisor suggests that those who do attempt to solicit hourly employees should avoid efforts to try to get hourly workers "to rally to the cause of free enterprise. Talk to them about concrete things—foreign competition,

---

[4] For a review see Edwin M. Epstein, "Labor and Federal Elections: The New Legal Framework," *Industrial Relations* 15, no. 3 (October 1976), pp. 257–74.

[5] Separate state laws cover candidates for state and local offices.

taxes, jobs and paychecks."[6] Nevertheless, corporate PACs have raised millions from executives and other non-hourly employees.

Because of the intricacies of adjusting to changes and the accounting practices required to conform to the law, local unions generally seek advice from their internationals when engaging in political fund raising and contributions.

Where the Bread is Buttered

Several features of the U.S. political system shape labor's political efforts. Some are long-standing features, others more recent.

Federalism. Authority in the U.S. system is divided among the federal government and the states (and, minimally, the municipal units of government). Since the New Deal of the 1930s, labor has preferred federal, as opposed to state, action on many programs and issues. The reasons for this preference lie in the sources of labor's advantage compared to those of its adversaries:

(1)   In most states business interests are better equipped than labor to exercise power in statehouses and state legislatures. The handful of part-time union lobbyists assigned to a legislature usually have little in the way of research support. Chambers of Commerce, on the other hand, often have staffs providing research and publicity backup. Sustained employer access to the branches of state government is thus likely to be greater than labor's.

(2)   Labor is strong in only a few states. Operating at the state level, then, labor's gains would at best be unevenly distributed. At worst, the states where labor is weak would exert a drag on further gains in progressive states.

(3)   Fragmenting labor's efforts into 50 different state campaigns makes uniformity of standards, concentration of limited political resources, legislative victory, and subsequent enforcement efforts difficult to achieve.

---

[6] Both quotes from John C. Perham, "Big Year for Company Political Action," *Dun's Review* 111, no. 3 (March 1978), p. 105. This advice confirms the notion of differential political assets discussed earlier—that corporations tend to rely on relatively large contributions from small numbers of wealthier individuals, while unions seek smaller sums from large numbers of workers.

(4) Labor's agenda consists of many issues. It is simply easier to keep issues in the public eye and build coalitions on a national than on a state-by-state basis.

Labor's stake in uniform federal action is evident in two major issues where it fell victim to the fragmentation associated with "states' rights" decentralization. The first instance was the passage of Section 14(b) of the Taft-Hartley Act and the subsequent passage of so-called right-to-work laws in more than 20 states.

The anti-union forces in Congress during the 1947 debates lacked the power to pass a national "right-to-work" law. But under the guise of "leaving it up to the states" they were able to include Section 14(b), with the result that 20 states now encourage the practice of *free-riding* (benefiting from union representation without contributing to the support of the union). While strong unions in these states approach 100 percent membership despite the laws, the provision against union security makes it extremely difficult for other unions to sustain themselves in the face of union-busting efforts by employers.

The second example is the Occupational Safety and Health Act, passed with a provision that enforcement could be taken over by the individual states should they so desire. While any state assuming this responsibility is required to "meet or exceed federal standards," there is no guarantee that enforcement will follow.

While the "leave it up to the states" rationale often appears democratic, it may mask a desire to undermine effective action and fragment labor's ability to achieve its goals.

The Party System. The 1970s saw a weakening of the major political parties by personal campaign organizations and single-issue politics. Formerly labor focused its efforts within the party structure at national and, in many instances, state levels. It now diffuses its efforts among a variety of political brokers, with lineups changing frequently.

The causes of the decline of the party system are debated. Some point to the breakup of the old city machines and the impact of television as a medium through which candidates can appeal directly to voters without the mediation of a party structure. Others suggest that the spread of the primary system is largely responsible. Regardless of the causes, the shift from comprehensive programs and platforms to personalities and single, often emotional, issues has not benefitted those forces like organized labor that seek to represent the interests of broad segments of the society on a full spectrum of issues. On balance, the new pattern probably makes pro-labor legislators more vulnerable to being "knocked off" because of their positions on one or two emotional issues.

Voter Participation Patterns. Voting research demonstrates a correlation between electoral participation, income, and education. The wealthier and more highly educated are more apt to vote than are working people. They are also more prone to vote against candidates representing working class interests. Thus labor interests usually suffer in low-turnout elections.

The percentage of people voting in elections has been declining for years, perhaps because many feel that major parties and candidates offer no genuine alternatives and because of the absence of strong party organizations to formulate consistent programs.

Labor thus has a clear stake in anything that makes it easier for people to register and vote, for example, mail-in registration systems and the elimination of deadlines and residency restrictions for registration. Similarly, labor stands to benefit from get-out-the-vote drives in working-class districts.

Political Action and Union Structure/Jurisdiction

Earlier in the chapter the industrial influence which leads unions to back certain job-related issues was noted. Thus it is not surprising to find unions pursuing political issues affecting regulation in, for instance, the transportation industry. The Teamsters in trucking; the Machinists, Transport Workers, Air Line Pilots and others in the airline industry; the seagoing unions in shipping; and the railroad unions in their industry are all vitally affected by the regulation (and deregulation) of common carriers and the distribution of freight and passengers among competing types of transport. Virtually every union has its unique cluster of industry and occupational concerns.

Other differences in political orientation roughly follow the distinction between factory and nonfactory unionism discussed in Chapter 6. Generally, major factory unions in national markets have political emphases different from nonfactory local market unions. The former are more likely to focus their efforts on the federal government, to promote issues that address the needs of their members (and nonmembers) as consumers, to enter coalitions with nonlabor groups, and to act in a more partisan fashion in their party affiliations. They are also more likely to engage in political education and electoral campaign activity than are local market, nonfactory unions.

While the building trades are not entirely representative of the nonfactory unions, their economic environments and their bargaining concerns suggest some reasons for their different political emphasis. To the extent their members are employed by contractors doing business within a local market of adjacent counties or within a single city, their primary political arena has been traditionally municipal and state, as opposed to national. At these levels building codes are developed and enforced, licenses granted, state and local prevailing wages enforced, and many government contracts awarded. Building trades leaders often form limited alliances with their employing contractors in order to channel more work to the unionized sector. Even profit-sector construction is likely to be heavily influenced by state and local politics.

To ally with a single party would leave these unions vulnerable to party turnover. As a result, building trades and most nonfactory local market unions are less likely to emphasize federal action or adopt broad ideological stances in politics and are more likely to try to develop influence in local politics.[7]

But lest this picture be exaggerated, it should be noted that the pattern is shifting, with increased emphasis on federal action or inaction by some building trades unions.

Union Political Activity: Modes and Means

Most of labor's political effort is directed toward three tasks: political research and education, electoral action, and lobbying. These activities are aimed at government action more favorable to working people, unions, and their allies.

Political Education. AFL-CIO and international union staffs conduct background research on issues and candidates, then disseminate the results in a variety of media. A key element of this research is analysis of voting records, especially of congressional votes, an effort in which the AFL-CIO Legislative Department and the Committee on Political Education (COPE) play a central role.

---

[7] For an analysis of this traditional pattern, see chapter 7, "Organized Labor in City Politics," Edward C. Banfield and James Q. Wilson, CITY POLITICS (Cambridge: Harvard University Press, 1965), pp. 487–500.

Union members and their families are reached through the labor press—notably international union papers and local union newspapers and newsletters. Political education is also conducted by means of speeches and discussion at union forums.

Electoral Action. A union's mode of electoral activity varies with the way it relates to the political party structure at each level. Where a union is closely tied to a political party, its electoral activity often lacks an independent identity. Where it supports candidates rather than party organizations, its efforts will be somewhat more visible and independent.

Union campaign activity begins with candidate endorsement. In a few cases unions will seek out desirable candidates and encourage them to run. More often unionists participate in the slating process within party organizations and in the union endorsement process at appropriate levels of union and AFL-CIO structure. The role of COPE committees in the endorsement process will be discussed shortly.

In the past, labor tried not to take sides in close primary campaigns but in the 1980s began to experiment with new strategies. Realizing that a "hands off primaries" policy often produces a candidate with little sympathy for labor, the Federation now encourages pre-primary and primary involvement where there are pro-labor candidates. The October 1983 endorsement of Walter Mondale for the 1984 Democratic presidential nomination was the first major application of this policy, popularly viewed as a high-risk tactic.

Labor often contributes much time and money to campaigns. In some cases union staffers devote full-time to a campaign in order to communicate with union members and their families. But the great bulk of the donated time is that of thousands of part-time volunteers. Some of these unionists are precinct and higher party officials who simply increase their efforts at campaign time. Others are mobilized for specific phases of the campaign such as voter registration, precinct canvassing, and voter turnout on election day.

Post-Election Activity. This effort is designed to enhance labor's influence with legislators and other officials. Despite stories and allegations of congressmen being "bought and paid for," however, it seems that the minimal goal of contributions and campaign work is *access*, the ability to get a hearing and serious consideration of labor's point of view from the supported candidate, once in office. Beyond access, backers hope for a voting record sympathetic to labor and, from those most supportive of labor positions, help in "lining up" and persuading fellow representatives to follow suit.

Lobbying extends well beyond the legislative branch. At the federal level, labor monitors and attempts to protect worker and union interests in the activities of many agencies. Presidential actions on wage-price controls, regulation, and other economic matters are clearly important to labor. So too are the activities of the Departments of Labor, Commerce, Housing and Urban Development, Education, and Health and Human Services. Many of these agencies maintain advisory committees drawn from groups affected by their actions. Special study committees have similar impact.

Congressional lobbying is pursued by the Legislative Department of the AFL-CIO, by the Federation's trade and industrial departments, and by legislative representatives of many international unions. While internationals often pursue the specific interests of their industry and jurisdiction, which sometimes bring them into conflict with other unions, the Federation attempts to coordinate lobbying activities among different unions in order to maximize labor's impact. This coordination includes formulating a legislative agenda, working with unions to publicize in a timely fashion information on specific issues, bringing union members and others to testify, stimulating mail campaigns, and engaging in many of the other actions needed to ensure or block legislation, appointments, or agency actions.

On certain issues union lobbyists work closely with their counterparts in civil rights, public interest, and consumer-oriented groups.

The importance of state government decisions to the lives of workers is often overlooked. But state federation and individual union lobbyists in most states are active in lobbying for improvements in workers' (injury) compensation, unemployment compensation benefits, and a variety of other issues. As noted earlier, the effectiveness of labor's state-level efforts varies immensely, but does not usually equal employer group activity.

COPE and Its International Union Counterparts

The umbrella political organization representing the majority of the labor movement, often working in cooperation with representatives of unaffiliated unions, is the Committee on Political Education (COPE). COPE and the Legislative Department encompass all three functions—education, electoral action, and lobbying—described above. Although it supports more Democrats than Republicans, COPE is officially nonpartisan.

COPE consists of a national structure, headed by the AFL-CIO Executive Council, and a network of state, city-county, congressional district, and local union COPE committees. State and local central bodies maintain COPE committees to coordinate endorsements and electoral activity within their corresponding government jurisdictions. Congressional district COPEs often combine several different central bodies and unions.

Candidate endorsement procedures under COPE rules operate essentially like this: national COPE endorses candidates for president and vice-president; state COPE committees (in reality the state AFL-CIO boards) make endorsements for all federal and statewide offices in their states, with the stipulation that they do so after considering input from national and local COPEs; COPE committees of local central bodies (mostly central body board members) endorse candidates for local office and recommend to the state COPE endorsements of candidates for state legislatures and for Congress.

COPE rules show a strong bias toward unity. Recommendations must be made on a two-thirds vote and local central bodies are required to support national and state endorsements, as state bodies are required to support national endorsements. This recalls the problems that have emerged in years such as 1972 when some central bodies and several internationals opposed national policy by supporting the presidential candidacy of George McGovern.

Most international unions maintain their own political education arms. Some coordinate their activities closely with COPE, while others take more independent paths.

A major activity of national COPE is the computerization of union membership. Begun in the 1960s, this massive task proceeded into the 1980s. It entails the collection of membership addresses from international unions and matching them to voting district information. The goal is to provide an up-to-date list of union members in each electoral unit, to be made available to subunits of COPE for mailing, canvassing, registration, voter turnout, and political education activities.

Labor's Electoral Impact

Do union members and their families make up a distinctive voting bloc? How do members view the political activity of their unions? Are their votes influenced by the candidate endorsements of their union? What is the impact of labor's political activity on election outcomes?

There are indeed some distinguishing characteristics of the "labor vote," taken as a whole and not broken down by occupation, class, or other traits. For example, union members are more apt to vote than are nonmembers, and since 1936 they are more inclined to register and vote Democratic in national elections. It is unclear how much of this behavior is attributable to factors other than union political activity, such as working-class identification or minority group status. Some evidence suggests that as unions organize more nonmanual workers, the distinctiveness of the labor vote may be lost.[8]

Members' views of their union's political activity vary according to:[9]

(1) Whether the union's preference agrees with their own. A staunch Republican is obviously more likely to object to union political efforts on behalf of Democratic candidates.

(2) The extent to which the union's efforts reflect the characteristics of its market. A local market unionist is probably more likely to be uninterested in union support of the broad social programs most characteristic of national market unions. The evidence here is incomplete, though, and the statement would probably not apply to municipal employee unions in major cities.

(3) The degree of activism and the efforts of the leadership to explain to members the rationale for union involvement.

(4) The extent to which the individual member identifies with the union in nonpolitical areas. Active unionists are more likely to support union political efforts.

Where all these factors combine in the same direction, individual members are likely to have clear-cut views on their union's political activities. And where the union endorsement does not run against the grain in terms of deep-seated candidate, party, or issue

---

[8] See Arthur C. Wolfe, "Trends in Labor Union Voting Behavior, 1948-1968," and Hamilton comment, in LABOR AND AMERICAN POLITICS, rev. ed., Rehmus, McLaughlin, and Nesbitt, eds. (Ann Arbor, Mi.: University of Michigan Press, 1978), pp. 368-83.

[9] See summary in LABOR AND AMERICAN POLITICS, pp. 359-62.

orientations of its members, union efforts to influence members are likely to meet with success.

Union campaign efforts are also likely to induce higher *turnout* among members who are initially uninformed and those who are already inclined to vote with the union endorsement. This is especially true where the union demonstrates a link between the vote and the economic welfare of the members.

The often heard statement that "nobody can tell me how to vote" usually misses the point in at least two ways. First, major vestiges of the "directed vote" disappeared with the old ward/machine politics. Secondly, although no group is likely to try to "tell" someone how to vote, voters are nevertheless targets of all sorts of efforts to convince them how to vote. Such persuasive efforts are the stuff of electoral campaigns and of politics itself.

The impact of labor on elections must be assessed largely on a case-by-case basis, since there are huge failures and major successes. John L. Lewis, splitting from the majority of the labor movement, was unable to swing the 1940 presidential election from Franklin Roosevelt to Wendell Wilkie. But labor backing played a key role in tipping the relatively close election of Kennedy in 1960 (although it was unable to prevent the Nixon victory in 1968). And there are a few instances where labor has successfully endorsed split tickets in statewide elections.

The above examples suggest some of the conditions for labor influence. Unity within the labor movement is one. Obviously, labor's total impact is seriously reduced when major unions back opposing candidates. In other cases labor involvement may halt the momentum of an opposition candidate. This was apparently the case in the 1968 presidential candidacy of George Wallace, which appeared to be gaining support among union members before several unions began a "stop-Wallace" campaign.

Perhaps the major impact is not labor's ability to change votes, but its ability to register voters and increase turnouts for its candidates. It is in this way that the large numbers of volunteers have their true impact. Many close elections are decided by size of the turnout. The pattern noted earlier, that a large turnout generally favors parties and candidates with a more progessive orientation, suggests the direction of union influence.

Labor is rarely able to determine the outcome of an election or a legislative vote solely on its own strength. To succeed, labor requires allies. It is through electoral and lobbying coalitions, longstanding or temporary, that the votes are amassed to elect officials and enact legislation sympathetic to its positions.

Labor in the Community

As on the national scene, the need for coalition-building exists in most communities. For in all but a few areas, labor cannot succeed solely through its own efforts. Community-level goals such as the prevention of plant closings, avoidance of interference in strikes, and better living conditions were discussed earlier. Here the role of the local central bodies and other union groups can be decisive. Labor strength is enhanced if councils are supported by a large proportion of affiliations, if the affiliates are active, and if the different groups cooperate with one another. Alliances with human rights groups, consumer coalitions, religious groups, and neighborhood bodies can increase the strength of all concerned.

Success in these efforts often requires overcoming local media blockages, for instance, newspapers that play up negative labor stories while omitting positive labor developments as unnewsworthy. Unions must also view coalition-building as a year-round endeavor, not merely a subject for lip-service during a major strike. These needs are particularly important for municipal employee unions, whose success or failure in bargaining is likely to be directly affected by their success in gaining community support.

Prospects

Labor has never had an easy time working through the U.S. political system. Despite their numbers, workers are often treated and have to operate much like a minority, building alliances with other groups and seeking a haven in what is often a reluctant party structure. Nationally this has often put labor in the position of trying to keep the Democrats in power in order to avoid something worse.

The traditional political party structure provided some measure of stability and a mechanism for labor influence, no matter how minimal at times. The fragmentation of this structure in recent decades has opened the door to all manner of do-it-yourself approaches—issue-by-issue, candidate-by-candidate, and interest-by-interest approaches—with little or no tie to traditional brokering mechanisms such as parties or coalitions.

This observation should not be taken to glorify the past. Even the hailed New Deal advances of the 1930s were largely efforts to preserve a crumbling system, not to promote labor advancement for its own sake. Yet during that decade labor issues were popularly seen as human and civil rights issues, much as discrimination against racial minorities became the civil rights issue of the 1960s.

In the 1980s labor retains the advantage of neither structure nor issue. Yet political effectiveness is now even more essential to the labor movement because of the increasing dependence of labor and the economy on government action or inaction in matters falling outside the scope of collective bargaining and also because bargaining is itself ever more regulated by government.

Organized labor, especially at the national level, continues to devote a large proportion of its resources to political action in the conventional sense of electoral and lobbying efforts played by the accepted rules of the game. Raising questions about the likely effectiveness of these conventional efforts are unfavorable shifts in labor's political strength reflected in the line-ups in Congress and the White House, increases in corporate power, and the climate of support for a variety of anti-union initiatives. Labor's congressional strength may sag further as the 1982 reapportionment takes effect, shifting representation away from areas of its traditional strength.

If conventional politics reverses the unemployment, inflation, and energy problems that are the major manifestations of the economic crisis, then the rules of that game are likely to remain intact. Conventional politics will be rewarded, in effect. If these efforts fail and the crisis deepens, however, then labor may be forced to abandon its reliance on conventional strategies and turn to new measures. One strategy would be for labor to rely on its latent ability to stop production in order to influence government through such tactics as political and general strikes. Commonly thought unworkable or ineffective, such tactics certainly run against the no-strike clauses found in most collective bargaining agreements. However, they have never really been tested in recent U.S. history under such general crisis circumstances. Political strikes or the threat of them have, however, proved useful in Great Britain where they were influential in blocking antilabor efforts in the early 1970s.

Under either scenario the prospect is for heightened class conflict. Thus far the government has found it easier to attempt to reduce inflation by increasing unemployment, rather than by controlling the institutions and economic sectors that are both the causes and beneficiaries of inflation. Employers seize the bargaining initiative with "takeback" proposals, and workers in many instances have their backs to the wall.

Much of labor's future will depend on its ability to expand through organizing and effective representation—efforts which must be supported by successes in the political arena. We can thus amplify the statement of an earlier chapter that "Where labor can't organize, it can't bargain, and where it can't bargain, it can't organize" by noting that political effectiveness is increasingly crucial to both endeavors.

Key Words and Phrases

Sons of Liberty	Federal Elections Campaign Act
Workingmen's Party	Political Action Committee
voluntarism	(PAC)
nonpartisanship	federalism
labor party	states rights
institutional issues	Section 14(b)
employment (jobs) issues	Occupational Safety and
class issues	Health Act
societal issues	common situs picketing
"American bottoms"	AFL-CIO Department of
unemployment compensation	Legislation
workers' compensation	Committee on Political
political assets	Education (COPE)
Business Roundtable	labor vote
labor law reform	coalition building
political money	conventional politics
voluntary ("free") dollars	free riding

Review and Discussion Questions

1. Present your own classification of political issues of concern to labor. This can be markedly different from either the bifocal or four-part schemes presented in the text.

2. Why does labor invest so many "political chips" in legislation that does not exclusively benefit union members? For example, social security, minimum wage, employment discrimination laws.

3. Other than those cited, what features of a union's structure and jurisdiction might influence its political orientation and activity? If possible, cite specific unions.

4. Are the laws regulating union and corporation political spending equitable? Why or why not?

5. What are the distinct functions performed by COPE and the Legislative Department? To what extent are these functions duplicated or amplified by international and local unions?

6. Specify the likely political concerns of each of the following unions: (a) A local of a national union operating under a national agreement; (b) A local of a municipal employees union; (c) A local building trades union; (d) A nonfactory local in a highly mixed jurisdiction.

Suggestions for Further Reading

The best source on labor's political activity is a reader edited by Rehmus, McLaughlin and Nesbitt, *Labor and American Politics*. For an excellent and thorough analysis of how labor relates to the party structure in four cities, how it mobilizes volunteers, and how unions are motivated to participate under different circumstances, see J. David Greenstone, *Labor in American Politics*.

Labor's political efforts at the state level are the subject of Melvin Kahn, *The Politics of American Labor: The Indiana Microcosm*, and Philip Taft, *Labor Politics American Style: The California State Federation of Labor*. Though both are somewhat outdated on particulars, they remain useful and relevant. For an urban emphasis see Gus Tyler, *Labor in the Metropolis*.

Classic examinations of union member views and voting behavior are, respectively, Joel Seidman, et al., *The Worker Views His Union*, and Arthur Kornhauser, et al., *When Labor Votes: A Study of Auto Workers*.

There are many books and articles devoted to labor's political activity during certain periods in history. Other works such as Bok and Dunlop, *Labor and the American Community*, have one or more chapters on the subject.

For current sources the *AFL-CIO News* and the newspapers of international unions, state federations, and other bodies present labor viewpoints.

Complete bibliographical information for the above titles can be found in the Bibliography.

10

Members and Leaders
Participation, Power, and
Performance

Most important of all, Brother Reuther, for eighteen years I work at the
Kelsey-Hayes foundry before the union, and for eighteen years they call
me dumb Polak. And then the union come along, and they call me
brother.

Letter to Walter Reuther, ca 1939

Union office is a calling, not a business. The morals of the marketplace
will not suffice. Those who enter that calling are, and should be, held to
a higher standard.

Lane Kirkland, 1981

A union is comprised of workers organized together for a purpose. The analysis of structures, roles, and positions that is essential
to understanding the union as an organization need not obscure the
people who make up the organization.

Earlier chapters discussed the attitudes and motivations of
workers toward participation and voting in union representation
elections and profiled the people of the labor movement in terms of
numbers—by union, state, economic sector, occupation, race, and
sex. This chapter will examine the people of the labor movement in
their capacities as rank-and-file members and as leaders, the modes
of their participation, and the power relationships that determine
who runs the union. This, in turn, will lead to discussion of three
issues in union governance: internal democracy, the representation
of women and minorities, and corrupt practices.

Concepts from previous chapters contribute to this discussion.
It therefore helps to know if we are talking about a factory or a non-

202

factory union or about the bargaining or internal dimension of a union's government. It may also be necessary to know the history and policies of a particular union and employer.

As a recent study stresses, there are two popular conceptions of unionism. The *monopoly view*, long maintained by economists and the press, emphasizes the impact of unions on wages and prices, and arrives at largely negative conclusions. The other view, that of the union as *collective voice*, sees unions more for their positive functions as expressions of workers' need in both economic and organizational affairs.[1]

The monopoly view is based largely on neoclassical economic assumptions that unions upset the working of capitalist labor markets. These assumptions include a reliance on individual decision making and an emphasis on "natural" mechanisms of adjustment, such as employment mobility and market-regulated wage setting. While not denying that unions often raise wages beyond their "free market" level, the collective voice perspective notes the many other positive functions performed by unions. These gains arise from the collective formulation and strengthening of worker demands through unionism and extend to unorganized workers and firms. They provide workers with a voice in both workplace and political arenas. This chapter analyzes some of the internal union conditions that influence the collective voice and the issues it addresses.

The Rank and File: Attitudes and Participation

Many stereotypes accompany the subject of internal union dynamics and the attitudes of rank-and-file members toward their unions. One such view, popularized by anti-union sources, suggests that within each union member there is a captive of "the labor bosses." That is, given a free choice, the members would turn not only against union leaders but against unionism itself.[2] A second and particularly self-defeating view is held by many unionists. This view maintains that those who fail to attend monthly meetings are, by virtue of their absence, apathetic. Since most members do not attend, most are therefore apathetic.

---

[1] Richard B. Freeman and James L. Medoff, WHAT DO UNIONS DO? (New York: Basic Books, 1984), compares these two perspectives in the light of research findings.

[2] For example, see Patrick Cox, "If Unions Cooperated, We Would All Benefit," *USA Today*, 19 May 1983. "Less than 20 percent of all private sector workers are represented by unions; none would be if they had a choice."

The experienced local union leader is sometimes the true expert on what makes a particular rank-and-file membership tick. Call it knowledge or intuition, this expertise is based on close day-to-day interaction with the members in a variety of capacities. But even these leaders sometimes miscalculate.

On the other hand some academic observers of attitudes and participation know only what can be learned from measures appropriate for questionnaires, interview guides, and statistical manipulation. Of the studies that result, some tell us only that their compilers are able to count. Others have greater value.

The study of unions, their members, and leaders was in academic vogue during the late 1940s and the 1950s. In 1960 Spinrad summarized the major findings on union participation.[3] He noted such measures of participation as meeting attendance, serving on committees, reading union newspapers, and holding union office. Despite differences among measures, however, Spinrad noted certain patterns of participation in well-established unions.

Certain *aspects of the job itself* were associated with higher participation. Working in a small plant, in a plant with a stable work force, and on the night shift seems to encourage participation by generating a greater sense of community among workers. In the building trades, union participation results from a sense of trade, from shared experiences and perspectives, and from a dependence on the union for information about work opportunities and developments in the industry.

Within many industrial shops participation is greater among those such as maintenance workers whose jobs permit them to move about and mingle with other workers rather than those whose jobs isolate them from others. Participation also correlates with membership in a group whose members work closely together and are relatively homogeneous in pay and skill level. And it associates with relatively higher paid and skilled jobs whose occupants are often the first to organize in a plant.

Residence seems to affect union participation. Workers who live in urban working-class communities are more active in their unions than those with either rural or middle-class suburban backgrounds. Those residing in "occupational communities" near their place of work often make up the most pro-union blocs. This has

---

[3] William Spinrad, "Correlates of Trade Union Participation: A Summary of the Literature," *American Sociological Review* 25 (April 1960), pp. 237–44.

been observed of miners, loggers and lumber-mill workers, fishermen, and sometimes steel and auto workers. Living near fellow workers facilitates union activity, while participation may be inhibited when the labor force of a plant or office is scattered over a 50-mile radius.

There is a question of causation—something of the chicken-egg dilemma—in these findings. Is a worker less active *because* he or she lives in a largely nonunion middle class suburb, far from the workplace and most fellow workers? Or is it the less union-oriented workers who elect to live there in the first place?

Findings on *personal associations* of workers suggest that in some cases the latter explanation may apply. Workers who associate with fellow workers in their leisure time tend to be more active, although clearly these social patterns are often conditioned by the nature of the job and by geographical considerations.

Certain other characteristics correlate with high union activism. These include union family backgrounds, minority, and Catholic backgrounds—all of which appear to have in common a tradition of reliance on collective, as opposed to individual, efforts for advancement. Ethnic work groups, be they "dominant" or "deprived" groups, tend toward higher participation, especially when occupational and community lines coincide.

Spinrad also noted findings of low union activity by workers who are related to or friendly with supervisors, those whose employers maintain a paternalistic atmosphere, and those who know few union activists.

Regarding *job orientations*, Spinrad cites several studies finding that union participation increases with job satisfaction, a pattern that may be explained by the high satisfaction of many skilled craft workers and the correlation of activism with higher pay and status in industrial locals. Nevertheless, Spinrad notes that even activists who are satisfied with the job itself may be indignant about particular aspects of the work environment such as favoritism by supervisors. This is also borne out by the finding that workers who emphasize the union's role in improving working conditions are more likely to be activists.[4] Considered as a whole, these patterns lead to the not surprising conclusion that workers who perceive a high stake in their jobs are apt to become union activists in order to protect that stake.

---

[4] Spinrad, "Trade Union Participation," p. 242.

Finally, studies show that active unionists tend to have a high sense of working-class identification and are highly class conscious. They emphasize collective over individual efforts for improvement, regardless of whether they hold *combative attitudes* toward management.

Union activity can serve a variety of functions for the individual. It can satisfy collective economic and political needs, thus accruing also to the benefit of individuals. And it serves as a mechanism for personal development and satisfaction for many with leadership talent, social needs, and a desire to have a say in decisions that affect their lives.

Recent Additions

What of the more than two decades since this research was conducted? Are union members different now? Have subsequent studies contributed to our knowledge?

Clearly, the membership of the labor movement has changed since the 1950s, and several of these changes reflect shifts in the makeup of the work force.

There are now relatively more members in low-paid jobs such as those found in the service sector. In the other direction, there is increasing unionization of professional occupations and office workers. Included are engineers and technicians, teachers, athletes, medical personnel, and air line pilots. Also, there are more women both in the work force and in unions, and some are working in so-called nontraditional jobs such as skilled trades.[5]

During the 1970s interest grew in studying these groups which make up what is sometimes called "the new unionism." But there was little reexamination of the more traditional groups. Because university faculty members are interested in themselves and find it convenient to study themselves, it is not surprising that much of the new attention was directed at faculty unions and their members, as well as at teachers in general.

Despite the imbalance in groups of workers studied, some modest advances over the knowledge of the 1950s occurred. Researchers now use more varied measures of union participation; distinguish among members on the basis of their desires to be included

---

[5] Mary Lindenstein Walshok, BLUE COLLAR WOMEN (Garden City, N.Y.: Anchor Books, 1981). Chapter 1 summarizes the data. The book is an in-depth examination of the backgrounds and job experiences of some of these women.

in union decision making; examine member expectations of their employers and their unions; and apply more sophisticated techniques to analyze results.[6]

This research will never yield a profile of a typical union member because there is no such person. But it does focus on important dimensions of structure, attitude, and participation—for the moment providing more questions than firm answers. The studies do not tell us, for example, how the "new" and the "traditional" members compare; nor do we know much about how the traditional group has changed over the years. Union leaders of long experience and great perception can tell us more about these changes, but few have the time or inclination to record their observations.

Another topic drawing increased attention from unions and researchers alike is that of union women, their participation and leadership activity. With women now comprising more than 43 percent of the work force and approaching one-third of union membership (with significant numbers of women in apprenticeship programs and others who hold journeymen [sic] cards), there is a need to learn more about the attitudes and needs of this pool of potential activists and leadership talent as well as about the barriers which face them.

A major survey of union women by Wertheimer and Nelson extended to 1500 women from 108 locals in New York City, but focused primarily on seven locals. The authors found women often more active than men, as measured by meeting attendance, grievance activity, voting, and other nonleadership activity, but underrepresented in leadership positions. They also found that activist women are typically older, single (often formerly married), and the sole support of their families, a finding that confirms the earlier suggestion that activists tend to be those with high stakes in their jobs.

Identified as barriers to increased union responsibilities by many women were family and home responsibilities, difficulties with supervisors encountered by activists, a need for greater competence in union matters, and a lack of self-confidence. Despite these barriers, the study suggested, there are many women available for greater union responsibilities. The study also pointed to the need for increased labor education for union women.[7]

---

[6] For sources the reader should refer to George Strauss, "Union Government in the U.S., Research Past and Future," *Industrial Relations* 16 (May 1977), pp. 217–23. For limited findings on these subjects, see Glick, Mirvis, and Harder, "Union Satisfaction and Participation," pp. 145–51, in the same issue.

[7] Barbara Wertheimer and Anne H. Nelson, TRADE UNION WOMEN: A STUDY OF THEIR PARTICIPATION IN NEW YORK CITY LOCALS (New York: Praeger, 1975), especially pp. 118–20 and chapter 6.

One result of the many studies of union participation is increased attention to the meaning of different forms of participation for the member and the union. Activities such as running for office, working on an active committee, or serving vigorously as a steward usually require greater effort and commitment of time from the member than do glancing through a union newspaper, voting in an election, or simply attending a meeting. But this distinction does not justify the conclusion that the member who simply glances through the union newspaper is less committed to union goals than one who runs for office.

All these forms of participation have been used as measures in one or more of the studies. Their significance needs to be explored further in different union settings. Attention also needs to be paid to the conditions under which people move from one level of activity to another level requiring greater effort.

Measuring interest in the union by the attendance at monthly meetings, regardless of their purpose, may mislead efforts to improve union effectiveness, especially in large locals where the meeting is more appropriately viewed as a delegate assembly for officers and activists.

There is clearly a need for closer examination of the day-to-day forms of union participation at the shop or office level. More specifically, what can unions do to involve members and represent them even more effectively in the workplace where there is little competition from home, social activities, television, and other "attractions"?

A second need is to identify the relationship between particular types of unions (e.g., factory/nonfactory, craft/industrial) and the attitudes and participation of their members. Efforts here could benefit not only organizing but the design of union organizations. While it is probably not true that a single form of unionism is "right" for each industry and environment, there is a need for more information on the subject.

Union Leaders: Recruitment and Progression

Because virtually all unionists participate before they assume leadership positions, the following treatment of leadership is a direct extension of the discussion of participation.

Leaders are typically bred and get their first experience in the workplace, where millions of union members have served as shop stewards. A minority, usually those in large industrial plants, work full-time on grievance handling and other bargaining activities, for which they are compensated by the employer. The majority work at their regular jobs, except for time spent in grievance handling.

The status and power of stewards varies. Where the position is full-time there is apt to be considerable status and reward, and hence competition in steward elections. But where the union is weak and shop-level activity appears to be ineffective, or where the aggravations exceed the rewards (gratification, esteem of fellow workers, time away from "the machine," as well as any remuneration), the job sometimes goes begging or is filled by anyone willing to take it. Between these extremes are all manner of situations. It is safe to say that most stewards are motivated to some degree by a desire to improve the conditions of fellow workers and achieve union goals.[8]

Turnover among stewards is typically high, especially when compared to the low turnover among international union officers. Nevertheless it is from the steward ranks that most higher level leaders are ultimately drawn, especially in factory unions.

Top local union office can lead to full-time staff representative or international representative positions. Some factory unions have a policy of promoting to staff only persons who have previously served as local presidents. Others will recruit staff representatives from outside the ranks or from offices other than local president.

A 1977–78 survey of international unions noted a growing number (28 percent of the respondents) looking outside their organizations for international representatives and organizers.[9] The study noted that these unions fall into two categories based on their membership type. Their members are either well-paid professional and technical workers or low-paid semiskilled and unskilled people. The former are presumed reluctant to assume union responsibilities because they are dedicated to their occupations; some unions representing the latter group report difficulties in recruiting "qualified" staff from the ranks.

The study also observes that unions sometimes begin with "outside" staff in the early stages of organization when pay is low

---

[8] Leonard R. Sayles and George Strauss, THE LOCAL UNION, rev. ed. (New York: Harcourt, Brace and World, 1964), chapter 8, and James Wallihan, "Workplace Politics and Leadership in a Chicago Printing Trades Union" (Ph.D. diss., Indiana University, 1974), chapter 9, find several relationships between workplace environments, workers' "union morale," and the selection and performance of stewards.

[9] Lois S. Gray, "Unions Implementing Managerial Techniques," *Monthly Labor Review* 104, no. 6 (June 1981), p. 4.

and the work permits little sleep. Similarly, unions undergoing rapid growth, such as public employee unions in the 1960s and 1970s, often look outside their ranks.

Top national union officers are a distinct group with respect to salaries, life style, and job security. Two surveys of international presidents, conducted more than two decades apart, are instructive. During the 1940s, C. Wright Mills compared the top leaders of the long established AFL affiliates with the "upstart" leadership of CIO unions, including leaders of state and local central bodies.

Mills found that in 1946 the average AFL union had been organized for 50 years and the average age of top leaders was 57. CIO unions had been organized for only 12 years and the average age of top leaders was 43. Associated with their relative youth, CIO leaders had more formal education. The two groups reflected the general population in their class origins. Three-fourths began as wage workers and about 60 percent had fathers who were wage workers. A sizable minority had fathers who were either farmers or small businessmen.[10]

Once elected, most top union officers enjoyed considerable job security. A survey of seven unions between 1910–1941 found that of 734 successful candidates for national office, 634 ran unopposed.[11]

A 1967 survey by Friedman updated Mills' earlier findings. Most of the differences between AFL and CIO leaders had evaporated over the intervening years, largely because of the continued tenure of many of the CIO leaders. Thus presidents, secretary/treasurers, and vice-presidents of former AFL unions average 56 years of age, while those of former CIO unions average 55. The two groups had also become quite similar in formal education, religious affiliation, and career mobility patterns.[12] The average leader began working at age 18, joined a union by 24, was first elected to union office at 28, and assumed his or her present position at about 43. The security of top leaders is suggested by subtracting the figure of 43 from the average age of 56, indicating an average tenure of 13 years in current positions.[13]

---

[10] Mills, C. W., THE NEW MEN OF POWER: AMERICA'S LABOR LEADERS (New York: Harcourt & Brace, 1948), chapter 5.

[11] Ibid., p. 64.

[12] Abraham Friedman, "The American Trade Union Leader: A Collective Portrait," in TRADE UNION GOVERNMENT AND COLLECTIVE BARGAINING, ed. Joel Seidman (New York: Praeger, 1970), pp. 230–35.

[13] The 13-year old difference is somewhat questionable because Friedman's data indicate that leaders have held their present positions for only 9.3 years. Friedman, "American Trade Union Leader," p. 217.

One exception to the pattern of top officials rising from workplace through local union office is found in the national AFL-CIO and its state and local central bodies, where many full-time officers have not previously performed major bargaining responsibilities or held top elective positions at other levels.

While firm patterns are difficult to find in such infrequent events, the 1979 transition in top AFL-CIO leadership shows a progression. The present leadership first entered labor leadership in the 1940s through staff appointment. President Lane Kirkland, a merchant marine deck officer and member of the Masters, Mates and Pilots union, joined the AFL staff in 1948; was appointed George Meany's executive assistant in 1960; and was elected secretary-treasurer in 1969, before assuming the presidency ten years later. Current Secretary-Treasurer Thomas Donahue followed a similar path. In 1949 he took a staff position with Building Service Employees Local 32B in New York City. He later served in appointed positions with the Service Employees International Union (SEIU) and the Labor Department before being elected first vice-president of the SEIU. In 1973 he became Meany's executive assistant, the post in which Kirkland had earlier served.[14] Both Kirkland and Donahue are college graduates.

The fact that top officers can move up through appointive positions in the Federation corresponds with the division of functions between the Federation and its international union affiliates. Thus one would expect top international officers to have held a number of previous elective positions with significant bargaining responsibilities. But the functions of federation leadership permit a different background.

The departure of the leadership shaped by events of the 1930s is now virtually complete. The union roots of the new leadership are in the post-World War II era.

This transition leads to speculation about the impact of the change in leadership:

> The earlier generation was idealistic, militant, and its quick success meant that it never had to learn the apple-polishing skills required to work one's way up the bureaucratic ladder. In many unions the large concentration of leadership in a comparatively narrow age bracket created a classic personnel problem during the fifties and sixties. Few of these leaders died, reached retirement age, or were defeated in elections. At the same time union growth slowed precipitously. Thus there

---

[14] *The Service Employee*, December, 1979, p. 5, and *CWA News*, December 1979, p. 8.

were few junior level openings which could be used to train replacements for the generation of the thirties when that generation reached retirement age. And in some unions an entire generation was skipped as men in their thirties replaced those retiring in their sixties.[15]

There is little doubt that a relatively abrupt generational shift has occurred in several unions. The consequences remain to be seen.

Issue: Democracy or Oligarchy

Having looked at rank-and-file and leadership roles we turn now to the relationship between the two. To what extent are unions internally democratic? Do members control leaders and policy? Are members able to progress into the ranks of leaders without coercive restriction? Or are unions little more than oligarchies, with a powerful few dominating a powerless rank and file? Or, at worst, autocracies run by a single tyrant, the "labor boss?"

This subject is often obscured by academics who adopt one-dimensional criteria, apply them to a single level of a single union, and then generalize their results to all levels of all unions; by employers wanting to deal with union leaders who can guarantee results from their members; and by the union leader who points to a constitutional provision as the equivalent of democracy or who denies that the subject is fit for inquiry by any but the leaders of his or her own union.

Prominent stereotypes and case histories on this subject are well known: John L. Lewis who brooked no opposition while running the United Mine Workers; the rank-and-file Teamster who doesn't care how Jimmy Hoffa got things done, only that he delivered results for the members; and such leaders as Arnold Miller of the Mine Workers, Edward Sadlowski of the Steelworkers, and others who tried to beat the odds by opposing incumbent-backed slates.

In 1925 A. J. Muste in a classic portrayal described unions as part armies and part town meetings.[16] The union is a democratic structure ultimately governed by the rank and file. But it is also a fighting organization, requiring solidarity and discipline to be effective with employers. The tension between these two premises is obvi-

---

[15] Strauss, "Union Government in the U.S.," p. 225.

[16] A. J. Muste, "Factional Fights in Trade Unions," in AMERICAN LABOR DYNAMICS, ed. J. B. S. Hardman (New York: Harcourt & Brace, 1928), p. 332.

ous, but to conclude that unions must always choose between democracy and effectiveness ignores other choices. In many cases the two go hand in hand.

Members themselves have diverse expectations of their unions and varying desires to participate in decisions made by their unions. At one extreme are those who view their union card like an insurance policy and have no more desire to participate in union affairs than in the management of their insurance carriers, especially when things are going reasonably well. At the other pole are those who expect to be consulted and to have an active voice in all matters affecting them. Perhaps in between are the majority who do not desire to participate routinely, but who want to retain the right to voice their opinion when they feel the need arises—when things are not going well, especially in collective bargaining matters.

Herein lies one of the difficulties for all organizations, especially largely voluntary bodies such as unions. It is nearly impossible to maintain a generally high level of mobilization and participation among all members. The active few tend to exercise power, with a variety of checks retained by the less active or the inactive majority. But when the checks are exercised infrequently there is a tendency for them to evaporate.

Definitions and Measures. One definition of union democracy can be labeled *formal or procedural.* It focuses on constitutional guarantees of the rights to free expression, the right to fair elections, and equal access to running for office. Some would include here all the guarantees and forms found in civil government, looking even for a formal two-party system.[17]

The 1959 Labor-Management Reporting and Disclosure Act (LMRDA, also known as the Landrum-Griffin Act) addressed this procedural version of union democracy when it set standards for protecting the rights of members and regulated the conduct of union elections and the use of trusteeships over subordinate bodies.

The *behavioral view* focuses less on formal and procedural measures, seeking instead evidence of high participation, electoral competition, and leadership turnover.

---

[17]This is the strong suggestion of an early study of the International Typographical Union. See Seymour Lipset, Martin Trow, and James Coleman, UNION DEMOCRACY (Glencoe, Ill.: The Free Press, 1956). This study is vulnerable on at least two points: The differences between the two parties in the ITU were arguably exaggerated and electoral opposition equivalent to parties in other unions is largely ignored. The essentials of this perspective are behavioral rather than formal-procedural.

A *substantive* definition of union democracy asks not *how* these leaders are selected or controlled or how membership desires are identified, but whether union leaders reflect the desires of members. This definition points to results, not methods.

If the procedural definition is open to criticism for emphasizing form over substance, the substantive view is vulnerable to the opposite—that it ignores democratic mechanisms in favor of sometimes less tangible evidence of responsiveness. The behavioral perspective often tends to equate mere competition or leadership change with democracy, regardless of substance.

Power Within Unions. Unions are not untouched by the tendency toward oligarchy (control by a few) in large organizations. Top international union leaders become set apart from the rank and file and are unlikely to be replaced through the electoral process. They wield the preponderance, if not all, of the power.

Perhaps the most comprehensive statement of the sources of oligarchy in unions is that of Lipset.[18] Lipset identifies *union communications* as a key power source for top leaders who can control access to publications and other channels of distribution to make their views known. In addition, communication between the international and locals is more easily accomplished than is communication among diverse locals. In most unions, especially those with largely manual worker memberships, union activity provides the opportunity to learn such *political skills* as communication, organization, and decision making. Top officers presumably have more of these skills, if not a monopoly, than do most members of the union. Lipset argues further that

> higher, more secure income, together with the different range of experience that is involved in being a union official—desk work, travel, association with business, government, and other union leaders—provides the basis and substance for a style of life markedly different from that of people in the shop.[19]

This leads, he says, to a desire of union officers to maintain this status which, while understandable, is inconsistent with the democratic expectation of insecurity in office. Since union leaders have fewer alternatives than high-status people in other walks of life, they strive harder to hold onto their offices.

---

[18] S. M. Lipset, POLITICAL MAN (Garden City, N.Y.: Anchor Books, 1960), chapter 12.
[19] Ibid., p. 399.

Lipset notes other factors that influence the extent of union democracy: the manner of the union's original organization, whether bottom-up or top-down; the pattern of succession following the departure of a dominant leader; the response to crisis situations; and the character of individual leaders. A prevailing influence, he suggests, is the philosophy of business unionism, a set of ideas justifying the narrowest definition of a union's role in society and limiting its area of membership service to collective bargaining matters. He asserts that this approach, by narrowing the grounds for internal conflict and by stabilizing bureaucracy, discourages widespread member participation and legitimates oligarchic leadership.

Though some of Lipset's generalizations may be overdrawn, it is clear that top officers are often able to draw on resources accruing from their positions to enhance their tenure in office and guide their unions in certain directions. But perhaps the most pervasive condition contributing to oligarchy in unions is the very consolidation of bargaining structure, and the accompanying centralization of internal structure, that unions must achieve to become effective. Under these conditions international officers play lead roles, while local union representatives participate in a more limited fashion.

By most *behavioral* measures—electoral opposition, closeness of elections, leadership turnover, and the like—union democracy is greatest at the shop and local union levels. The progression from the local level to full-time staff and top national office is often controlled by the top leadership's patronage. Staff positions in many unions are easily awarded to political allies whose loyalty can be assured. Yet there is a countervailing force—the need of national officers to satisfy constituents and a variety of power centers in the union—which can stem pressures toward oligarchy, machine politics, and strict conformity.

Countertrends—Sources of Democracy. A number of enduring mechanisms in unions often limit the excesses of oligarchy. Less visible than elections is bargaining *within* both internal and collective bargaining governments. Leaders of power blocs within a union, for instance, may mobilize members and local leaders for a variety of purposes that result in changes short of turnover in top offices. Some changes reflecting pressure from below may occur in secondary leadership, in bargaining practices and structures, and in the terms of major contracts.

While it is seldom easy to "beat city hall," these internal rivalries sometimes emerge into full-blown insurgent candidacies for top office. Examples are the campaigns of Arnold Miller and the Miners for Democracy in the United Mine Workers and Edward Sadlowski in the Steelworkers. To be successful, such candidacies usually require an overwhelming popular base in the union, a number of strong issues, and a top leadership that is ineffective and has lost touch with the membership. But even when all of these factors were not present, insurgencies sometimes have polled 30 to 40 percent despite the obvious advantages enjoyed by incumbents.

Formal constraints, such as those provided for in the LMRDA, provide limited safeguards for some forms of expression and for election procedures, thus making the advantages of incumbency less formidable. Sadlowski, for instance, would not have been elected director of District 31 of the Steelworkers (Chicago and Northwest Indiana) in 1974 had not the Secretary of Labor intervened to force a rerun after the original election was "won" by his administration-backed opponent.

In the collective bargaining government, legal regulation can play a role in checking certain excesses and discouraging job harassment of political opponents within the union. While frequently abused, the requirement of the Labor Management Relations Act (LMRA) for fair representation of all members of a bargaining unit in negotiations and grievances is perhaps a major example.

There are additional constraints on leaders in particular segments of the labor movement. In the building trades, for example, local union size, homogeneity, and the nature of the industry itself are observed to contribute to representative leadership.[20]

Unions never conform entirely to the ideal model of democracy. No organization does. But compared to other institutions in the United States, and despite some exceptions, they remain among the most democratic. This is surprising when one considers that most unions must adapt to an institution—the corporation—whose operating model is authoritarian as opposed to democratic and whose power is, if not unlimited, certainly great.

The Representation of Minorities and Women

Chapter 3 examined the composition of the work force and of union membership by race and sex. Considering their percentages

---

[20] See George Strauss, "Control by the Membership in Building Trades Unions," in LABOR AND TRADE UNIONISM, eds. Galenson and Lipset (New York: John Wiley & Sons, 1960), pp. 282-291.

in the work force, women are the least likely and black males most likely to be union members.

These figures mirror unionization differences in the industries in which the groups are employed. For example, significant numbers of women work in the less-organized service and office sectors. But the figures for black males may also reflect the fact that blacks are significantly more likely to vote for unions in representation elections.

Figure 6 demonstrates that within each category of race and sex, the earnings of unionized workers are substantially greater than those of nonunion workers. Nevertheless there remain major

Figure 6.   Usual Weekly Earnings of Employed Full-Time Wage and Salary Workers by Labor Organization Representation, May 1977

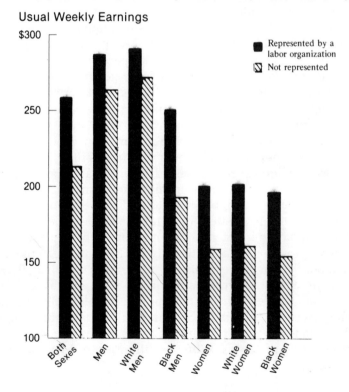

Source: Bureau of Labor Statistics, Earnings and Other Characteristics of Organized Workers, May 1977, Report 556 (Washington, D.C.: Government Printing Office, 1979), p. 4.

differences between groups. While women appear to benefit more substantially from union representation, women of both races are still paid less than are males of either race. For all groups, however, joining a union appears to be a rational choice. To the extent that blacks, though their earnings still lag behind those of whites of the same sex, benefit even more than whites, their strong preference for unionization seems especially rational.[21]

The fact that the earnings of blacks and women trail those of whites and males has several explanations. Both groups are over-represented in less-skilled and lower-paid classifications. How much of this is attributable to direct, and how muct to broader, institutional discrimination is uncertain, but despite the entry of some women and blacks to positions previously denied them, both are clearly factors. Many women have the additional barrier during child-bearing and child-rearing years of reduced ability to establish themselves in job ladders.

In the light of publicity about discrimination in building trades unions during the late 1960s and the 1970s, it is interesting to compare Labor Department figures on the percentages of blacks in union and nonunion segments of the construction industry in 1977. Of the workers represented by unions 8.8 percent were blacks, while 8.7 percent of those in nonunion construction were black.[22]

While these percentages appear low in either case and while they certainly mask major differences among trades and unions (e.g., there are more blacks in the trowel trades than the mechanical trades), the figures seem to belie the claim that discrimination in the industry is a uniquely union-inspired problem. The percentages also counter the belief that minorities and women seeking entry to the industry will find greater opportunities in the nonunion sector.

Discrimination in internal union government is addressed under general provisions such as those in LMRDA that ban the denial of union political rights regardless of the criteria on which discrimination is practiced. Discrimination in the workplace is a different matter, falling under Taft-Hartley and the Equal Employment Opportunity Acts. In most industries hiring is done by the employer, not the union. Nevertheless, unions can contribute to discrimination by exerting pressures, subtle or otherwise, or by failing to op-

---

[21] For additional evidence on the antidiscrimination impact of unionization, see Richard B. Freeman and James L. Medoff, "The Two Faces of Unionism," *The Public Interest* 57 (Fall 1979), pp. 87–8.

[22] Bureau of Labor Statistics, *Earnings and Other Characteristics of Organized Workers, May 1977*, Rept. 556 (Washington, D.C.: Government Printing Office, 1979).

pose discriminatory hiring practices. But their real impact in factory and most nonfactory settings is felt after hiring, when bargaining agreements and grievance representation have a direct impact on job rights and benefits. Some unions now emphasize antidiscrimination measures in the workplace and in collective bargaining agreements.

Leadership Patterns. Work force participation and union membership rates are one standard for comparing race and sex representation in union leadership. Many unions with substantial membership of blacks and women have little or no representation from these groups in top national leadership positions. As of 1980 three internationals, each with over 100,000 women making up at least 25 percent of the membership, had no women as international officers or board members.

In 1980 the AFL-CIO Executive Council, with one black and no women members, moved to increase representation from these groups, which meant breaking the tradition of selecting members only from the ranks of international union presidents. In that year it appointed its first woman member, a vice president from the Clothing and Textile Workers Union. The following year the Executive Council added a black woman vice president of the Government Employees who had first joined that union four years earlier. These additions at least reflect recognition of a problem. They do not, however, alter the patterns of leadership progression in the internationals which indirectly determine most of the membership of the Executive Council.

Factors that might explain some of the underrepresentation of minorities and women in higher level union positions include the following:

(1) Because leadership emerges disproportionately from among higher skilled workers and since minorities and women are underrepresented in these groups, it follows that they might be underrepresented in leadership positions.

(2) There is a time lag between the appearance of new groups in the work force and their emergence in leadership positions.

But sometimes the lag is severly extended, an indicator that other barriers are operating. An example is found in the garment industry. When the garment unions were first organized in the early part of the century, many of the workers were of Jewish and Italian descent, and the leadership of the garment unions reflected this composition, especially in the number of Jewish officers. But for decades there have been large numbers of blacks and Hispanics in the membership, with few emerging in top leadership. This is especially true of the International Ladies Garment Workers Union (ILG), less so of the Clothing and Textile Workers (ACTWU) where a broader spectrum of ethnic groups is represented on its executive board.

(3) Locals with substantial minority or female membership may elect black or women leaders, but this strength is dissipated in intermediate body and international union elections. This point deserves closer examination, for it involves the electoral arena, where no form of regulation governs the criteria by which members decide for whom to vote in union elections.

The number and distribution of women and minorities at each level of a union's structure affect the chances of finding these groups represented at different levels of leadership. Race and sex criteria often affect these chances, but are not always key factors. No simple generalization holds up.

During the 1950s Greer studied leadership patterns in 21 Los Angeles locals, focusing on proportions of minority membership, the types of jobs held by minorities, and the impact of factory and nonfactory settings.[23] He noted that the strong steward systems of industrial locals offer leadership opportunities that are not available where the first significant unit of collective bargaining government is localwide, as in many nonfactory and craft unions. In addition Greer noted that once in office black union leaders are both "race leaders" and union leaders, with little conflict between the two roles.

A 1975 study by Lamm reports similar findings that are more impressionistic, because it involves only three San Francisco locals, profiling 18 black union leaders. Blacks comprised over 20 percent of the unionized work force in the area but only 10 percent of the full-time leadership. In the three locals, each with a different proportion of black members, several electoral strategies were observed.

Lamm points out that, in the locals studied, slate-balancing appeared most effective in obtaining leadership posts for blacks, especially where they are a minority of the local membership. Race unity strategies may fail even where blacks are a majority because "black members are just as likely to divide on such job-related lines as age, if the issue has to do with pensions, or job classification, if it has to do with pay."[24]

---

[23] Scott Greer, Last Man In (Glencoe, Ill.: The Free Press, 1959).

[24] Roger Lamm, "Black Union Leaders at the Local Level," *Industrial Relations* 14 (May 1975), p. 223.

Lamm's findings, though based on limited data, also seem to confirm our suggestion that race is less important as a criteria in small units where candidates are more apt to be known personally by the electorate and to be judged on relevant criteria. Thus race probably becomes a more significant factor as one moves toward higher positions and broader election units.

Also significant is Lamm's finding that the leaders studied, while committed to improvement for blacks, were also committed unionists who easily reconciled their roles as black leaders and as union leaders. Almost all strongly identified with the working class, as opposed to the black middle class.

There are multiple connections among race and sex proportions of membership, union structure, electoral strategy and outcome, with much depending on how strategies are implemented and responded to by different groups. The only pattern seems to be that race becomes a more conscious criteria in the largest locals—and there are clear exceptions even to this generalization.

Union Corruption

Simply put, union corruption is the misuse of union position or power for private gain. Private gain can be taken to include retention of union office by corrupt means, such as buying support or suppressing opposition. But the focus of this section is financial abuse—that is, the improper diversion of employer or union funds to personal use.

There is often an assumed coincidence between corruption and oligarchy in unions, the presumption being that most democratically controlled unions will not sanction the misuse of union funds. Indeed, in most of the more prominent cases, the two seem to go hand in hand, but there are examples of almost autocratic (one person) rule with no hint of financial scandal, and of corrupt individuals in democratic unions.

"Prominent" is a key word because publicity about the relatively small number of corrupt leaders or corrupt unions often casts suspicion on all. While there are no firm statistics on this elusive subject, one can suspect that, in recent decades noted for corporate abuses, executive "crime in the suites," and Watergate, unions emerge clean by comparison. Indeed, the AFL-CIO reports 1977–78 data showing unions to be one of the lowest bonding risks. During those years unions paid $6.8 million in premiums but were reimbursed only $2.3 million to cover losses, a 33.6 percent ratio even

222 / Union Government and Organization

lower than the ratio for civil government units. Financial institutions were reimbursed 60 percent of premiums while other businesses posted losses amounting to 51 percent of premiums.[25]

Several distinctions are useful. There are differences between amateur, individual, or "penny ante" theft and professional or entrenched corruption. The former are of the type that afflict most organizations, be they little leagues, churches, or businesses, at one time or another, and occur where people handle money.

In unions, individual or small time theft occurs when someone falsifies an expense account, fails to turn in all money collected for a raffle, or "borrows" small amounts from treasury funds. While faulty internal procedures may contribute, the problem is usually random, not endemic. The overwhelming majority of union members and leaders are honest in their union dealings, but now and then one will "tap the till." As an example, in a 1,000-member local of which the author was a member, he was aware of two such incidents over a 10-year period. In one instance a shop steward disappeared with $300 in dues money he had collected. In another, employer dues check-off payments were diverted, though it was never proven whether the office secretary, the secretary-treasurer, or both were responsible. Each case was an aberration and was dealt with quickly.

The more serious abuses are of the professional, entrenched variety where one or more leaders systematically divert union resources to personal use. Here the link between corruption and union governance is often explicit. In the case of Tony Boyle of the United Mine Workers, for instance, the use of union funds for personal enrichment was coupled with ruthless suppression of opposition, including the imposition of trusteeships over dissident districts and the murder of opposition leader Jock Yablonski and his family. Related practices in a few unions that surfaced during the McClellan hearings of the 1950s included the solicitation of kickbacks from employers in return for "sweetheart" contracts, denial of job referrals to opponents, beatings and other forms of intimidation, and the rigging of union elections through such devices as the manufacture of votes from "paper" local unions.

Corruption in high union places does not always infect the entire leadership. During the mid-1970s, for instance, when the president of one major industrial international was discovered to have

---

[25] National Organizing Committee, AFL-CIO, Statistical and Tactical Information Report, no. 1 (November 1980), p. 1.

diverted about a quarter of a million dollars, the international moved quickly, replaced the president, and there has been no hint of scandal since.

By and large, corruption is more likely to become entrenched in industries with characteristics that make them vulnerable to penetration by organized crime. Most unions targeted by the McClellan committee were nonfactory unions, including locals of the Teamsters, Bakery Workers, and the Restaurant Workers. As nonfactory unions, these organziations share environments characterized by relatively small employers operating labor-intensive business in local and regional markets. Even in the absence of unions, firms of this sort are more apt to become targets for racketeers than are corporations in national markets. Hence, in the first instance it is the nature of the industry and not the presence of a union that is attractive to racketeers.

Where corrupt practices involve unions or organizations which masquerade as unions (such as "racket locals" or "paper locals" set up to extort employers), they thrive on employers who seek an edge on their competitors by obtaining lower labor costs. This atmosphere is more receptive to "sweetheart contracts," bribes to union officials for "looking the other way" at contract violations, and other forms of union malpractice.

Many nonfactory locals invest substantial authority in the business agent in order to enforce contracts efficiently. When a problem arises it must be dealt with expeditiously, because prolonged dispute resolution procedures are less workable in industries where employer and employee turnover is high and where employers are relatively small. While this practice may be necessary, it does not always afford as many internal checks as do elaborate systems in which several people are involved.

Major abuses have declined substantially since the 1950s and many of the unions whose locals were cited then are now largely free of corruption. This is arguably attributable to at least four developments:

(1) The reporting and disclosure requirements of the LMRDA, while they have not eliminated the sources of corruption, have made its detection and prosecution simpler. At the same time the election provisions and other safeguards have established firmer standards for the conduct of internal union government.

(2) The labor movement itself, both before and after the pas-

sage of LMRDA, has taken steps to force unions to clean up their houses. George Meany had an especially strong record in this area during the 1950s, including a key role in the expulsion of violators.[26]

(3) The adverse publicity of the McClellan hearings, while largely antiunion in its animus, no doubt provoked a defensive reaction among many unionists and created an awareness of the need to root out corruption in order to maintain a strong image, as well as for more altruistic reasons.

(4) Since that time many internationals have introduced tighter financial controls, including better auditing procedures, bookkeeping, and constitutional provisions to deal with local unions and leaders at all levels.

The AFL-CIO faces a dilemma in its efforts to eliminate corruption among affiliates. The Federation is haunted to this day by the 1957 expulsion of the Teamsters, a last resort that symbolizes the inadequacy and likely futility of applying this ultimate weapon against corrupt affiliates. The weapon is potentially more damaging to the user than to the target.

We have alluded at several points in the book to elements of the Landrum-Griffin Act, properly titled to the Labor-Management Reporting and Disclosure Act of 1959. This legislation addresses many of the areas covered in this chapter. Its main provisions are:

(1) Title I, the Bill of Rights, requires that members have equal rights to participate and to vote and protects their freedoms of speech and of assembly within the union. It also requires local union dues increases to be approved by a secret ballot vote of membership.

(2) Title II establishes a number of annual reporting requirements for unions and union officers. The emphasis of the reports is on finances, both union finances and exchanges of money with employers.

(3) Title III sets certain standards governing trusteeships. The purpose of a trusteeship is set forth in a union's constitution, permitting the international to administer a local that has engaged in financial malpractice or corruption or that has failed to carry out its bargaining duties.

---

[26] John Hutchinson, THE IMPERFECT UNION (New York: Dutton, 1970), pp. 387–89.

Title III is designed to eliminate possible misuse of trusteeships to suppress dissident locals or milk local union assets. Trusteeships must be reported to the Department of Labor and are presumed valid for the first 18 months, after which the international must justify continuing its control of local union affairs.

(4) Title IV establishes minimum standards for the conduct of union elections. Locals must elect officers at least once every three years, internationals at least once every five. There must be equal opportunity to nominate candidates, and union funds may not be used for campaigning purposes.

(5) Title V, Safeguards for Labor Organizations, deals with the financial responsbilities of union officers and requires bonding for those who handle funds. It also contains miscellaneous provisions such as one prohibiting convicted felons from holding union office for five years after their imprisonment.

Enforcement of Title I occurs through the individual filing a civil suit in federal court. Enforcement of Titles II, III, and IV rests with the Secretary of Labor, who can bring suit if he or she believes a violation has occurred. For obvious reasons this provision has led to controversy and allegations that politics governs administration of the LMRDA.

Traditionally opposed to such government efforts to legislate controls of its internal government, labor has preferred self-policing, despite its minimal ability to enforce sanctions against violators. Meanwhile there have been a few voices in the labor movement supporting legislative initiatives against racketeering and other forms of union corruption. Perhaps in recognition of all these factors, the AFL-CIO in 1981 backed measures in a proposed Racketeering Act that would increase the penalties for union leaders convicted of receiving payoffs and require their removal from union office upon first conviction, not after exhaustion of all appeals.

Conclusion

This chapter has reviewed the internal governance of unions, specifically some characteristics of the leaders and the led and the relationships among the two as they determine who runs the union and in whose interests.

Participation in union affairs is influenced by such factors as skill, family background, and orientations toward the job. Recruitment to leadership positions beyond the local level occurs through appointment and election, with most unions advancing top local union officers to a variety of staff positions. This progression can be viewed as an extension of the participation patterns, with many of the same determinants operating. Once in office, top international union leaders benefit from incumbency, with defeat possible but unlikely.

Minorities and women generally seem to fare better at the local level where their numbers are sometimes more substantial or their talents better known. At the international union level both groups are more underrepresented.

There are different measures of union democracy. Procedural, substantive, and behavioral measures each focus on certain dimensions to the exclusion of others. Similarly, there are different ways to view corruption, with the type and the extent to which it is ingrained being significant. Participation, leadership, and governance patterns vary among unions, often along factory and nonfactory lines. Federal law regulates member participation, the conduct of elections, the imposition of trusteeships, and certain financial and reporting practices.

Key Words and Phrases

monopoly view of unions	union democracy
collective voice	formal, procedural democracy
union participation	behavioral democracy
job orientation	substantive democracy
barriers to participation	slate balancing
recruitment	union corruption
incentives/rewards	bonding
progression	individual corruption
turnover oligarchy	entrenched corruption
autocracy	McClellan Committee

Review and Discussion Questions

1. Observe your own local union or interview an activist or leader from another. Compile a list of the ways in which rank-and-file members partic-

ipate in union affairs, both internal government and collective bargaining. Which seem to be most essential to the strength and effectiveness of the local union? To democratic union governance?

2. Based on your observation or interview construct a list showing the approximate amount of time devoted to different matters at monthly meetings. Which meetings are best attended and why? Which are most poorly attended and why? Does attendance have anything to do with the size of the local? With its structure? With the agenda?

3. What forms of union service and participation do you think are valued most highly by the members? Why?

4. Survey the leaders in both internal and collective bargaining offices. What are their job classifications, seniority dates, prior offices held? How long have they held their present positions? What are the turnover rates at different levels? Identify any patterns that emerge from your survey.

5. What participation patterns exist among women and minorities? Discuss this question in terms of the material in the chapter and any other criteria you deem significant.

6. What are the leadership patterns within the international union with respect to the dimensions mentioned in the questions above—origins, tenure, turnover, race, sex, etc. (Note: You may have to study union publications closely or talk to old-timers or otherwise knowledgeable people in the leadership to obtain the necessary information.)

Suggestions for Further Reading

The Spinrad and Strauss articles cited in the chapter are excellent reviews of the literature on union participation. The interested reader can refer to them for further readings.

There are a number of books on union democracy. Joel Seidman, ed., *Trade Union Government and Collective Bargaining* contains several contributions on internal politics, discrimination, and rank-and-file insurgency. Burton H. Hall, ed., *Autocracy and Insurgency in Organized Labor* includes several debates over internal problems in specific unions. J. David Edelstein and Malcolm Warner, *Comparative Union Democracy: Organization and Opposition in British and American Unions* is a major and more recent study focusing on behavioral measures of democracy. A classic statement of the position implied in its title is John R. Coleman, "The Compulsive Pressures of Democracy in Unionism," in Galenson and Lipset, eds., *Labor and Trade Unionism*.

In addition to the items noted at the end of Chapter 3 on black and women workers, see Ray Marshall and Vernon Briggs, Jr., *The Negro and Apprenticeship*, and William H. Harris, *The Harder We Run: Black Workers Since the Civil War*. A comprehensive historical sourcebook on working women is Rosalyn Baxandall, Linda Gordon, and Susan Reverby, eds., *America's Working Women*. See also the sources by Wertheimer and Nelson and by Walshok footnoted in the chapter. During the late 1970s and the early 1980s a number of new works in this area appeared.

Complete bibliographical information for the above titles can be found in the Bibliography.

11

Closing Statements

The coal operators would think they got the union crushed, but just like putting out a fire you can go out and stomp on it and leave a few sparks and here comes a wind and it's going to spread again.

Hobart Grills, 1931

This chapter has three aims: to summarize the earlier chapters in the form of some general statements describing the organization of the labor movement, its structures, functions, and activities; to examine some current problems and issues faced by workers and their unions; and to project, somewhat speculatively, some likely directions for labor over the balance of the century. In brief, the chapter is designed to formulate our knowledge of the past and present to understand and perhaps influence the future.

From Description to Explanation

The content of this book is divisible into three categories of knowledge—*terminology*, *description*, and *explanation*. Terminology, which establishes the language from which the other two follow, consists of identifying and naming unions, their structures, functions, personnel, and the features of their environments. The distinction between description and explanation is the distinction between "what is" and "why." Descriptive propositions identify characteristics, while explanatory propositions assert cause-effect relationships.

A simple example illustrates these categories. We assert that "Union functions are to varying degrees carried out at both local union and workplace levels." This is a purely descriptive statement that says nothing with regard to what way or why one union would

229

operate more on one level than another. But if we assert that "Unions in employment situations characterized by small employers and mobile worksites will operate primarily at the local union level, with little or no permanent structure in the workplace" we are moving toward explanation. Explanatory propositions relate two or more phenomena, or variables, to one another in an attempt to identify cause and effect. In the example above we are suggesting that employer size and employment situation cause variation in union structure at the local level.

Terminology and description help in finding one's way around the labor movement. They are the raw material that must be processed into broader concepts that are then related to one another in comprehensive statements of cause-effect relationships.

A useful tool in the early processing of this raw material is *classification*, used frequently in this book. Classification can be simple and descriptive, as in classifying unions according to size. Or it can be more complex, as in the factory/nonfactory scheme incorporating several dimensions of environment into an explanation of union structure and behavior. At its best classification tells us something new about what is being examined.

In order to be useful a classification need not explain everything. Because of the variety and complexity of structures and functions within the labor movement, we must settle for imperfect typologies and propositions that add to our understanding without completing it.

In assessing the propositions put forth in the next section, several cautions should be borne in mind:

(1) The precision of the physical and biological sciences is seldom attainable in studying human institutions such as the labor movement. Conclusions are more apt to be limited.

(2) Because of the multiple influences shaping an organization and the behavior of its participants, one can rarely predict that a given set of causes will produce precisely the same effects in different situations.

(3) Similarly, we should be wary of assertions of single causation. Statements that "if this (singular), then that" may shed light on a relationship but ignore other equally important factors.

(4) Finally, we need to avoid the knee-jerk determinism that at one extreme leads to fatalism and inaction and at the other to a sterile form of organizational engineering. Such determinism assumes, for instance, that there is a single

best form of union structure for each set of conditions and
that these conditions are unchangeable.

This book has argued that environment, including the employment setting and bargaining situation in which unionists find themselves, influences union structure. Unions are, or should be, flexible
organizations shaped by the needs and by the imaginations of their
members and leaders. Unionists play an active part in building their
organizations and often in changing the very conditions that make
up their environments.

Summary Propositions

Bearing in mind the cautions discussed above, the following
statements are offered to summarize selected points developed in
this book. Some are primarily descriptive, others explanatory. They
should, of course, be examined critically and tested against experience and knowledge from other sources.

Union Origins, Goals, Philosophy. Unions are collective responses by workers to problems of compensation, job security,
working conditions, and authority that arise in the employment relationship and the society. More specific attributions of origin seldom hold up. Some unions arose in craft employment conditions
that preceded industrialism; others appeared in response to
changes in markets and distribution or to mass production; yet
other unions show no relationship to developments in the general
economy but seem to arise from changed employer policy, the passage of legislation, changes in technology, or in imitation of workers
in other situations. Yet it is safe to say that the formation of a national labor movement as a coherent network spanning localized elements was possible only with industrialism.

Most unions are at once dedicated to the *protection* of their
members' skills, income, and conditions, and to the *advancement*
of their collective interests. In both defensive and offensive modes,
workers and unions seek to counteract the one-directional nature of
formal authority in capitalist enterprises and other bureaucratic organizations whose labor relations policies are modeled on those of
capitalist enterprise.

Unions adjust to their main adversaries—employers—and to
the assumptions of capitalism. Some of these accommodations are
structural, others philosophical. The majority of U.S. workers,
though by no means all, currently accept the right of employers to

appropriate some measure of their labor as profit. In particular instances, of course, there is disagreement over the definition of "reasonable" as opposed to "excess" profits. The grant of the employer's right to exercise authority is reflected in collective bargaining agreements preserving management's rights in exchange for concessions in wages, benefits, and conditions.

Another premise of many unionists is that no grant of pay or conditions is secure as long as ultimate power rests with the employer. Consequently within the collective bargaining framework conflict exists regarding management prerogatives, with a trend over the past 40 years toward limiting the employers' ability to make decisions without involving those affected. A related principle is that of fairness—equity among workers. Labor generally holds that fairness is not protected where employers make decisions without limitation.

Labor's program is also based significantly on the insecurity of employment. The drive to preserve and expand collective work opportunities takes many forms. Sometimes it leads unions to become closely allied with employers. In some industries unions and employers jointly lobby various levels of government in support of new projects. In other industries the alliances are more occasional and often arise in response to economic difficulties, as in the auto, rubber, and steel industries, where at least a limited identification is perceived between the employment future of workers and the business future of some employers.

Union Composition and Jurisdiction. The trend in many unions is toward heterogeneity in membership and jurisdiction. The explanations for this trend are several:

(1) Corporate and technological changes alter skills and the organization of work, forcing unions to organize new types of workers to remain relevant to their industries or to organize new members from other industries to maintain their organizational ability to represent current members.

(2) Bargaining effectiveness often requires vertical or horizontal inclusion to "protect one's flanks."

(3) The trend toward corporate concentration and conglomeration leads unions to organize on broader scales and to merge.

(4) A handful of jurisdictions are already largely unionized. This forces growth-oriented unions to look elsewhere for new members.

(5)   In some instances jurisdictional diversity results because
one industry and union dominate a geographic area. Unrelated units of workers want to affiliate with that union,
rather than one without other locals in the vicinity even
though it specializes in their industry.

The labor movement includes a growing percentage of minorities and women. Blacks are now more likely to be represented by
unions than any other racial or sex grouping. Nevertheless, blacks
as well as women and Hispanics remain underrepresented in leadership positions.

Organizational Structure and Function. Union organization
consists of structures designed to perform functions. The form of a
particular union is largely a product of two forces: The first is *environment*, which shapes the union's bargaining functions and structures. The second force is the *effort of workers and union leaders* to
shape their organizations so as to maximize their effectiveness.

Salient features of the environment include the nature of the
industry, its product market and technology and the employment
patterns associated with it. Union structure and function are influenced by such features as employer size and concentration, employment stability, compensation patterns, and variability of employment location and conditions. Depending on how its environment
and structure exhibit these characteristics, a union will be classified
as either factory or nonfactory.

All unions perform two distinct governmental functions, often
with separate structures for each. These are the government of the
collective bargaining relationship and the internal union government. The collective bargaining government structure consists of
those positions that arise within the union in order to deal with employers. Examples are stewards, negotiating committee members,
and business agents. The internal government bodies have no direct
relationship with the employer. They are structures and functions
that exist in all manner of organizations other than unions. Secretaries and treasurers, and often presidents and vice-presidents, are
examples of officers in internal government positions.

The difference in structures and functions between bargaining
government and internal government is most evident in the nonfactory local union where internal government is the primary responsibility of one set of officers, headed by the president, and collective
bargaining the province of another set—the business agent and assistants. As a rule, power in the union gravitates to those with responsibility for the collective bargaining government.

Executive officers perform similar tasks in the internal govern-ment at both local and international levels in most unions. Bargain-ing governments and functions, however, exhibit tremendous varia-tion among unions and are most apt to change in response to new circumstances, though often with considerable lag. Thus bargain-ing government is the more dynamic of the two dimensions.

History shows structural adaptation of union organization to changes in bargaining environment. Waves of employer expansion were followed, with some delay, by union catchup. Early unions were local organizations of largely skilled workers formed to deal with relatively small, local employers. As markets, technology, and transportation expanded, employers grew in size. While local unions sometimes federated into national organizations, those rep-resenting employees of the new giants in steel and transportation equipment were outmatched in bargaining power. The prevailing mode of organization was still the craft model of the AFL, whose membership failed to encompass the millions of new industrial workers.

The union catchup eventually came in the 1930s with the spread of the industrial model of organization in basic manufactur-ing industries. In this model, union jurisdiction was aligned with the industry instead of organizing an occupation across industry lines.

In recent decades a new lag has emerged as a result of the third wave of changes in corporate organization—the emergence of con-glomerate and multinational corporations. This wave has outpaced both industrial and craft models of union organization. While many unions have diversified their membership, the membership fails to coincide with that of conglomerates. Nor does the largely national scope of U.S.-based unions begin to reach the international opera-tions of the multinationals.

Relatively untouched by the new corporate forms as yet are the local market unions—those facing local employers in local product and service markets—with strong traditions of local union auton-omy. Examples are many of the building trades unions and state and municipal workers' unions such as the Fire Fighters. But even here there are broader influences emerging as seen in the centraliza-tion of some construction industry bargaining.

These examples show at another level how unions address em-ployer structure. Where employers have substantial leverage in their product markets (usually in industries with a few large corpo-rations which operate as monopolies or oligopolies) unions, in order to maximize their effectiveness, have centralized their bargaining efforts and structures. Their local unions then play more limited roles.

Another type of evidence of employer structure influencing union structure is found in the structures and practices of individual employers and unions. For instance, the many levels of authority found in the hierarchies of major corporations are reflected in the multistep grievance procedures and elaborate bargaining organizations which unions must staff to be effective. The five- and six-step procedures in large industrial contracts contrast sharply with the essentially two-step procedures negotiated by many nonfactory locals.

Size and permanency of employment in a workplace influence union structure. Thus, the larger and more fixed the workplace, the greater is the tendency for union structure to be anchored within it, rather than at a union hall.

In addition there are a number of behavioral ways in which unions reflect their industries. One observer notes, for instance, the penchant of federal employees to sprinkle some of their union communications with "as per" and other jargon characteristic of bureaucratic employment. Another suspected that a series of color-coded education pamphlets produced by the Communications Workers union reflected the prevalence of color-coding in the telephone industry.

The economics of a decentralized industry (clothing and trucking, for example) have also led unions, paradoxically perhaps, to centralize their structures in order to bargain effectively.

Either way, the evidence points to one of the most significant generalizations about unions as organizations—that they do tend to follow and address the organization of their industries and employers.

Power Within Unions. The logic that leads unions to become, through organizing and mergers, larger and, for bargaining reasons, more centralized, poses dilemmas for union democracy and membership participation. Compounding this difficulty is the tendency for bargaining to become heavily legalized and routinized. Local union officers and members have some input but the decisions are increasingly framed by national officers and their staffs of experts.

Modes of Organizational Change

Environmental influences on union structure are not inconsistent with changes being made consciously and democratically.

In practice there are a number of methods in which union structures have been fashioned:

(1) *The piecemeal or evolutionary method.* The initial structure is gradually modified to meet needs. In doing so it is often adapted to address important changes in corporate structure.

(2) *Formalization of informal structures.* New structures sometimes result from informal bodies that achieve some influence or serve a need. The Machinists state councils, for example, began informally in some states, and were then incorporated into the International's constitution. Local industry or service councils have often emerged in the same way. Several unionists decide to meet periodically to exchange information and develop common goals, eventually to formalize these mechanisms.

(3) *Imitation, transplant.* Appropriately or not, some newly organized unions are patterned on the structures of other unions, typically those assisting in their organization. Thus the Textile Workers union, organized in the 1930s with the help of the Clothing Workers, imitated the joint board unit and other characteristics of the Clothing Workers, despite major differences in the industries of the two unions. Similarly the organizational structure of the Steelworkers union reveals the influence of the United Mine Workers, whose leaders and staff helped in its formative stages.

(4) *Conscious, comprehensive creation or reorganization.* Union leaders fashion a new structure to meet what they consider to be the peculiar needs of an industry. Or, as seldom occurs, they radically revise their current structures.

Issues and Questions

This section summarizes several of the issues and unanswered questions facing the labor movement.

Labor's Image. During the 1930s, some have noted, labor issues were civil rights questions. Workers and unions received much support on that basis.

In the 1980s this perception no longer prevails. The labor movement is clearly a subject of misinformation, much of it slanted toward the needs of labor's opponents.

To what extent is labor able to affect the images others hold of it? Must labor resign itself to broad cycles in which workers and unions are viewed alternately as underdogs, then as "too successful?" Do union actions form the basis for negative images or do the images emerge simply because of ineffective public education by unions about their goals and accomplishments?

Organizing Effectiveness. Union ability to organize is challenged on many fronts. Changing technology and corporate formations that undermine union bargaining effectiveness in turn sap union ability to expand membership. Conversely, the inability to organize undermines the ability to bargain effectively on behalf of workers already organized.

What adaptations in structure, policy, program, and organizing techniques will enhance union ability to organize unrepresented workers? How can the labor movement neutralize those corporations, consultants, and political groups that have thwarted union efforts? Must fundamentally different appeals, with internal consequences for union programs, be developed to reach workers in the white-collar and service sectors?

To what extent do the attitudes of union leaders and members encourage aggressive efforts to overhaul structures that are less effective than they once were and to undertake aggressive new organizing efforts and policy directions? Are union structures and policies, including patterns of leadership selection and progression, conducive to union goals? If not, are there options that are consistent with legitimate principles of unionism and of rank-and-file control?

Before all the questions on organizing can be answered, another might have to be posed. What are the ideal and practical limits of unionism? What is its effective scope? With the extension of union representation into so-called professional occupations a number of questions about union substance and appeal are raised. Should the labor movement of the future, like the Knights of Labor a century ago, attempt to extend unionism to the self-employed? Should its efforts include casual "day workers," the unemployed, and other nonstrategic or hard-to-organize groups? At the other extreme should it extend to nonexecutive salaried personnel, to concerted efforts to organize supervisors?

These are not, in most cases, immediate issues since there are many categories of employees within the scope of conventional unionism who are as yet unorganized. But the examples tickle the limits of unionism—and there are in fact those of the opinion that the absolute or proportional size of the labor movement does not matter. As long as core occupational groups are organized, they feel, 10 or 20 percent of the work force is an acceptable figure.

To the extent that the labor movement expands its scope at either end of the occupational spectrum, or that it includes groups of workers who do not share "traditional" characteristics, union programs and even structures may have to be retailored to be effective.

Structure and Function.   Overlapping some of the questions posed above are those of organizational design and administration. What structures are best for which workers? How can more effective structures be identified? Who should create and "install" them? Are any of the discarded models of the past, such as the assemblies of the Knights of Labor or the "one big union" notion of the Wobblies, worth reexamination? Or are the effective structures of the future yet to be discovered?

To what extent can unions maintain traditional notions of jurisdiction, focusing their efforts within closely allied industries and occupations? Given the growth of conglomerates and multinationals, can labor "match up" with only slight variations in its present structures? Or are radical new forms necessary to gain an equal footing with the corporate giants?

What are the advantages and disadvantages of different forms of factory and nonfactory union structures for various combinations of workers? Is there an optimum relationship between locals, internationals, and other bodies in each case? Who determines what it is?

Will the merger trend leading to larger international unions bring about new needs for structural adjustment to cope with the tensions between control from the top and local self-governance? As it stands, many unions resemble the federal system, with the internationals paralleling the federal government and the locals paralleling cities and states. Once a union passes a certain size, internal governance and administration may require significant adjustment.

Related to the above are questions such as "what is the ideal role of the local in organizing?" The local, even the factory local, may be able to perform as the key unit in new-member organizing. This would require the creation of new incentives for factory locals to engage in organizing. Another question has to do with the appropriate levels and forms of membership participation at the local level. Much here depends on the type of local in question, be it factory, nonfactory, or some variant. Many locals have the potential for creating new forums for participation that are closer to the worker and the workplace. With these forums vitalized, the monthly meeting might become more like an executive board meeting or a delegate assembly.

Early in the 1980s the AFL-CIO took up some of its long-standing problems, among them the chronic weakness of many of its state and local central bodies and the paucity of women and minorities in high positions. It may play an increasingly strong role in determining the future shape of the movement. This is seen in its encouragement of certain mergers among affiliates.

Politics. The 1980 elections crystallized for labor some fundamental problems in the area of legislation and political action. A number of issues may be rethought during the 1980s. One of these is the question, "what are labor's interests in politics?" Do they extend to spending political "chips" for social legislation that benefits nonmembers as much or more than members? It seems unlikely, despite the call of some to retreat to purely self-interest issues, that labor will back off entirely from its traditional broad scope efforts.

Labor's strategy, however changed, is likely to retain its electoral and lobbying emphasis. Within this framework the AFL-CIO is attempting modest changes. Dissatisfied with the results of its traditional "hands-off primaries" practice because it often gives labor little say in shaping general election choices, affiliates and the federation will take on an expanded role in primaries, seeking out candidates sympathetic to their views. A number of other problem areas include restrictions on raising political funds, an area where labor is typically overmatched by the growing number of corporate, and other, PACs.

Leadership. Leadership recruitment policies are not always effective in advancing aggressive and imaginative leaders within union structures. Unions, like other institutions, have their share of sponsored functionaries who advance through loyalty with minimum performance. But, for a political institution like a union, to abandon the combination of election and appointment currently in place in favor of a "merit system" or some other method would probably create more problems than it would solve. Despite its imperfections, election is one mechanism that maintains accountability of leaders to rank-and-file members.

The imperfections are most obvious in those occasional instances where autocracy and unscrupulous neglect of workers' interests prevails. In the end an aroused rank and file often take care of such problems, but the end is often too long in coming. In the meantime the union is set back decades and many members suffer.

Out-of-touch leadership is replaced largely in two ways in the labor movement. Often it is replaced through election, retirement, or death, with the replacements sometimes being of a more innovative bent. But in the past, when the dominant element in organized labor has collectively been out of touch, it has been replaced or at least shaken-up by the emergence of a rival group with a rival philosophy and organizational model, as in the case of the CIO challenge to the aging leadership of the AFL in the 1930s.

Tied in part to the question of recruitment and leadership is the status of minorities and women. While there are some structural explanations for the failure of representatives of these groups to move to top positions, most of these explanations assume some level of discrimination. This is notable in the explanation that black strength at the local level is often dissipated in the larger unit elections for national offices. The AFL-CIO, sensitive to the absence of any women on the Executive Council (because none were presidents of major affiliates), moved in 1980–81 to by-pass the normal process by appointing two women to the Council, because it could not influence the internal affairs of affiliates and voting patterns that would move women up by conventional means.

The Balance of the Century: Prospects

As it moves toward the turn of another century, organized labor faces several difficulties. The U.S. economy is no longer what it was when labor made its last major breakthroughs. It is now predominantly a service, not a manufacturing, economy. Its center is shifting from the industrialized snow belt, traditional source of union strength, to the sun belt.

Unable to "defeat its enemies" in the 1980 and 1984 elections, labor faces an aggressive national administration determined to scrap the programs of the previous 40 years. It also faces a fleet of "union busters," some of whom ply their trade as employer consultants while others occupy key spots in government. Federal labor laws increasingly make labor's most effective economic weapons illegal. And, as key industries undergo fundamental change, unions are confronted with "concession" or "give back" bargaining.

Organized labor has not slept through all this. The increased number of union mergers has significantly altered the jurisdictional scope of several unions. Marginal adjustments have served to keep some union structures and policies relatively up to date.

On the other hand, organized labor has not yet realized the organizing and political successes necessary to achieve the quantum leap forward that the movement has enjoyed every few decades in its past. Electoral defeats, to the extent they reduce the number of political arrows in labor's quiver, hinder its ability to make gains on all fronts.

Should organized labor's reliance on the traditional methods of electoral action and lobbying prove unsuccessful, it may be forced to explore other methods or lose ground to groups that do. In the United Kingdom during the 1960s and early 1970s, for instance, a combination of irrelevant union structures and political onslaughts by conservative governments led to the growth of a nationwide shop stewards movement that for a time appeared to substitute workplace organization for that nation's equivalent of our local union and even national union structure. If, however, the Reagan administration, like the Nixon administration, falls of its own excesses, policy, or character faults, there may be a new lease for the traditional political methods, slightly updated.

More fundamental changes in labor's approach would seem to involve, at a minimum, a different relationship between labor, the political parties, and the government, which in turn would entail a substantial ideological shift. While each of the alternatives identified in Chapter 9 has its advocates, a shift of this magnitude is unlikely unless what we have termed the "conventional approach" is seen as unworkable, the economy is unable to rebound from the fundamental dislocations it experienced, or the international situation collapses.

With corporations increasingly disregarding national boundaries and loyalties, labor will have to develop allies on both domestic and international fronts. Efforts thus far have been little more than token.

In order to restore its lost political strength, labor may first have to make breakthroughs on the economic front through a combination of organizing, structural change, and bargaining successes. Whether it will take a fundamentally different organizational model to make these changes remains to be seen.

Currently there are no sharply posed organizational alternatives such as existed in the years of industrial union competition with craft unionism. If such alternatives emerge they might entail changes in the structure of ownership and management initiated through the political system, possibly with worker and union backing. At the moment no such alternatives have received significant trials or backing in the United States. They exist as a gleam in the eyes of academics studying European models or in this country as scattered experiments. Examples include codetermination in Germany and "worker self-management" in Yugoslavia, schemes in which workers exercise varying degrees of ownership and control of the enterprises in which they are employed.

Because the major alternatives require fundamental change in the ownership of, and/or the making of authoritative decisions within, a society, industry, or enterprise, they alter traditional labor and management powers and identities. Because unions as they are now structured "grew up with" and are geared to these traditional roles, the question is raised whether they could adapt to these new configurations of identity and power.

If uncertainty lies behind the skepticism of some labor leaders toward such participatory arrangements, there is also a more immediate concern: that many of the participatory schemes now being floated about the United States by corporations would in fact make no changes in either the ownership or control of industry. Instead, many participatory schemes are thinly disguised devices to raise capital from workers or to boost worker productivity and take advantage of worker knowledge and creativity while leaving basic power relationships unchanged.

More genuine innovations have tended to arise as products of adversity and are limited to troubled plants or corporations in troubled industries. We refer here to the reopening of a closed plant under worker/community ownership, the seating of the UAW president on the Chrysler board of directors in response to that corporation's difficulties, the creation of worker-owned plywood factories in the northwest, and so on. These innovations typically result from job-threatening calamity, not from the national political process.

The effectiveness of labor's conventional structures and weapons during the 1980s may determine whether there is a shift to basically new forms of economic organization and worker organization by the turn of the century. Meanwhile the movement remains a fascinating mix of structural and functional arrangements that changes with fits and starts at times and at others with amazing creativity and permanency.

Selected Bibliography

AFL-CIO. *Right to Work*. Special Report. Washington, D.C.: AFL-CIO, 1977.

_____. *Statistical and Tactical Information Report*. Washington, D.C., 1980.

_____. *Union Membership and Employment, 1959–1979*. Washington, D.C., 1980.

Alexander, Kenneth O. "Union Structure and Bargaining Structure." *Labor Law Journal* 24 (March 1973): 164–172.

Allison, Elizabeth K. "Financial Analysis of the Local Union." *Industrial Relations* 14 (May 1975): 145–155.

Andrews, Mary A. "Housestaff Physicians and Interns Press for Bargaining Rights." *Monthly Labor Review* 101 (August 1978): 30.

Applebaum, Leon, and Blaine, Harry R. "Compensation and Turnover of Union Officers." *Industrial Relations* 14 (May 1975): 156–67.

Banfield, Edward C., and Wilson, James Q. *City Politics*. Cambridge: Harvard University Press, 1965.

Banks, Robert F., and Steiber, Jack, eds., *Multinationals, Unions, and Labor Relations in Industrialized Countries*. Ithaca: New York State School of Industrial & Labor Relations, 1977.

Barbash, Jack. *American Unions: Structure, Government and Politics*. New York: Random House, 1967.

Barbash, Jack. *Labor's Grass Roots*. Westport, Conn.: Greenwood Press, 1961.

Barry, John, ed. *Proceedings of the Twelfth Constitutional Convention of the AFL-CIO, 1977*. Washington, D.C.: AFL-CIO, 1978.

_____. *Proceedings of the Fourteenth Constitutional Convention of the AFL-CIO, 1981*. Washington, D.C.: AFL-CIO, 1982.

Baxandall, Rosalyn; Gordon, Linda; and Reverby, Susan, eds. *America's Working Women*. New York: Random House, 1976.

Bendiner, Burton, B. "A Labor Response to Multinationals: Coordination of Bargaining Goals." *Monthly Labor Review* 101 (July 1978): 9–13.

Bennett, John W. "Using Union Memorabilia as a Teaching Aid." *Labor Studies Journal*, 13 (Fall 1978): 114–30.

Berenbeim, Ronald. "The Declining Market for Unionization." *Information Bulletin*, No. 44, New York: The Conference Board, 1978.

Bok, Derek C., and Dunlop, John T. *Labor and the American Community*. New York: Simon & Schuster, 1970.

Boyer, Richard, and Morais, Herbert. *Labor's Untold Story*. 3rd ed. Chicago: United Electrical Workers, 1970.

Braverman, Harry. *Labor and Monopoly Capital: The Degradation of Work in the*

Twentieth Century. New York: Monthly Review Press, 1974.

Bromwich, Leo. *Union Constitutions*. New York: Fund for the Republic, 1959.

Brooks, Thomas R. *Communications Workers of America: The Story of a Union*. New York: Mason Charter, 1977.

Cebula, James E. *Glory and Despair: A History of the Molders Union*. Cincinnati: International Molders and Allied Workers Union, 1976.

Chaison, Gary N. "A Note on Union Merger Trends, 1900–1978." *Industrial and Labor Relations Review* 34 (October 1980): 114–20.

Chitayat, Gideon. *Trade Union Mergers and Labor Conglomerates*. New York: Praeger Publishers, 1979.

Christie, Robert A. *Empire in Wood*. Ithaca, N.Y.: Cornell University Press, 1956.

Coleman, John R. "The Compulsive Pressures of Democracy in Unionism." In *Labor and Trade Unionism*, edited by Galenson and Lipset. New York: John Wiley & Sons, 1960.

Cook, Alice H. "Dual Government in Unions: A Tool for Analysis." *Industrial and Labor Relations Review* 15 (April 1962): 323–49.

———. *Union Democracy: Practice and Ideal*. Ithaca, New York: Cornell University Press, 1963.

Cook, Stephen, and Stanley, Miles. *Making It Go: A Handbook for Local Central Bodies*. Information Series 8. Morgantown, W. Va.: Institute for Labor Studies, West Virginia University, 1970.

Craypo, Charles. *The Economics of Collective Bargaining*. Washington, D.C.: The Bureau of National Affairs, Inc., forthcoming.

Dunlop, John T. "What's Ahead in Union Government." In *Trade Union Government and Collective Bargaining*, edited by Joel Seidman. New York: Praeger Publishers, 1970.

Edelstein, J. David, and Warner, Malcolm. *Comparative Union Democracy: Organization and Opposition in British and American Unions*. New York: John Wiley & Sons, 1975.

Epstein, Edwin M. "Labor and Federal Elections: The New Legal Framework." *Industrial Relations* 15 (October 1976): 257–74.

Estey, Martin S. "The Strategic Alliance as a Factor in Union Growth." *Industrial and Labor Relations Review* 9 (October 1955): 41–53.

Filippelli, Ronald. *Labor in the U.S.A.: A History*. New York: John Wiley & Sons, 1984.

Fink, Gary. "The Rejection of Voluntarism." *Industrial and Labor Relations Review* 26 (January 1973): 805–19.

Finley, Joseph E. *White Collar Union*. New York: Octagon Books, 1975.

Freeman, Richard B., and Medoff, James L. *What Do Unions Do?* New York: Basic Books, 1984.

Friedlander, Peter. *The Emergence of a UAW Local, 1936–1939*. Pittsburgh: University of Pittsburgh Press, 1975.

Friedman, Abraham. "The American Trade Union Leader: A Collective Portrait." In *Trade Union Government and Collective Bargaining*, edited by Joel Seidman. New York: Praeger Publishers, 1970.

Gagala, Kenneth. *Union Organizing and Staying Organized*. Reston, Va.: Reston Publishing Co., Inc., 1983.

Gamm, Sara. "The Election Base of National Executive Boards." *Industrial and Labor Relations Review* 32 (April 1979): 295–311.

Getman, Julius; Goldberg, Stephen; and Herman, Jeanne. *Union Representation Elections: Law and Reality*. New York: Russell Sage, 1976.

Glick, W.; Mirvis, P.; and Harder, D. "Union Satisfaction and Participation." *Industrial Relations* 16 (May 1977): 145–51.

Gifford, Courtney D., ed. *Directory of U.S. Labor Organizations, 1982–83 Edition*. Washington, D.C.: The Bureau of National Affairs, Inc., 1982.

Goldberg, Arthur. *AFL-CIO: Labor United*. New York: McGraw-Hill, 1956.

Goldfield, Michael. "The Decline of Organized Labor: NLRB Union Certification Election Results." *Politics and Society* 11 (1982): 167–209.

Gray, Lois S. "Unions Implementing Managerial Techniques." *Monthly Labor Review* 104 (June 1981): 3–21.

Greenstone, J. David. *Labor in American Politics*. Chicago: University of Chicago Press, 1977.

Greer, Scott. *Last Man In*. Glencoe, Ill.: Free Press, 1959.

Hall, Burton H., ed. *Autocracy and Insurgency in Organized Labor*. New Brunswick, N.J.: Transaction Books, 1972.

Harris, William H. *The Harder We Run: Black Workers Since the Civil War*. New York: Oxford University Press, 1982.

Hershfield, David C. *The Multinational Union Challenges the Multinational Company*. New York: The Conference Board, 1975.

Hickman, Charles W. "Labor Organization Fees and Dues." *Monthly Labor Review* 100 (May 1977): 21.

Hoxie, Robert. *Trade Unionism in the United States*. New York: Appleton, 1917.

Hutchinson, John. *The Imperfect Union*. New York: Dutton, 1970.

Craypo, Charles. "The Impact on Labor of Changing Corporate Structure and Technology." *Labor Studies Journal* 3 (Winter 1979): 3.

James, Ralph, and James, Estelle. *Hoffa and the Teamsters*. New York: Van Nostrand, 1965.

Janus, Charles J. "Union Mergers in the 1970s." *Monthly Labor Review* 101 (October 1978): 13–23.

Kahn, Melvin. *The Politics of American Labor: The Indiana Microcosm*. Carbondale: Southern Illinois University Press, 1964.

Kennedy, Van Dusen. *Nonfactory Unionism and Labor Relations*. Berkeley: Institute of Industrial Relations, University of California, 1955.

Kennedy, Van Dusen, and Krauss, Wilma Rule. *The Business Agent and His Union*. Rev. ed. Berkeley: Institute of Industrial Relations, University of California, 1964.

Kochan, Thomas A. "How American Workers View Labor Unions." *Monthly Labor Review* 102 (April 1979): 23–31.

Kornhauser, Arthur, and Sheppard, Harold. *When Labor Votes: A Study of Auto Workers*. New York: University Books, 1956.

Kovner, Joseph, and Lahne, Herbert. "Shop Society and the Union." *Industrial and Labor Relations Review* 7 (October 1953): 3–14.

Kuhn, James. *Bargaining in Grievance Settlement*. New York: Columbia University Press, 1961.

Lahne, Herbert J. "The Intermediate Union Body in Collective Bargaining." *Industrial and Labor Relations Review* 6 (January 1953): 163–79.

Lahne, Herbert J., and Kovner, Joseph. "Local Union Structure: Formality and Reality." *Industrial and Labor Relations Review* 9 (October 1955): 24–31.

Lamm, Roger. "Black Union Leaders at the Local Level." *Industrial Relations* 14 (May 1975): 220–32.

Leiserson, William. *American Trade Union Democracy*. Cambridge, Mass.: Harvard University Press, 1959.

Livernash, E. Robert. "New Developments in Bargaining Structure." In *Trade Union Government and Collective Bargaining*, edited by Joel Seidman. New York: Praeger Publishers, 1970.

Lipset, S. M. *Political Man*. Garden City, N.Y.: Anchor Books, 1960.

Marshall, Ray. *The Negro and Organized Labor*. New York: John Wiley & Sons, 1965.

Marshall, Ray, and Briggs, Vernon, Jr. *The Negro and Apprenticeship*. Baltimore: Johns Hopkins Press, 1967.

Marshall, Ray, and Rungeling, Brian. *The Role of Unions in the American Economy*. New York: Joint Council on Economic Education, 1976.

Mathewson, Stanley B. *Restriction of Output Among Unorganized Workers*. New York: Viking Press, 1931.

Mills, C. Wright. *The New Men of Power*. New York: Harcourt, Brace, 1948.

Muste, A. J. "Factional Fights in Trade Unions." In *American Labor Dynamics*, edited by J. B. S. Hardman, New York: Harcourt & Brace, 1928.

Rayback, Joseph. *A History of American Labor*. New York: Free Press, 1966.

Rehmus, Charles M.; McLaughlin, Doris B.; and Nesbitt, Frederick H. *Labor and American Politics*. Rev. ed. Ann Arbor: University of Michigan Press, 1978.

Roomkin, Myron, and Juris, Harvey A. "Unions in the Traditional Sectors: The Mid-Life Passage of the Labor Movement." In *Thirty-First Annual Proceedings of the Industrial Relations Research Association*, edited by Barbara D. Dennis. Madison, Wis.: Industrial Relations Research Association, 1978.

Sayles, Leonard. *Behavior of Industrial Work Groups: Prediction and Control*. 1958. Reprint. New York: Arno Press, 1977.

Sayles, Leonard R., and Strauss, George. *The Local Union*. Rev. ed. New York: Harcourt, Brace, and World, 1967.

Schlossberg, Stephen I., and Scott, Judith A. *Organizing and the Law*. 3rd ed. Washington, D.C.: The Bureau of National Affairs, Inc., 1983.

Seidman, Joel, et al. *The Worker Views His Union*. Chicago: University of Chicago Press, 1958.

Siegel, Abraham J., ed. *The Impact of Computers on Collective Bargaining*. Cambridge, Mass.: MIT Press, 1969.

Spinrad, William. "Correlates of Trade Union Participation: A Summary of the Literature." *American Sociological Review* 25 (April 1960): 237–44.

Strauss, George. "Union Government in the U.S.: Research Past and Future." *Industrial Relations* 16 (May 1977): 215–42.

Strauss, George. *Unions in the Building Trades.* Buffalo, N.Y.: University of Buffalo, 1958.

Sykes, A. J. M. "Trade-Union Workshop Organization in the Printing Industry—The Chapel." *Human Relations* 13 (February 1960): 49–65.

Taft, Philip. *Labor Politics American Style: The California State Federation of Labor.* Cambridge: Harvard University Press, 1968.

_____. *The Structure and Government of Labor Unions.* Cambridge, Mass.: Harvard University Press, 1954.

Tannenbaum, Arnold S. "Unions." In *Handbook of Organizations,* edited by James G. March. Chicago: Rand McNally, 1965.

Tyler, Gus. *Labor in the Metropolis.* Columbus, Ohio: Charles E. Merrill Publishing Co., 1972.

Ulman, Lloyd. *The Rise of the National Trade Union.* Cambridge, Mass.: Harvard University Press, 1955.

U.S. Department of Labor. *Directory of National Unions and Employee Associations, 1979.* Bulletin 2079. Washington, D.C.: Government Printing Office, 1980.

_____. *Earnings and Other Characteristics of Organized Workers.* Bulletin 2105. Washington, D.C., 1980.

_____. *Perspectives on Working Women: A Data Book.* Bulletin 2080. Washington, D.C., 1980.

_____. *The American Worker,* edited by Richard B. Morris. Washington, D.C., 1976.

Wallihan, James. "Workplace Politics and Leadership in a Chicago Printing Trades Union." Ph.D. diss., Indiana University, 1974.

Walshok, Mary Lindenstein. *Blue Collar Women.* Garden City, N.Y.: Anchor Books, 1981.

Webb, Sidney, and Webb, Beatrice. *History of Trade Unionism.* London: Longmans, Green, 1911.

Wertheimer, Barbara. *We Were There: The Story of Working Women in America.* New York: Pantheon Books, 1977.

Wertheimer, Barbara, and Nelson, Anne H. *Trade Union Women: A Study of Their Participation in New York City Locals.* New York: Praeger Publishers, 1975.

Wolfe, Arthur C. "Trends in Labor Union Voting Behavior, 1948–1968." In *Labor and American Politics,* edited by Charles M. Rehmus and Doris B. McLaughlin. Rev. ed. Ann Arbor: University of Michigan Press, 1978.

Topical Index

Boyle, Tony 222
Bribery 128, 223
Broadcast Employees (NABET), *see* National Association of Broadcast Employees and Technicians
Brotherhood of Locomotive Engineers (BLE) 52
Brotherhood of Maintenance of Way Employees (BMWE) 52
Brotherhood of Railway, Airline and Steamship Clerks, Freight Handlers, Express and Station Employees (BRAC) 145, 166
Budgeting 120
Building Service Employees 211
Building Trades Councils 106, 132, 162
Business agent 8, 80, 82, 102–104, 136, 143, 233

C

California Faculty Association 167
California State Employees Association (CAL-SEA) 167
Canadian Railway Labor Association 171
Capitalism 184–185, 203
Carlough, Edward 116
Carpenters (CJA), *see* United Brotherhood of Carpenters and Joiners of America
Central labor bodies 132, 163
Central Labor Councils 132
Chamber of Commerce 187, 189
Chapels 17, 102
Checkoff provisions 174
Chrysler Corporation 184, 187, 242
Civil Service Employees Association, Inc. (CSEA), *see* American Federation of State, County, and Municipal Employees
Classification 230
Clothing and Textile Workers (ACTWU), *see* Amalgamated Clothing and Textile Workers Union
Coalition of Black Trade Unionists 166
Coalition of Labor Union Women (CLUW) 166
Collective bargaining 4, 14, 21, 34, 63, 69, 147, 179–180, 185, 233
Committee on Political Education 164, 194–195
Communications 15, 72
Communications Workers of America 56, 62, 92, 133, 155, 235
Communist Party 154

Conditions of employment 4
Conglomerates 37, 140–141, 144, 232
Congress of Industrial Organizations 35–37, 79
Contracts 140, 144
  administration 14, 96
  negotiation 14, 72, 89, 96
  proposals 100
  sweetheart 223
  votes 100
Cook, Alice 74, 79
Coopers' International Union of North America (CIU) 66
Coordinated bargaining 138
Corruption 202, 221–225
Craft unions 6

D

Debs, Eugene V. 178
Department of Labor 51, 225
Depression 47
Discrimination
  race 218–220
  sex 52, 218–220
District assembly 33
Donahue, Thomas 211
Dues 31, 100, 122, 123
Dunlop, John T. 175

E

Economic organizations 16
Education 15–16, 195, 235
Elections 27, 29, 56, 67, 215, 225, 241
  campaign tactics 29–30, 216
  local 100
  representation 22, 68
Electoral impact 195–197
Electrical Workers (UE), *see* United Electrical, Radio and Machine Workers of America
Electronic Workers 134
Embezzlement 128
Employment patterns 58
Energy problems 199
Equal employment opportunity 185, 218, 224
Executive board 134
Executive officers 234

About the Author

Jim Wallihan is Associate Professor of Labor Studies at Indiana University. Since 1974 he has worked with the University's Division of Labor Studies at Indiana University–Purdue University at Indianapolis (IUPUI), where he teaches and coordinates programs with unions in the area.

Jim's first union experience came in his hometown of Riverside, California, where in 1957 at age 16 he joined the former Retail Clerks Union. He later worked for five years as a paperhandler in Chicago, serving in several capacities in his local of the former Printing Pressmen's union. His Ph.D. dissertation at Indiana University deals with shop level organization and grievance representation in several units of that local union. Additionally, he recently completed two terms as president of American Federation of Teachers Local 3950.

Jim and his wife Charlene have four children, Christina, Daniel, Rebecca, and John.